Oxford Early Christian Texts

General Editor: Dr. Henry Chadwick, Dean of Christ Church, Oxford

THEOPHILUS OF ANTIOCH

THEOPHILUS OF ANTIOCH
AD AUTOLYCUM

TEXT AND TRANSLATION
BY
ROBERT M. GRANT

OXFORD
AT THE CLARENDON PRESS
1970

Oxford University Press, Ely House, London W. 1

GLASGOW NEW YORK TORONTO MELBOURNE WELLINGTON
CAPE TOWN SALISBURY IBADAN NAIROBI DAR ES SALAAM LUSAKA ADDIS ABABA
BOMBAY CALCUTTA MADRAS KARACHI LAHORE DACCA
KUALA LUMPUR SINGAPORE HONG KONG TOKYO

© OXFORD UNIVERSITY PRESS 1970

PRINTED IN GREAT BRITAIN

PREFACE

THIS text and translation of Theophilus is a result of long-extended but intermittently advanced studies begun at the Harvard Divinity School in 1942 under the direction of Professors A. D. Nock and H. J. Cadbury. Since that date my work has benefited from the advice and criticisms of Professors A. S. Pease, J. H. Waszink, W. C. van Unnik, and G. Quispel. My most recent advisers have been Professors B. Einarson and C. Trypanis of the University of Chicago, and Dr. Henry Chadwick of Oxford. Needless to say, none is responsible for my errors of commission or omission.

I should also express my gratitude to three foundations which provided assistance at various points: the Carnegie Foundation for the Advancement of Teaching, the United States Educational Foundation in the Netherlands, and the John Simon Guggenheim Memorial Foundation.

My special thanks are due to Mme. Zeegers-Vander Vorst for reading the proofs.

ROBERT M. GRANT

Chicago
May 1970

CONTENTS

INTRODUCTION

Theophilus of Antioch	ix
The Arrangement of the Work	x
Non-Biblical Sources	xi
The Old Testament	xii
The New Testament	xiii
Biblical Exegesis	xiv
Theology	xv
Theophilus as a Jewish Christian	xvii
Transmission of Theophilus' Books	xix
Editions	xxi
The Chronology of Theophilus	xxiii
ABBREVIATIONS AND EDITIONS	xxvii
SIGLA	xxix
AD AUTOLYCUM	1
INDEX OF BIBLICAL QUOTATIONS AND ALLUSIONS	148
INDEX OF NON-BIBLICAL SOURCES AND PARALLELS	151

INTRODUCTION

THEOPHILUS OF ANTIOCH

AMONG the Greek Christian writers of the second century a prominent place belongs to the Apologists, at least a dozen in number, who addressed defences of Christianity to the emperors, to 'the Greeks' in general, and in at least two instances to private individuals. Some of the apologists were teachers within the Christian communities; at least four of them were bishops. The three books *To Autolycus* by Theophilus of Antioch thus fall within known categories; they were produced by a bishop for a private individual (as well as for a wider audience) in defence of the Christian faith. The church historian Eusebius calls the work 'elementary' (*Historia ecclesiastica* iv. 24) and so it is, as compared with other Christian writings of Theophilus' own time. It has the merit, however, of showing the approach being taken toward theology and culture at Antioch in the latter years of the second century, and of indicating the remarkable diversity in Christian ideas. It is strikingly more prosaic and, indeed, banal than the letters of Ignatius, bishop of Antioch more than half a century earlier. Presumably the church enjoyed greater tranquillity under Theophilus than under his predecessor.

The date of Theophilus can be determined only from his reference to the death of Marcus Aurelius, which occurred on 17 March 180 (III. 28). His reference to the Tigris and the Euphrates (II. 24) may show that he lived nearer the Tigris and the Euphrates than the Nile. What we know of his life is that he was brought up to speak Greek and at school acquired some acquaintance with Greek literature. He was a slow learner (II. 25), not eager to spend all his time in a library (III. 4), probably married (II. 28). Presumably under the influence of Jewish Christians, he encountered the Greek Old Testament and became a Christian (I. 14). According to the

Chronicon of Eusebius he became bishop of Antioch in 169, and this date may be approximately correct.

THE ARRANGEMENT OF THE WORK

The arrangement of the first book is rather remarkable and suggests that catechetical materials on various subjects have been rearranged in order to provide an apologetic discussion. The first chapter on the name 'Christian' finds its complement and conclusion in the twelfth; the second chapter on the vision of God is naturally balanced by the fifth on God's invisibility. Chapters three and four on the nature of God lead appropriately through chapter five on invisibility to chapters six and seven on God the creator, thence to chapters eight and thirteen on resurrection. Chapters nine to eleven, on idolatry and emperor-worship, constitute a unified group, but chapters eight and fourteen, both on faith, are not clearly related to the rest. One hesitates to say what an ancient author should have written, but it would appear that a more logical sequence would be provided if one followed the order 2, 5, 3–4, 6–7, 9–11, 8, 13–14, 1, 12. This is not to say that any such order ever existed. It is merely to note that the materials employed doubtless existed independently before Theophilus wrote this book.

The second book consists of a preface (c. 1), attacks on idolatry and mythology (2–3; 34), and criticisms of philosophers (4), poets (5–6), and historians (7). The inconsistent poets (8) are then contrasted with the consistent prophets (9–10). The bulk of the book consists of an exegetical treatment of the early chapters of Genesis (11–32), which must have existed separately. It concludes with another statement about the truth of prophets and Christians (33). At this point idolatry is attacked again (34), and the book ends with a description of Christian morality as based on the Old Testament, consistent in itself (35), with the *Sibylline Oracles* (36), and with certain Greek poets (37–8).

The third book contrasts the futility and inconsistency of Greek poets, historians, and philosophers (1–8; cf. II. 1–8) with

the consistency and high morality of the law, the prophets, and the gospels, all reflected in Christian life (9–15). At this point Theophilus turns to history again; the latter half of the book is devoted to showing how ancient and accurate Christian history is. Since what Theophilus means is Old Testament history, he relies chiefly on Jewish sources. He begins by criticizing Plato's ideas about the deluge (16–18) as contrasted with the true account in Genesis (19). The exodus and other events can be dated correctly from pagan accounts—taken from Josephus (20–3). He then relies on the Old Testament or on a secondary source in order to set forth a chronological scheme running from Adam to Cyrus, king of Persia (24–6). By correlating Cyrus' death with the reign of Tarquin at Rome he is able to move to the work of Chryseros the Nomenclator on Roman chronology and to reach the death of Marcus Aurelius (27), finally adding up the figures he has provided (28). An appendix contains recalcitrant materials not used earlier, as well as a final exhortation (29–30).

Theophilus' arrangement of his materials thus leaves something to be desired, and his insistently didactic tone often fails to retain the reader's interest. His style, though correct, is monotonous because he constantly repeats words and expressions.

NON-BIBLICAL SOURCES

At first glance the second and third books suggest that his reading of non-Christian writings was extensive, but such an impression is modified by a closer look. The list of Greek authors he provides in III. 2 is probably based on a school catalogue like the Alexandrian list of 'great books'. Theophilus' quotations from the poets, however, are largely derived from an anthology which also underlies the fourth-century collection of Johannes Stobaeus. The only poets whose works Theophilus probably knew directly were Homer and Hesiod; he would have read *Iliad*, *Odyssey*, and *Theogony* at school.[1] As for

---

[1] Cf. H.-I. Marrou, *Histoire de l'éducation dans l'antiquité* (Paris, 1950), 226–7. For Theophilus' use of anthologies and the *Sibylline Oracles* see Nicole Zeegers-Vander Vorst, 'Les Citations des poètes grecs chez les apologistes chrétiens du ii[e]

philosophy, he probably read some, or parts of some, of the dialogues of Plato; everything else comes from the handbooks highly popular in the second century, and to them he has added his own errors. His concern for history, at least outside the Old Testament, did not go very deep. He had certainly read Josephus' apologetic treatise *Contra Apionem* with care, and he knew something about Herodotus and Thucydides (III. 26). He could copy chronological information out of the works of Thallus and Chryseros the Nomenclator, and a rather lengthy (and rather irrelevant) passage from Satyrus *On the Demes of the Alexandrians*. This last passage, quoted in II. 7, looks like a bit of erudition for erudition's sake, as do his references to Apollonides Horapius and Apollonius the Egyptian.

THE OLD TESTAMENT

The Old Testament was written by prophets who were inspired by God, and it consists of history, dealing with the past, law, dealing with the present, and prediction, dealing with the future. The most important parts of their message, now contained in the holy or divine scriptures, are the creation narrative in Genesis—which is not merely historical but contains theological and moral meanings as well—and the legislation promulgated in Exodus, with which the teaching of all the prophets and of the gospels is in agreement.

The story in Genesis is significant theologically because it describes the creation of the universe by the one God and also implies that he used his Logos as the instrument of creation and revelation. The various days of creation provided settings for events related to human nature and destiny, for the goal of creation was man, made in God's image and set in the earthly paradise to obey God's will. Man's disobedience brought the penalty of death upon him, but God always desires his repentance and, indeed, the whole subsequent history can be viewed

siècle' (Diss. Louvain, 1968), 144–91; also H. Chadwick, 'Florilegien', *Reallexikon für Antike und Christentum*, vii. 1131–59 (on Theophilus, 1143–4).

INTRODUCTION

as the story of God's reiterated calls to man to repent. Theophilus identifies Noah with Deucalion, not only to find the Greeks involuntarily agreeing with Genesis but also to point out that the Greek name contains an allusion to repentance (III. 19). 'Our patriarch' or 'forefather' Abraham (III. 24, 28) actually obeyed God (III. 9). Moses was the servant of God and delivered the law to the whole world, though especially to the Hebrews, also called Jews (III. 9). Later on, God's will was obeyed and proclaimed by David, 'our ancestor' and 'the patriarch' (III. 25, 28), and by Solomon, both king and prophet (III. 13). The reason for Theophilus' emphasis on David and Solomon is that their writings, the Psalms and the book of Proverbs, contain not only moral teaching but also doctrinal implications concerning the Logos and the Sophia of God. From the writings of the later prophets Theophilus provides quotations from Hosea, Joel, Habakkuk, Zechariah (the last of the prophets, III. 23), Malachi, Isaiah, Jeremiah (with an allusion to Baruch in III. 11), and Ezekiel. In III. 29 he mentions Daniel along with Jeremiah. All these men were prophets of the truth; all were 'illiterate men and shepherds and uneducated' (II. 35).

Revelation was not restricted to the Hebrew prophets, however, even though they were chronologically prior to all other writers. There was also the (Hellenistic Jewish) Sibyl, who was 'a prophetess for the Greeks and the other nations' (II. 36; cf. II. 3, 31). The quotations Theophilus provides from the *Sibylline Oracles* show that his own theology was deeply influenced by them. She too proclaimed the one God as creator, denounced idolatry, and called upon men to repent in order to escape judgement.

THE NEW TESTAMENT

All three books *Ad Autolycum* contain rather frequent allusions to the New Testament writings, but Theophilus' view of them becomes clear only in the second and the third. In II. 10 he clearly alludes to Luke 1: 35 as providing a title by which

the Logos is known, and in II. 22 he says that John (the evangelist) was inspired by the Spirit, presumably as the author of a book included in 'the holy scriptures'. This point is confirmed in III. 12, where the prophetic writings and the gospels are described as inspired by the one Spirit of God. The gospel from which Theophilus provides quotations is Matthew (III. 13–14). In addition, what has been commanded by the divine Word (or Logos) includes the content of 1 Timothy, Titus, and Romans (III. 14). It is therefore evident that Theophilus' New Testament canon includes not only at least three gospels but also the Pauline epistles including the Pastorals. He does not mention Paul any more than he mentions Jesus.[1]

BIBLICAL EXEGESIS

Theophilus' exegesis of the Old Testament is essentially Jewish in nature. It is primarily literal and, when it goes beyond the letter, looks for moral meanings and, in some instances, for prefigurations of Jewish and Christian teachings. The creation story in Genesis is literally true except in so far as it ascribes to God what must be meant in regard to God's Logos. Some of the prefigurations point toward baptism (II. 16) or toward the future resurrection (II. 14; cf. 26). Others contain theological meanings having to do with the triad God–Logos–Sophia (II. 15) or the sole rule of God (II. 28). We shall later discuss the way in which the decalogue is revised.

Like Philo, Theophilus also provides etymological explanations supposedly based on Hebrew words; thus Sabbath means 'seventh' (II. 12), Eden means 'delight' (II. 24), and Noah means 'rest' (III. 19). He goes beyond the Old Testament, however, in the direction of popular Greek etymologies when he explains the meaning of *theos* (I. 4), *thēria* (II. 17), Eva (II. 28), *drakōn* (II. 28), Orpheus (II. 30), and Deucalion (III. 19). Such etymologies go back to the *Cratylus* of Plato and—wherever Theophilus got them—were popular in his time.

[1] For other books see the index of Biblical Quotations and Allusions.

His exegetical methods, therefore, like his thought in general, reflect a confluence of Greek and Jewish ideas on the common ground of Hellenistic Judaism and Christianity.

THEOLOGY

The theology of Theophilus, as Lortz remarked, is the most radically monotheistic to be found among the Greek Christian apologists.[1] In part this feature is due to his attack on idolatry and polytheism; in part it is due to his rejection of Marcionite doctrines, notable in the second book; in part, and most important, it is due to his proximity to Hellenistic Judaism, with which most of his doctrine has close affinities.

His doctrine of God, set forth most fully in the first book, is largely philosophical and specifically Middle Platonic in content. God is described largely in negative terms; he is uncreated, immortal, immutable, incomprehensible, invisible, and not to be identified with his appellations. At the same time, he is the active and almighty creator who exercises providential care. Theophilus is willing to uphold biblical teaching against philosophers not only in regard to God as creator (II. 4) but also in regard to his anger and his goodness, kindness, and mercy (I. 3).

A philosophical axiom provides a bridge from the doctrine of God to the doctrine of the Logos or 'word' of God. Since a container must be greater than what it contains, God has no locus but is the locus of everything (II. 3, 22). Therefore if God is described as being in a place the description must refer to his Logos, not to him.

Theophilus' doctrine of the Logos is derived from Hellenistic Jewish sources and further developed in the light of Stoic and rhetorical refinements. A thought (*logos*) when expressed becomes a word (*logos*). Theophilus thus speaks of the Logos *endiathetos*, 'innate' in the bowels (II. 10) or heart (II. 22) of God as his Counsellor, Mind, and Intelligence (II. 22). Before creation the Logos as thought became the Logos *prophorikos*,

[1] J. Lortz, *Tertullian als Apologet*, ii (Münster, 1930), 5.

'expressed' as word (II. 10, 22). It was now Beginning, Spirit of God, Wisdom (Sophia), Power of the Most High, minister of creation, Light, Voice, Son, and Power of God. It is obvious that these titles are derived from the Old Testament, the gospels, and 1 Corinthians, and that the Logos is the pre-existent Christ.[1] As in the case of his doctrine of God, Theophilus is interpreting traditional Jewish and Christian materials in a framework provided by Philo and other Hellenistic Jews and further developed chiefly by his predecessor the apologist Justin. At a later date his interpretation was to prove unsatisfactory. When Paul of Samosata, bishop of Antioch, also held that originally the Logos was 'in God' (II. 22), his view was condemned as 'Jewish'.[2]

The extent to which Theophilus' theology actually was Jewish is indicated by the difficulties he experienced in finding a function for the Sophia or Wisdom of God. Sophia has no function distinct from that of the Logos, though it is one of the two 'hands of God' (II. 18) and with God and the Logos constitutes a triad (II. 15). Perhaps he uses the term because it is scriptural, but avoids developing it because it was being discussed at great length by contemporary Gnostics. Sometimes he identifies Sophia with the Holy Spirit (I. 7, 13), sometimes with the Logos (II. 10). To say that 'the essence of the Logos is the Spirit'[3] is to make his doctrine of the Spirit clearer than it is. Indeed, like other apologists he knows of two spirits: one is the Holy Spirit; the other is a more generalized *anima mundi* (cf. I. 5, 7; II. 13).

In the books to Autolycus Theophilus has little to say about either demons or angels. In part his silence is probably due to his emphasis on monotheism, in part to the fact that he has discussed them elsewhere. Thus he says that the gods of the pagans are demons (I. 10) and that the Muses who inspired the poets are demons too; demons in his own time have been exorcized (II. 8). The chief of the demons is Satan, who was originally an angel (II. 28). Theophilus thus knows a spiritual

---

[1] II. 10, 13, 22. [2] Epiphanius, *Haer.* lxv. 3.
[3] T. Rüsch, *Die Entstehung der Lehre vom Heiligen Geist* (Zurich, 1952), 79.

INTRODUCTION xvii

world of which he makes little mention in his apologetic books.

THEOPHILUS AS A JEWISH CHRISTIAN

Theophilus was undoubtedly a Christian, as is shown by his use of the word and by his references and allusions to New Testament books. He refers to 'holy churches' (II. 14) and to baptism as the 'bath of regeneration' which produces repentance, remission of sins, and God's blessing (II. 16). He speaks of 'gospels' (III. 12) and says that the evangelist John, like the prophets, was inspired by the Spirit (II. 22). His doctrine of the Logos, though essentially derived from Hellenistic Judaism, is related to Christian teaching about Christ (II. 10).

His understanding of the work of Jesus Christ can be recovered only from allusions, for like other apologists of his time he never openly speaks of him. Apparently he viewed Jesus as a second Adam, for of the first Adam he says that God intended him to progress, grow and become mature, ascend into heaven, and become God (II. 24). This picture may reflect the advancement and growth of Jesus (Luke 2: 40, 52), who was the mature or perfect man (Eph. 4: 13). Conceivably Theophilus made use of the Christological hymn in Philippians 2: 5–11: because of his obedience Jesus was exalted, perhaps reversing the disobedience and fall of Adam. For Theophilus, however, there is no special emphasis on the redemptive work of Christ. By disobedience Adam obtained death; by obedience to the will of God 'whoever will can obtain eternal life for himself' (II. 27; cf. Rom. 5: 14). Jesus was not the only prophet foretold by Moses (III. 11), nor was he the only Jewish leader who could heal all diseases (III. 21). His gospel was fully in accord with the law and the prophets (III. 12–15). His work was therefore like that of the other prophets inspired by the Spirit, sent to 'teach and remind' (John 14: 26) men of the content of the law (III. 11).

On the other hand, the primary statement of the law—the decalogue—has been tacitly modified, presumably in relation

to Jesus' teaching (III. 9). Theophilus omits the third and fourth commandments (though he alludes to their content elsewhere, II. 10, 12) and adds some 'judgements' from Exodus 21-3. The principle he must be applying is expressed in the *Epistle of Barnabas* x. 12: 'We are speaking [the commandments] as the Lord desired.' He may even share the view of the *Clementine Homilies* (iii. 49): 'By relying on the teaching of Jesus one will be able to differentiate what is true from what is false in the writings of the Old Testament.' Jesus had been condemned for blasphemy and criticized for violating the Sabbath rest. Theophilus therefore omitted the commandments in question.

In spite of this radical approach to the law Theophilus was strongly sympathetic with the Jewish people. The Hebrews, also called Jews, were the legitimate descendants of the patriarchs (III. 9), though they are under foreign domination because they did not repent (III. 11). The temple in Jerusalem was originally built in accordance with God's will (III. 25); priests were associated with it by God's command (III. 21). This is not to say that Theophilus would have favoured Jewish revolt against Roman authority. He insisted upon obedience to the emperor (I. 11) and claimed that Roman power was due to God (III. 27). But when Theophilus says that only Christians possess the truth (II. 33), the line between Christians and Jews is not absolutely fixed. In almost every respect his apology is a defence of Hellenistic Judaism as well as of Jewish Christianity.

One more point at which the close proximity of Judaism and Christianity at Antioch in his time is evident is in the praises of God as creator (I. 6-7). This passage consists almost entirely of biblical allusions, while at the same time it resembles the eucharistic thanksgiving to be found in the *Apostolic Constitutions* (vii. 34-5). We may venture to suppose[1] that Theophilus is echoing the eucharistic prayer which, as bishop of Antioch, he was accustomed to offer,[2] and that like the

---

[1] Cf. *Anglican Theological Review* xxx (1948), 91-4.
[2] For the thanksgiving cf. Justin, *Dial*. xli. 1.

prayers of the *Apostolic Constitutions* it is thoroughly Jewish in origin.[1]

TRANSMISSION OF THEOPHILUS' BOOKS

Within a very few years after Theophilus wrote, echoes of his second book occur in the treatise *Adversus haereses* by Irenaeus, bishop of Lyons. Thereafter, the second and third books were used by Tertullian of Carthage in his *Apologeticum* (197) and *Adversus Marcionem* (213). The first book is reflected in Novatian's treatise *De trinitate* (c. 255), while Methodius, toward the end of the third century, made use of the second. The second and third books are used by Lactantius, early in the fourth century, while Eusebius of Caesarea explicitly refers to the three books *To Autolycus*.[2] As far as our evidence goes, we can say that they were popular among early Christian writers, although there is no trace of their use at Alexandria.

Several excerpts from the treatise are to be found in a catena ultimately dependent upon Procopius of Gaza (5th–6th century)[3] and in the *Sacra parallela* ascribed to John of Damascus (8th century).[4] These excerpts contain theological modifications of what Theophilus wrote, however, and are of no value in establishing his text. For this we are dependent upon a single manuscript now at Venice and once the property of Cardinal Bessarion. This is Codex Marcianus gr. 496 (folios 160 verso—185 recto), written in the late tenth century or the early eleventh, and later corrected for orthography. Two sixteenth-century copies of this manuscript provide no independent testimony. One, now at Paris in the Bibliothèque nationale (Cod. Paris. gr. 887), contains only the third book, found in a collection of treatises on the Trinity. It is fairly likely that the copyist, the monk Pachomius (Constantinus

[1] On this point cf. W. Bousset in *Nachrichten . . . Göttingen, phil.-hist. Klasse* (1915), 435–85; E. R. Goodenough, *By Light Light* (New Haven, 1935), 306–58.
[2] For details cf. *Vigiliae Christianae* vi (1952), 146–59.
[3] M. Richard in *Revue biblique* xlvii (1938), 387–97.
[4] K. Holl in *Texte und Untersuchungen* xx. 2 (1899), 56–7 (nos. 131–4).

Palaeocappa), was instructed to copy the second book, with its reference to the triad (II. 15), but made a mistake. The manuscript comes from the year 1540. The other, now in the Bodleian Library at Oxford (Bodl. MS. Auct. E. I. 11), is complete; it was probably copied between 1541 and 1546 by Bartholomaios Brixianos. The first edition of Theophilus' work in 1546 was based on a copy of the Venice manuscript, perhaps the one made by Brixianos.

Since the only primary source for Theophilus' text is provided by the Venice manuscript, it is unfortunate that omissions from it are obvious at several points. At the beginning of II. 11, for example, eleven words from Genesis are missing, as we know because a comment on them is then provided. At the end of II. 37 or the beginning of II. 38 a quotation or two from the poets seems to have dropped out. In III. 12 the promised quotations from the gospels are lacking, and in III. 16 the quotation from Plato as given in the manuscript does not prove Theophilus' point. As a less significant example of the same tendency we may note the quotation from Isaiah at the beginning of II. 38: the full text of the prophet proves Theophilus' point, not what is in the Venice manuscript.

Because all these omissions occur in regard to quotations, it is possible that they are due not to later copyists of his work but to scribal assistants who, like those of Eusebius of Caesarea,[1] supplied some or all of the quotations. We do not know enough about Theophilus' method of composition to be sure. Copyists certainly made mistakes, for example at the end of II. 6. Not surprisingly, many errors occur toward the end of the third book, especially in III. 27, where the lengths of the reigns of the Roman emperors are being listed. An editor is tempted to let the figures stand as they are in the Venice manuscript, but the presence of six correct totals (Augustus, Otho, Vespasian, Nerva, Hadrian, Marcus Aurelius) and of four more figures where emendations are obvious (Tiberius, Galba, Titus, Antoninus Pius) suggests that further emending

[1] Cf. H. J. Lawlor–J. E. L. Oulton, *Eusebius: the Ecclesiastical History* (London, 1928), ii. 24–7.

INTRODUCTION   xxi

should be undertaken.[1] In addition, the whole chronological scheme of Theophilus makes emendation necessary. It seems fairly clear that Theophilus' authority Chryseros did not correlate the kinds of calculations used in his sources. Sometimes the length of a reign is determined by subtracting the beginning date from the end; sometimes this figure is stated 'inclusively', with the days at the beginning and the end; sometimes it is given 'exclusively', with both such days left out.[2] Thus in the case of Julius Caesar the emended figure (3 years, 7 months, 6 days) is based on the 3 years, 4 months, 6 days of the manuscript but changed to allow for simple subtraction when moving from Pharsalus (9 August 48) to the Ides of March in 44 (without allowing for the calendar change in 46). The figure of 56 years, 4 months, 1 day for Augustus is the 'exclusive' total from his acclamation as *imperator* on 16 April 43 to his death on 19 August, A.D. 14. We have provided another 'exclusive' figure for Tiberius, and then figures derived by subtraction for the later emperors to Vitellius. The manuscript itself provides an 'exclusive' and correct figure for Vespasian. From Titus to Trajan obvious errors are based on 'inclusive' figures; the reigns of Hadrian and Antoninus Pius must be 'exclusive'; and the reign of Marcus Aurelius is based on subtraction. It may be surprising to find all three methods being used in the same work, but both Josephus and Dio Cassius reflect similar inconsistencies.

EDITIONS

The first edition of Theophilus was published at Zurich in 1546 by Joannes Frisius, who used a manuscript supplied by Conrad Gesner and a Latin version made by Conrad Clauser. The Latin title of his book is this: *Hoc volumine continentur: Sententiarum sive capitum . . . Tomi tres, per Antonium et Maximum monachos olim collecti . . . Theophili sexti Antiochensis episcopi de*

[1] It might be supposed that the text could be corrected from the similar list in Clement, *Str.* i. 144. 4; but that list itself requires emendation.
[2] Cf. L. Holzapfel, 'Römische Kaiserdaten', *Klio* xii (1912), 483-93; xiii (1913), 289-304; xv (1918), 99-121; xvii (1921), 74-93.

Deo et fide Christianorum contra Gentes Institutionum libri tres aa Autolycum . . . The book also contained the first edition of Tatian.

Another important edition, full of conjectural readings generally regarded as excessively ingenious, was made by John Fell, bishop of Oxford, and published at Oxford in 1684. Its title is *S. Theophili Episcopi Antiocheni ad Autolycum libri III recogniti et notis illustrati*.

At Hamburg in 1724 there appeared the excellent edition of J. C. Wolf, *Theophili, Episcopi Antiocheni, Libri III Ad Autolycum graece ad fidem Ms. Bodleiani et ex parte Regii Parisiens. denuo recogniti, et pluribus in locis castigati, versione latina, frequenter emendata, notisque tum aliorum tum suis instructi*. . . . Eighteen years later Prudentius Maran at Paris included the work of Theophilus in his valuable *S. P. N. Justini philosophi et martyris opera quae exstant omnia*, though he did not make direct use of the manuscripts.

The edition by W. G. Humphry, *Theophili Episcopi Antiochensis libri tres ad Autolycum* (Cambridge, 1852), is significant chiefly for its acceptance of conjectures made by Wolf.

Up to this time the Venice manuscript had not been employed by any editor of Theophilus, and the edition of J. C. T. Otto, published at Jena in 1861, thus marked a significant forward step. As the eighth volume of Otto's *Corpus apologetarum christianorum saeculi secundi*, it bears the title *Theophili episcopi Antiocheni Ad Autolycum libri tres*. It is marked by judicious use of all the earlier materials and remains permanently valuable because of the editor's accuracy and his thorough acquaintance with the Christian apologists. His reliance on the Venice manuscript was not misplaced.

Three relatively modern editions are based on Otto's text. These were produced by S. Frasca (*S. Giustino Martire, Apologie*; *S. Teofilo Antiocheno, I Tre Libri Ad Autolico*, in the collection *Corona Patrum Salesiana*, Serie greca, iii, Torino, 1938), by E. Rapisarda (*Teofilo di Antiochia, I Tre Libri ad Autolico*, in the series *Scrittori greci commentati per le scuole*, 97, Torino, 1939, with a few readings from the Venice manuscript), and by

G. Bardy (*Théophile d'Antioche, Trois Livres à Autolycus*, in the series *Sources chrétiennes*, 20, Paris, 1948, with a French translation based on Maran's Latin version).

The present edition follows Otto in large measure, though use has been made throughout of the Venice manuscript by means of photographs. The editor has ventured to accept a considerable number of emendations, especially in the third book, in order to make sense of what Theophilus wrote. No attention is paid to the correction of errors due to itacism, faulty word-division, and the like. The readings of the Bodleian and Paris manuscripts have rarely been mentioned because they are secondary to the Venice manuscript. The readings found in catenas have no value for restablishing Theophilus' text.

The headings supplied for various chapters have no manuscript authority but follow the model provided in the English translation by Marcus Dods in the *Ante-Nicene Christian Library* (edited by A. Roberts and J. Donaldson), iii, Edinburgh, 1868.

THE CHRONOLOGY OF THEOPHILUS

A. From the creation to the deluge, 2,242 years

Adam	230	Gen. 5: 3
Seth	205	Gen. 5: 6
Enos	190	Gen. 5: 9
Kainan	170	Gen. 5: 12
Maleleel	165	Gen. 5: 15
Iareth	162	Gen. 5: 18
Enoch	165	Gen. 5: 21
Mathousala	167	Gen. 5: 25 (Cod. A, first hand)
Lamech	188	Gen. 5: 28
Noah	600	Gen. 7: 6

B. From the deluge to the time when Abraham had issue, 1,036 years

Arphaxath	135	Gen. 11: 12
Sala	130	Gen. 11: 14
Heber	134	Gen. 11: 16
Phaleg	130	Gen. 11: 18
Ragau	132	Gen. 11: 20
Seruch	130	Gen. 11: 22

xxiv INTRODUCTION

Nachor	75	Gen. 11: 24 (Lucianic text)
Tharra	70	Gen. 11: 26
Abraham	100	Gen. 21: 5

C. From Isaac to the death of Moses, 660 years (III. 28)

Isaac	60	Gen. 25: 26
Jacob	130	Gen. 47: 28
Sojourn in Egypt	430	Exod. 12: 40 (Cod. A)
Wilderness	40	Num. 14: 33; Deut. ii. 7

D. From the rule of Joshua to the death of David, 498 years (III. 28)

Joshua	27	Clement, *Str.* i. 109. 3
K. of Mesopotamia	8	Judges 3: 8
Gothoneel	40	Judges 3: 11
Eklon (of Moab)	18	Judges 3: 14
Aoth	8	Cf. Judges 3: 30 (80 years of peace)
Foreigners	20	Judges 4: 3
Deborra	40	Judges 5: 31
Midianites	7	Judges 6: 1
Gideon	40	Judges 8: 28
Abimelech	3	Judges 9: 22
Thola	23	Judges 10: 2
Iair	22	Judges 10: 3
Philistines	18	Judges 10: 8
Iephtha	6	Judges 12: 7 (Cod. A)
Esbon	7	Judges 12: 9
Ailon	10	Judges 12: 11
Abdon	8	Judges 12: 14
Foreigners	40	Judges 13: 1; Josephus, *Ant.* v. 275
Samson	20	Judges 16: 31; Josephus, *Ant.* v. 316
Peace	40	(See Eli and Saul below)
Samera	1	Cf. Samegar, Judges 3: 31
Eli	20	1 Reg. (1 Sam.) 4: 18 (40: Hebrew and Josephus, *Ant.* v. 359)
Samuel	12	Josephus, *Ant.* vi. 294
Saul	20	Josephus, *Ant.* vi. 378 (40: Acts 13: 21)
David	40	3 Reg. (1 Kings) 2: 11; Josephus, *Ant.* vii. 389

E. From the death of David to the Babylonian exile, 518 years, 6 months, 10 days

Solomon	40	3 Reg. 11: 42 (80: Josephus, *Ant.* viii. 211)
Roboam	17	3 Reg. 14: 21; 2 Paral. (2 Chron.) 12: 13
Abias	7	3 Reg. 15: 2 (6 years); 2 Paral. 13: 2 (3 years)

Asa	41	3 Reg. 15: 10; 2 Paral. 16: 13 (Cod. A)
Iosaphat	25	3 Reg. 16: 28; 2 Paral. 20: 31
Ioram	8	4 Reg. 8: 17; 2 Paral. 21: 5, 20
Ochozias	1	4 Reg. 8: 26; 2 Paral. 22: 2
Gotholia	6	4 Reg. 11: 3; 2 Paral. 22: 12
Ioas	40	4 Reg. 12: 1; 2 Paral. 24: 1
Amesias	39	4 Reg. 14: 2 (29 years); so 2 Paral. 25: 1
Ozias	52	4 Reg. 15: 2; 2 Paral. 26: 3
Ioatham	16	4 Reg. 15: 33; 2 Paral. 27: 1
Achaz	17	4 Reg. 16: 2 (16 years); so 2 Paral. 28: 1
Ezechias	29	4 Reg. 18: 2; 2 Paral. 29: 1
Manasses	55	4 Reg. 21: 1; 2 Paral. 33: 1
Amos	2	4 Reg. 21: 19; 2 Paral. 33: 21
Iosias	31	4 Reg. 22: 1; 2 Paral. 34: 1
Ochas	3 months	4 Reg. 23: 31; 2 Paral. 36: 2
Ioakeim	11	4 Reg. 23: 36; 2 Paral. 36: 5
Another I.	3 months, 10 days	2 Paral. 36: 9; cf. 4 Reg. 24: 8
Sedekias	11	4 Reg. 24: 18; 2 Paral. 36: 11
Exile	70	2 Paral. 36: 21

F. From the reign of Cyrus to the death of Marcus Aurelius, 741 years

To death of Cyrus	28
Reign of Tarquin	25
Annual magistrates	463

Julius Caesar	3+	7 months	+	6 days	
Augustus	56+	4	+	1	
Tiberius	22+	6	+	26	
Gaius	3+	10	+	7	
Claudius	13+	8	+	20	
Nero	13+	7	+	27	
Galba	—	7	+	6	
Otho	—	3	+	5	
Vitellius	—	8	+	2	
Vespasian	9+	11	+	22	
Titus	2+	2	+	20	
Domitian	15	—	+	5	
Nerva	1+	4	+	10	
Trajan	19+	6	+	14	
Hadrian	20+	10	+	28	
Antonius Pius	22+	7	+	26	
Verus = M. Aurelius	19	—	+	10	
	217+100		+235	= 225+11+25	

ABBREVIATIONS AND EDITIONS

Alexandre: as cited by Geffcken (q.v.).
Bergk, T., *Poetae Lyrici Graeci*, ed. 5, i, Leipzig, 1900.
Castalio: as cited by Geffcken (q.v.)
Clauser, C. Latin version in edition of 1546; see page xxi.
Diels, H., *Doxographi Graeci*, Berlin, 1879; or cited by Nauck (q.v.).
Ducaeus (Fronto Le Duc): as cited by Otto (q.v.).
Einarson, B. Emendations in correspondence with Grant.
Fell, J. Edition of 1684; see page xxii.
FGrHist See Jacoby.
FHG C. Müller, *Fragmenta Historicorum Graecorum*, 5 vols., Paris, 1848–74.
Friedlieb: as cited by Geffcken (q.v.).
Geffcken, J., *Die Oracula Sibyllina*, Leipzig, 1902.
Gesner, C. Edition of 1546; see page xxi.
Grant, R. M., 'The Textual Tradition of Theophilus of Antioch', *Vigiliae Christianae*, vi (1952), 146–59; 'Notes on the Text of Theophilus Ad Autolycum III', ibid., xii (1958), 136–44.
Humphry, W. G. Edition of 1852; see page xxii.
Jacoby, F., *Die Fragmente der griechischen Historiker*, Berlin, 1923–30; revised edition, Leiden, 1957– .
Kern, O., *Orphicorum Fragmenta*, Berlin, 1922.
Kock, T., *Comicorum Graecorum Fragmenta*, Leipzig, 1884.
Loofs, F., *Theophilus von Antiochien adversus Marcionem und die anderen theologischen Quellen bei Irenaeus (Texte und Untersuchungen*, xlvi. 2), Leipzig, 1930.
Maran, P. Edition of 1742; see page xxii.
Meineke, A., *Fragmenta Comicorum Graecorum*, i, Berlin, 1839.
Nauck, A., *Tragicorum Graecorum Fragmenta*, ed. 2, Leipzig, 1889.
Nautin, P., 'Notes critiques sur Théophile d'Antioche, Ad Autolycum Lib. II', *Vigiliae Christianae*, xi (1957), 212–25.
Nolte, J. H., 'Conjecturae et emendationes ad Theophili Libr. ad Autolyc.', Migne, *Patrologia Graeca* vi. 1759–62.
Opsopoeus: as cited by Geffcken (q.v.).
Otto, J. C. T. Edition of 1861; see page xxii.

RE Pauly–Wissowa, *Realencyclopädie der classischen Altertumswissenschaft.*

Roscher, W. H.: as cited by O. Gross, *Die Gotteslehre des Theophilus von Antiocheia*, Chemnitz, 1896.

Rzach: as cited by Geffcken (q.v.).

Stob. C. Wachsmuth–O. Hense, *Joannis Stobaei Anthologium*, 5 vols., Berlin, 1884–1912.

SVF H. von Arnim, *Stoicorum Veterum Fragmenta*, 3 vols., Leipzig, 1903–5.

Thienemann: as cited by Otto (q.v.).

Usener, H., *Epicurea*, Leipzig, 1887.

Valckenaer: notes in 1546 edition in the University Library, Leiden.

Wilamowitz: as cited by Geffcken (q.v.).

Wolf, J. C. Edition of 1724; see page xxii.

Zeegers-Vander Vorst, N., 'Les Citations des poètes grecs chez les apologistes chrétiens du iie siècle', Diss. Louvain, 1968.

SIGLA

V   Cod. Marcianus (Venetus graecus) 496, s. xi
V² corrector of Cod. Marcianus 496, s. xv
B   Cod. Bodleianus Auct. E. 1. 11, s. xvi
P   Cod. Parisinus graecus 887, anno 1540

TEXT AND TRANSLATION

ΘΕΟΦΙΛΟΥ ΠΡΟΣ ΑΥΤΟΛΥΚΟΝ

τὸ α'[1]

1. Στωμύλον μὲν οὖν στόμα καὶ φράσις εὐεπὴς τέρψιν παρέχει καὶ ἔπαινον πρὸς κενὴν δόξαν ἀθλίοις ἀνθρώποις ἔχουσι τὸν νοῦν κατεφθαρμένον· ὁ δὲ τῆς ἀληθείας ἐραστὴς οὐ προσέχει λόγοις μεμιαμμένοις, ἀλλὰ ἐξετάζει τὸ ἔργον τοῦ λόγου τί καὶ ὁποῖόν ἐστιν. ἐπειδὴ οὖν, ὦ ἑταῖρε, κατέπληξάς με λόγοις κενοῖς καυχησάμενος ἐν τοῖς θεοῖς σου τοῖς λιθίνοις καὶ ξυλίνοις, ἐλατοῖς τε καὶ χωνευτοῖς καὶ πλαστοῖς καὶ γραπτοῖς, οἳ οὔτε βλέπουσιν οὔτε ἀκούουσιν (εἰσὶ γὰρ εἴδωλα καὶ ἔργα χειρῶν ἀνθρώπων), ἔτι δὲ φής με καὶ χριστιανὸν ὡς κακὸν τοὔνομα φοροῦντα, ἐγὼ μὲν οὖν ὁμολογῶ εἶναι χριστιανός, καὶ φορῶ τὸ θεοφιλὲς ὄνομα τοῦτο ἐλπίζων εὔχρηστος εἶναι τῷ θεῷ. οὐ γὰρ ὡς σὺ ὑπολαμβάνεις, χαλεπὸν εἶναι τοὔνομα τοῦ θεοῦ, οὕτως ἔχει· ἴσως δὲ ἔτι αὐτὸς σὺ ἄχρηστος ὢν τῷ θεῷ περὶ[1] τοῦ θεοῦ οὕτως φρονεῖς.

2. Ἀλλὰ καὶ ἐὰν φῇς· "Δεῖξόν μοι τὸν θεόν σου", κἀγώ σοι εἴποιμι ἄν· "Δεῖξόν μοι τὸν ἄνθρωπόν σου κἀγώ σοι δείξω τὸν θεόν μου." ἐπεὶ δεῖξον βλέποντας τοὺς ὀφθαλμοὺς τῆς ψυχῆς σου, καὶ τὰ ὦτα τῆς καρδίας σου ἀκούοντα. ὥσπερ γὰρ οἱ βλέποντες τοῖς ὀφθαλμοῖς τοῦ σώματος κατανοοῦσι τὴν τοῦ βίου καὶ ἐπίγειον πραγματείαν, ἅμα δοκιμάζοντες τὰ διαφέροντα, ἤτοι φῶς ἢ σκότος, ἢ λευκὸν ἢ μέλαν, ἢ ἀειδὲς ἢ εὔμορφον, ἢ εὔρυθμον καὶ εὔμετρον ἢ ἄρυθμον καὶ ἄμετρον ἢ ὑπέρμετρον ἢ κόλουρον, ὁμοίως δὲ καὶ τὰ ὑπ' ἀκοὴν πίπτοντα, ἢ ὀξύφωνα ἢ βαρύφωνα ἢ ἡδύφωνα, οὕτως ἔχοι ἂν καὶ περὶ τὰ ὦτα τῆς καρδίας καὶ τοὺς ὀφθαλμοὺς τοὺς τῆς ψυχῆς δύνασθαι θεὸν θεάσασθαι. βλέπεται γὰρ θεὸς τοῖς δυναμένοις αὐτὸν ὁρᾶν, ἔπαν ἔχωσι τοὺς ὀφθαλμοὺς ἀνεῳγμένους τῆς ψυχῆς. πάντες μὲν γὰρ ἔχουσι τοὺς ὀφθαλμούς, ἀλλὰ ἔνιοι ὑποκεχυμένους καὶ μὴ βλέποντας τὸ φῶς τοῦ ἡλίου. καὶ οὐ παρὰ τὸ μὴ βλέπειν τοὺς τυφλοὺς ἤδη καὶ οὐκ ἔστιν τὸ φῶς τοῦ ἡλίου φαῖνον, ἀλλὰ ἑαυτοὺς

---

[1] τὸ α'] Otto; cf. II. 1; III. 18: om. V   **1.** [1] περὶ] V²: om. V

THEOPHILUS TO AUTOLYCUS

Book I

1. Fluent speech and euphonious diction produce delight and praise—resulting in empty glory, among wretched men who have a depraved mind [cf. 2 Tim. 3: 8].[1] The man who loves truth, however, pays no attention to defiled language but examines the fact behind the word to see what it is and what it means. Since you, my friend, have attacked me with empty words by boasting of your gods of stone and wood, forged and cast and moulded and painted—which *neither see nor hear*, for they are *idols* and the *works of men's hands* [Ps. 113: 12–14]—and furthermore you call me a Christian as if I were bearing an evil name, I acknowledge that I am a Christian. I bear this name beloved by God in the hope of being useful[2] to God [cf. Philemon 11]. It is not the case, as you suppose, that the name of God is offensive. Perhaps you yourself are of no use[2] to God and therefore think about God in this way.

The Vision of God

2. But if you should say, 'Show me your God', I may reply to you, 'Show me your man and I will show you my God.' You must show me that the eyes of your soul can see and that the ears of your heart can hear. For just as those who see with bodily eyes contemplate the affairs of life on earth and distinguish things that differ [cf. Rom. 2: 18; Phil. 1: 10], such as light from darkness, white from black, ugly from beautiful, rhythmical and metrical from unrhythmical and unmetrical, beyond the metre from truncated; and similarly with things that fall under the sense of hearing, sounds that are shrill or deep or sweet; just so, the ears of the heart and the eyes of the soul are potentially capable of beholding God. For God is seen by those who are capable of seeing him, once they have the eyes of the soul opened. All men have eyes, but some have eyes which are hooded by cataracts and do not see the light of the sun. Just because the blind do not see, however, the light of

---

1. [1] Theophilus begins with a typical rhetorician's flourish but turns it into a typical early Christian condemnation of rhetoric.

[2] This is a play on words including *chrēstos*, pronounced like *christos*.

αἰτιάσθωσαν οἱ τυφλοὶ καὶ τοὺς ἑαυτῶν ὀφθαλμούς. οὕτως καὶ σύ, ὦ ἄνθρωπε, ἔχεις ὑποκεχυμένους τοὺς ὀφθαλμοὺς τῆς ψυχῆς σου ὑπὸ τῶν ἁμαρτημάτων καὶ τῶν πράξεών σου τῶν πονηρῶν. Ὥσπερ ἔσοπτρον ἐστιλβωμένον, οὕτως δεῖ τὸν ἄνθρωπον ἔχειν καθαρὰν ψυχήν. ἔπαν οὖν ᾖ ἰὸς ἐν τῷ ἐσόπτρῳ, οὐ δύναται ὁρᾶσθαι τὸ πρόσωπον τοῦ ἀνθρώπου ἐν τῷ ἐσόπτρῳ· οὕτως καὶ ὅταν ᾖ ἁμαρτία ἐν τῷ ἀνθρώπῳ, οὐ δύναται ὁ τοιοῦτος ἄνθρωπος θεωρεῖν τὸν θεόν. δεῖξον οὖν καὶ σὺ σεαυτόν, εἰ οὐκ εἶ μοιχός, εἰ οὐκ εἶ πόρνος, εἰ οὐκ εἶ κλέπτης, εἰ οὐκ εἶ ἅρπαξ, εἰ οὐκ εἶ ἀποστερητής, εἰ οὐκ εἶ ἀρσενοκοίτης, εἰ οὐκ εἶ ὑβριστής, εἰ οὐκ εἶ λοίδορος, εἰ οὐκ ὀργίλος, εἰ οὐ φθονερός, εἰ οὐκ ἀλαζών, εἰ οὐχ ὑπερόπτης, εἰ οὐ πλήκτης, εἰ οὐ φιλάργυρος, εἰ οὐ γονεῦσιν ἀπειθής, εἰ οὐ τὰ τέκνα σου πωλεῖς. τοῖς γὰρ ταῦτα πράσσουσιν ὁ θεὸς οὐκ ἐμφανίζεται, ἐὰν μὴ πρῶτον ἑαυτοὺς καθαρίσωσιν ἀπὸ παντὸς μολυσμοῦ.

Καὶ σοὶ οὖν ἅπαντα ἐπισκοτεῖ, καθάπερ ὕλης ἐπιφορὰ ἐπὰν γένηται τοῖς ὀφθαλμοῖς πρὸς τὸ μὴ δύνασθαι ἀτενίσαι τὸ φῶς τοῦ ἡλίου· οὕτως καὶ σοί,[1] ὦ ἄνθρωπε, ἐπισκοτοῦσιν αἱ ἀσέβειαι πρὸς τὸ μὴ δύνασθαί σε ὁρᾶν τὸν θεόν.

3. Ἐρεῖς οὖν μοι· "Σὺ ὁ βλέπων διήγησαί μοι τὸ εἶδος τοῦ θεοῦ." ἄκουε, ὦ ἄνθρωπε· τὸ μὲν εἶδος τοῦ θεοῦ ἄρρητον καὶ ἀνέκφραστόν ἐστιν, μὴ δυνάμενον ὀφθαλμοῖς σαρκίνοις ὁραθῆναι. δόξῃ γάρ ἐστιν ἀχώρητος, μεγέθει ἀκατάληπτος, ὕψει ἀπερινόητος, ἰσχύϊ ἀσύγκριτος, σοφίᾳ ἀσυμβίβαστος, ἀγαθωσύνῃ ἀμίμητος, καλοποιΐᾳ ἀνεκδιήγητος. εἰ γὰρ φῶς αὐτὸν εἴπω, ποίημα αὐτοῦ λέγω· εἰ λόγον εἴπω, ἀρχὴν αὐτοῦ λέγω· νοῦν ἐὰν εἴπω, φρόνησιν αὐτοῦ λέγω· πνεῦμα ἐὰν εἴπω, ἀναπνοὴν αὐτοῦ λέγω· σοφίαν ἐὰν εἴπω, γέννημα αὐτοῦ λέγω· ἰσχὺν ἐὰν εἴπω, κράτος αὐτοῦ λέγω· δύναμιν ἐὰν εἴπω, ἐνέργειαν αὐτοῦ λέγω· πρόνοιαν ἐὰν εἴπω, ἀγαθωσύνην αὐτοῦ λέγω· βασιλείαν ἐὰν εἴπω, δόξαν αὐτοῦ λέγω· κύριον ἐὰν εἴπω, κριτὴν αὐτὸν λέγω· κριτὴν ἐὰν εἴπω, δίκαιον αὐτὸν λέγω· πατέρα ἐὰν εἴπω, τὰ πάντα αὐτὸν λέγω· πῦρ ἐὰν εἴπω, τὴν ὀργὴν αὐτοῦ λέγω.

Ἐρεῖς οὖν μοι· " Ὀργίζεται θεός;" μάλιστα· ὀργίζεται τοῖς τὰ φαῦλα πράσσουσιν, ἀγαθὸς δὲ καὶ χρηστὸς καὶ οἰκτίρμων ἐστὶν ἐπὶ τοὺς ἀγαπῶντας καὶ φοβουμένους αὐτόν· παιδευτὴς γάρ ἐστιν τῶν θεοσεβῶν καὶ πατὴρ τῶν δικαίων, κριτὴς δὲ καὶ κολαστὴς τῶν ἀσεβῶν.

2. [1] σοί] Gesner: σύ V

the sun does not fail to shine; the blind must blame themselves and their eyes. So you also, O man, have cataracts over the eyes of your soul because of your sins and wicked deeds.

Just as a man must keep a mirror polished, so he must keep his soul pure. When there is rust on a mirror, a man's face cannot be seen in it; so also when there is sin in a man, such a man cannot see God.[1] So show yourself to me. Are you not an adulterer? a fornicator? a thief? a swindler? a robber? a pederast? insolent? a reviler? quick-tempered? envious? a braggart? disdainful? a bully? avaricious? disobedient to parents? one who sells his children? God does not become visible to those who do such things unless they first *cleanse themselves from all defilement* [2 Cor. 7: 1].

All this brings darkness upon you, just as when a flux of matter comes over the eyes and they cannot see the light of the sun. So also, O man, your ungodliness brings darkness upon you and you cannot see God.

The Nature of God

3. You will say to me, then, 'Since you see, describe the form of God to me.' Hear me, O man: the form of God is ineffable and inexpressible, since it cannot be seen with merely human eyes. For he is in glory uncontainable, in greatness incomprehensible, in loftiness inconceivable, in strength incomparable, in wisdom unteachable, in goodness inimitable, in beneficence inexpressible. For if I call him Light, I speak of his creature; if I call him Logos, I speak of his beginning; if I call him Mind, I speak of his intelligence; if I call him Spirit, I speak of his breath; if I call him Sophia (Wisdom), I speak of his offspring; if I call him Strength, I speak of his might; if I call him Power, I speak of his energy; if I call him Providence, I speak of his goodness; if I call him Kingdom, I speak of his glory; if I call him Lord, I speak of him as judge; if I call him Judge, I speak of him as just; if I call him Father, I speak of him as all things; if I call him Fire, I speak of his wrath.

You will say to me, then: 'Is God angry?' Certainly: he is angry with those who do evil deeds, but good and kind and merciful toward those who love and fear him. He is the instructor of the godly and the father of the righteous, but the judge and punisher of the ungodly.

2. [1] The 'pure in heart', therefore, can 'see God' (Matt. 5: 8).

4. Ἄναρχος δέ ἐστιν, ὅτι ἀγένητός ἐστιν· ἀναλλοίωτος δέ, καθότι ἀθάνατός ἐστιν. θεὸς δὲ λέγεται διὰ τὸ τεθεικέναι τὰ πάντα ἐπὶ τῇ ἑαυτοῦ ἀσφαλείᾳ, καὶ διὰ τὸ θέειν· τὸ δὲ θέειν ἐστὶν τὸ τρέχειν καὶ κινεῖν καὶ ἐνεργεῖν καὶ τρέφειν καὶ προνοεῖν καὶ κυβερνᾶν καὶ ζωοποιεῖν τὰ πάντα. κύριος δέ ἐστιν διὰ τὸ κυριεύειν αὐτὸν τῶν ὅλων, πατὴρ δὲ διὰ τὸ εἶναι αὐτὸν πρὸ τῶν ὅλων, δημιουργὸς δὲ καὶ ποιητὴς διὰ τὸ αὐτὸν εἶναι κτίστην καὶ ποιητὴν τῶν ὅλων, ὕψιστος δὲ διὰ τὸ εἶναι αὐτὸν ἀνώτερον τῶν πάντων, παντοκράτωρ δὲ ὅτι αὐτὸς τὰ πάντα κρατεῖ καὶ ἐμπεριέχει.

Τὰ γὰρ ὕψη τῶν οὐρανῶν καὶ τὰ βάθη τῶν ἀβύσσων καὶ τὰ πέρατα τῆς οἰκουμένης ἐν τῇ χειρὶ αὐτοῦ ἐστιν, καὶ οὐκ ἔστιν τόπος τῆς καταπαύσεως αὐτοῦ. οὐρανοὶ μὲν γὰρ ἔργον αὐτοῦ εἰσιν, γῆ ποίημα αὐτοῦ ἐστιν, θάλασσα κτίσμα αὐτοῦ ἐστιν, ἄνθρωπος πλάσμα καὶ εἰκὼν αὐτοῦ ἐστιν, ἥλιος καὶ σελήνη καὶ ἀστέρες στοιχεῖα αὐτοῦ εἰσιν, εἰς σημεῖα καὶ εἰς καιροὺς καὶ εἰς ἡμέρας καὶ εἰς ἐνιαυτοὺς γεγονότα, πρὸς ὑπηρεσίαν καὶ δουλείαν ἀνθρώπων· καὶ τὰ πάντα ὁ θεὸς ἐποίησεν ἐξ οὐκ ὄντων εἰς τὸ εἶναι, ἵνα διὰ τῶν ἔργων γινώσκηται καὶ νοηθῇ τὸ μέγεθος αὐτοῦ.

5. Καθάπερ γὰρ ψυχὴ ἐν ἀνθρώπῳ οὐ βλέπεται, ἀόρατος οὖσα ἀνθρώποις, διὰ δὲ τῆς κινήσεως τοῦ σώματος νοεῖται ἡ ψυχή, οὕτως ἔχοι ἂν καὶ τὸν θεὸν μὴ δύνασθαι ὁραθῆναι ὑπὸ ὀφθαλμῶν ἀνθρωπίνων, διὰ δὲ τῆς προνοίας καὶ τῶν ἔργων αὐτοῦ βλέπεται καὶ νοεῖται. ὃν τρόπον γὰρ καὶ πλοῖον θεασάμενός τις ἐν θαλάσσῃ κατηρτισμένον καὶ τρέχον καὶ κατερχόμενον εἰς λιμένα δῆλον ὅτι ἡγήσεται εἶναι ἐν αὐτῷ κυβερνήτην τὸν κυβερνῶντα αὐτό, οὕτως δεῖ νοεῖν εἶναι τὸν θεὸν κυβερνήτην τῶν ὅλων, εἰ καὶ οὐ θεωρεῖται ὀφθαλμοῖς σαρκίνοις διὰ τὸ αὐτὸν ἀχώρητον εἶναι. εἰ γὰρ τῷ ἡλίῳ ἐλαχίστῳ ὄντι στοιχείῳ οὐ δύναται ἄνθρωπος ἀτενίσαι διὰ τὴν ὑπερβάλλουσαν θέρμην καὶ δύναμιν, πῶς οὐχὶ μᾶλλον τῇ τοῦ θεοῦ δόξῃ ἀνεκφράστῳ οὔσῃ ἄνθρωπος θνητὸς οὐ δύναται ἀντωπῆσαι; ὃν τρόπον γὰρ ῥόα, ἔχουσα φλοιὸν τὸν περιέχοντα αὐτήν, ἔνδον ἔχει μονὰς καὶ θήκας πολλὰς διαχωριζομένας διὰ ὑμένων καὶ πολλοὺς κόκκους ἔχει τοὺς ἐν αὐτῇ κατοικοῦντας, οὕτως ἡ πᾶσα κτίσις περιέχεται ὑπὸ πνεύματος θεοῦ, καὶ τὸ πνεῦμα τὸ περιέχον σὺν τῇ κτίσει περιέχεται ὑπὸ χειρὸς θεοῦ· ὥσπερ οὖν ὁ κόκκος τῆς ῥόας

4. He has no beginning because he is uncreated; he is immutable because he is immortal. He is called God because he established everything on his own *steadfastness* [Ps. 103: 5] and because he runs; the word 'run' means to run and set in motion and energize and nourish and provide and govern everything and to make everything alive. He is Lord because he is master of the universe, Father because he is before the universe, Demiurge and Maker because he is creator and maker of the universe, Most High because he is above everything, Almighty because he controls and surrounds everything.

For *the heights* of the heavens and the depths of the abysses and *the ends* of the world are *in his hand* [Ps. 94: 4], and there is no *place of* his *rest* [Isa. 66: 1]. The heavens are his work, earth is his creation, the sea is of his making, man is his fabrication and image, sun and moon and stars are his elements, created *for signs and for seasons and for days and for years* [Gen. 1: 14], for service and *slavery to men* [Ps. 103: 14; 146: 8].

God made everything *out of what did not exist* [2 Macc. 7: 28], bringing it into existence so that his greatness might be known and apprehended through his works.

The Invisibility of God

5. Just as the soul in a man is not seen, since it is invisible to men, but is apprehended through the movement of the body, so it may be that God cannot be seen by human eyes but is seen and apprehended through his providence and his works. As when one observes a ship at sea, fitted out and cruising and returning to port, one will obviously infer that in her there is a pilot who steers her, so one must suppose that the pilot of the universe is God, even if he is not visible to merely human eyes because he is unconfined. If a man cannot stare at the sun, though it is a very small star, because of its overwhelming heat and power, how much more is it the case that a mortal man cannot view the glory of God which is inexpressible! As a pomegranate, with a rind surrounding it, has inside many cells and cases, separated by membranes, and has many seeds dwelling in it, so the whole creation is surrounded by the spirit of God and the surrounding spirit, along with the creation, is enclosed by the hand of God. As the pomegranate seed, dwelling inside,

ἔνδον κατοικῶν οὐ δύναται ὁρᾶν τὰ ἔξω τοῦ λέπους, αὐτὸς ὢν ἔνδον, οὕτως οὐδὲ ἄνθρωπος ἐμπεριεχόμενος μετὰ πάσης τῆς κτίσεως ὑπὸ χειρὸς θεοῦ οὐ δύναται θεωρεῖν τὸν θεόν.

Εἶτα βασιλεὺς μὲν ἐπίγειος πιστεύεται εἶναι, καίπερ μὴ πᾶσιν βλεπόμενος, διὰ δὲ νόμων καὶ διατάξεων αὐτοῦ καὶ ἐξουσιῶν καὶ δυνάμεων καὶ εἰκόνων νοεῖται. τὸν δὲ θεὸν οὐ βούλει σὺ νοεῖσθαι διὰ ἔργων καὶ δυνάμεων;

6. Κατανόησον, ὦ ἄνθρωπε, τὰ ἔργα αὐτοῦ, καιρῶν μὲν κατὰ χρόνους ἀλλαγὴν καὶ ἀέρων τροπάς, στοιχείων τὸν εὔτακτον δρόμον, ἡμερῶν τε καὶ νυκτῶν καὶ μηνῶν καὶ ἐνιαυτῶν τὴν εὔτακτον πορείαν, σπερμάτων τε καὶ φυτῶν καὶ καρπῶν τὴν διάφορον καλλονήν, τήν τε πολυποίκιλον γονὴν κτηνῶν τετραπόδων καὶ πετεινῶν καὶ ἑρπετῶν καὶ νηκτῶν, ἐνύδρων τε καὶ ἐναλίων, ἢ τὴν ἐν αὐτοῖς τοῖς ζώοις δεδομένην σύνεσιν πρὸς τὸ γεννᾶν καὶ ἐκτρέφειν, οὐκ εἰς ἰδίαν χρῆσιν, ἀλλὰ εἰς τὸ ἔχειν τὸν ἄνθρωπον, τήν τε πρόνοιαν ἣν ποιεῖται ὁ θεὸς ἑτοιμάζων τροφὴν πάσῃ σαρκί, ἢ τὴν ὑποταγὴν ἣν ὥρικεν ὑποτάσσεσθαι τὰ πάντα τῇ ἀνθρωπότητι, πηγῶν τε γλυκερῶν καὶ ποταμῶν ἀενάων ῥύσιν, δρόσων τε καὶ ὄμβρων καὶ ὑετῶν τὴν κατὰ καιροὺς γινομένην ἐπιχορηγίαν, τὴν οὐρανίων παμποίκιλον κίνησιν, Ἑωσφόρον ἀνατέλλοντα μὲν καὶ προσημαίνοντα ἔρχεσθαι τὸν τέλειον φωστῆρα, σύνδεσμόν τε Πλειάδος καὶ Ὠρίωνος, Ἀρκτοῦρόν τε καὶ τὴν λοιπῶν ἄστρων χορείαν γινομένην ἐν τῷ κύκλῳ τοῦ οὐρανοῦ, οἷς ἡ πολυποίκιλος σοφία τοῦ θεοῦ πᾶσιν ἴδια ὀνόματα κέκληκεν.

Οὗτος θεὸς μόνος ὁ ποιήσας ἐκ σκότους φῶς, ὁ ἐξαγαγὼν φῶς ἐκ θησαυρῶν αὐτοῦ, ταμεῖά τε νότου καὶ θησαυροὺς ἀβύσσου καὶ ὅρια θαλασσῶν χιόνων τε καὶ χαλαζῶν θησαυρούς, συνάγων ὕδατα ἐν θησαυροῖς ἀβύσσου καὶ συνάγων τὸ σκότος ἐν θησαυροῖς αὐτοῦ καὶ ἐξάγων τὸ φῶς τὸ γλυκὺ καὶ τὸ ποθεινὸν καὶ ἐπιτερπὲς ἐκ θησαυρῶν αὐτοῦ, ἀνάγων νεφέλας ἐξ ἐσχάτου τῆς γῆς καὶ ἀστραπὰς πληθύνων εἰς ὑετόν, ὁ ἀποστέλλων τὴν βροντὴν εἰς φόβον καὶ προκαταγγέλλων τὸν κτύπον τῆς βροντῆς διὰ τῆς ἀστραπῆς, ἵνα μὴ ψυχὴ αἰφνιδίως ταραχθεῖσα ἐκψύξῃ, ἀλλὰ μὴν καὶ τῆς ἀστραπῆς τῆς κατερχομένης ἐκ τῶν οὐρανῶν τὴν αὐτάρκειαν ἐπιμετρῶν πρὸς τὸ μὴ ἐκκαῦσαι τὴν γῆν· εἰ γὰρ λάβοι τὴν κατεξουσίαν ἡ ἀστραπή, ἐκκαύσει τὴν γῆν, εἰ δὲ καὶ ἡ βροντή, καταστρέψει τὰ ἐν αὐτῇ.

cannot see what is outside the rind since it is itself inside, so man, who with the whole creation is enclosed by the hand of God, cannot see God.

A king on earth is believed to exist even if he is not seen by all; he is apprehended by means of his laws and commands and authorities and powers and images. Are you unwilling to apprehend God through his works and powers?

God the Creator

6. Consider his works, O man: the periodic alternation of the seasons and the changes of winds, the orderly course of the stars, the orderly succession of days and nights and months and years, the diversified beauty of seeds and plants and fruits, the variegated offspring of quadrupeds and birds and reptiles and fishes in rivers and seas, or the instinct provided to animals themselves for generating and nourishing offspring (not for their own use but for man to have), and the providential care which God exercises in preparing nourishment for all flesh, or the subjection in which he decreed all things to be subject to mankind; the flow of fresh springs and ever-flowing rivers, the seasonal supply of dews and showers and rains, the complex movement of the heavenly bodies, with the morning star rising and giving notice of the coming of the perfect luminary, *the conjunction of the Pleiades and Orion* [Job 38: 31], *Arcturus* [Job 9: 9], and the chorus of the other stars in the orbit of heaven, to all of which *the manifold Sophia of God* [Eph. 3: 10] *gave* individual *names* [Ps. 146: 4].

It is this God alone who *made light from darkness* [Job 37: 15], who brought light out of his treasuries, the *storehouses of the south wind* [Job 9: 9] and the *treasuries of the abyss* [Ps. 32: 7] and the limits of the seas [cf. Job 38: 10] and the *treasuries of snow and hail* [Job 38: 22], collecting the waters in the treasuries of the abyss and collecting the darkness in his treasuries [cf. Isa. 45: 3] and *bringing forth* the sweet, desirable, and lovely *light* [cf. Eccl. 11: 7] *from his treasuries* [Jer. 10: 13] and *leading forth clouds from the end of the earth* and multiplying *lightnings into rain* [Jer. 10: 13; Ps. 134: 7]. It is he who sends the thunder [cf. Job 38: 35] to terrify and through the lightning announces the crash of the thunder in advance so that the soul may not faint at the sudden tumult. It is he who limits the power of the lightning as it comes down from the heavens so that it will not burn up the earth. For if the lightning got complete control it would burn up the earth; if the thunder did so, it would overturn everything on it [cf. Job 21: 15].

7. Οὗτός μου θεὸς ὁ τῶν ὅλων κύριος, ὁ τανύσας τὸν οὐρανὸν μόνος καὶ θεὶς τὸ εὖρος τῆς ὑπ' οὐρανόν, ὁ συνταράσσων τὸ κύτος τῆς θαλάσσης καὶ ἠχῶν τὰ κύματα αὐτῆς, ὁ δεσπόζων τοῦ κράτους αὐτῆς καὶ τὸν σάλον τῶν κυμάτων καταπραΰνων, ὁ θεμελιώσας τὴν γῆν ἐπὶ τῶν ὑδάτων καὶ δοὺς πνεῦμα τὸ τρέφον αὐτήν, οὗ ἡ πνοὴ ζωογονεῖ τὸ πᾶν, ὃς ἐὰν συσχῇ τὸ πνεῦμα παρ' ἑαυτῷ ἐκλείψει τὸ πᾶν. Τοῦτον λαλεῖς, ἄνθρωπε, τούτου τὸ πνεῦμα ἀναπνεῖς, τοῦτον ἀγνοεῖς. τοῦτο δέ σοι συμβέβηκεν διὰ τὴν τύφλωσιν τῆς ψυχῆς καὶ πήρωσιν[1] τῆς καρδίας σου. ἀλλὰ εἰ βούλει, δύνασαι θεραπευθῆναι· ἐπίδος σεαυτὸν τῷ ἰατρῷ καὶ παρακεντήσει σου τοὺς ὀφθαλμοὺς τῆς ψυχῆς καὶ τῆς καρδίας. τίς ἐστιν ὁ ἰατρός; ὁ θεός, ὁ θεραπεύων καὶ ζωοποιῶν διὰ τοῦ λόγου καὶ τῆς σοφίας. ὁ θεὸς διὰ τοῦ λόγου αὐτοῦ καὶ τῆς σοφίας ἐποίησε τὰ πάντα· τῷ γὰρ λόγῳ αὐτοῦ ἐστερεώθησαν οἱ οὐρανοὶ καὶ τῷ πνεύματι αὐτοῦ πᾶσα ἡ δύναμις αὐτῶν. κρατίστη ἐστὶν ἡ σοφία αὐτοῦ· ὁ θεὸς τῇ σοφίᾳ ἐθεμελίωσε τὴν γῆν, ἡτοίμασε δὲ οὐρανοὺς φρονήσει, ἐν αἰσθήσει ἄβυσσοι ἐρράγησαν, νέφη δὲ ἐρρύησαν δρόσους.

Εἰ ταῦτα νοεῖς, ἄνθρωπε, ἁγνῶς καὶ ὁσίως καὶ δικαίως ζῶν, δύνασαι ὁρᾶν τὸν θεόν. πρὸ παντὸς δὲ προηγείσθω σου ἐν τῇ καρδίᾳ πίστις καὶ φόβος ὁ τοῦ θεοῦ, καὶ τότε συνήσεις ταῦτα. ὅταν ἀπόθῃ τὸ θνητὸν καὶ ἐνδύσῃ τὴν ἀφθαρσίαν, τότε ὄψῃ κατὰ ἀξίαν τὸν θεόν. ἀνεγείρει γάρ σου τὴν σάρκα ἀθάνατον σὺν τῇ ψυχῇ ὁ θεός· καὶ τότε ὄψῃ γενόμενος ἀθάνατος τὸν ἀθάνατον, ἐὰν νῦν πιστεύσῃς αὐτῷ καὶ τότε ἐπιγνώσῃ ὅτι ἀδίκως κατελάλησας αὐτοῦ.

8. Ἀλλὰ ἀπιστεῖς νεκροὺς ἐγείρεσθαι. ὅταν ἔσται, τότε πιστεύσεις θέλων καὶ μὴ θέλων· καὶ ἡ πίστις σου εἰς ἀπιστίαν λογισθήσεται, ἐὰν μὴ νῦν πιστεύσῃς. πρὸς τί δὲ καὶ ἀπιστεῖς; ἢ οὐκ οἶδας ὅτι ἁπάντων πραγμάτων ἡ πίστις προηγεῖται; τίς γὰρ δύναται θερίσαι γεωργός, ἐὰν μὴ πρῶτον πιστεύσῃ τὸ σπέρμα τῇ γῇ; ἢ τίς δύναται διαπερᾶσαι τὴν θάλασσαν, ἐὰν μὴ πρῶτον ἑαυτὸν πιστεύσῃ τῷ πλοίῳ καὶ τῷ κυβερνήτῃ; τίς δὲ κάμνων δύναται θεραπευθῆναι, ἐὰν

7. [1] πήρωσιν] V: πώρωσιν Wolf

7. This is my God, the Lord of the universe, who *alone spread out the heaven* [Job 9: 8] and *determined the breadth of what is under heaven* [Job 38: 18], who *stirs up the deep of the sea and makes its waves resound* [Ps. 64: 8], who *rules over its power and pacifies the movement of the waves* [Ps. 88: 10], who *established the earth upon the waters* [Ps. 23: 2] and gave a spirit to nourish it [cf. Gen. 1: 2]. His breath gives life to everything; *if he held back his spirit by himself everything would fail* [Job 34: 14 f.].

You speak of him, O man; you breathe his breath; you do not know him. This has happened to you because of the blindness of your soul and your heart, but if you will you can be cured. Deliver yourself to the physician, and he will couch the eyes of your soul and heart. Who is the physician? He is God, who heals and gives life through Logos and Sophia. God made everything through Logos and Sophia, for *by his Logos the heavens were made firm and by his Spirit all their power* [Ps. 32: 6]. His Sophia is most powerful: *God by Sophia founded the earth; he prepared the heavens by intelligence; by knowledge the abysses were broken up and the clouds poured forth dews* [Prov. 3: 19 f.].

If you know these things, O man, and live in purity, holiness, and righteousness, you can see God. But before all, faith and the fear of God must take the lead in your heart; then you will understand these things. When you put off what is mortal and put on imperishability [cf. 1 Cor. 15: 53 f.], then you will rightly see God. For God raises up your flesh immortal with your soul; after becoming immortal you will then see the Immortal, if you believe in him now. Then you will know that you unjustly spoke against him.

Belief in Resurrection

8. But you do not believe that the dead are raised. When the event takes place, you will believe whether you wish or not; your faith will be reckoned as unfaith unless you believe now. But why do you disbelieve? Do you not know that faith leads the way in all actions?[1] What farmer can harvest unless he first entrusts the seed to the earth? Who can cross the sea unless he first entrusts himself to the ship and the pilot? What sick man can be cured unless he first entrusts himself to the physician? What art or science can

8. [1] Possibly a known axiom; cf. H. Chadwick, *The Sentences of Sextus* (Cambridge, 1959), no. 166.

μὴ πρῶτον ἑαυτὸν πιστεύσῃ τῷ ἰατρῷ; ποίαν δὲ τέχνην ἢ ἐπιστήμην δύναταί τις μαθεῖν, ἐὰν μὴ πρῶτον ἐπιδῷ ἑαυτὸν καὶ πιστεύσῃ τῷ διδασκάλῳ; εἰ οὖν γεωργὸς πιστεύει τῇ γῇ καὶ ὁ πλέων τῷ πλοίῳ, καὶ ὁ κάμνων τῷ ἰατρῷ, σὺ οὐ βούλει ἑαυτὸν πιστεῦσαι τῷ θεῷ, τοσούτους ἀρραβῶνας ἔχων παρ' αὐτοῦ; πρῶτον μὲν ὅτι ἐποίησέν σε ἐξ οὐκ ὄντος εἰς τὸ εἶναι. εἰ γὰρ ὁ πατήρ σου οὐκ ἦν οὐδὲ ἡ μήτηρ, πολὺ μᾶλλον οὐδὲ σὺ ἦς ποτε. καὶ ἔπλασέν σε ἐξ ὑγρᾶς οὐσίας μικρᾶς καὶ ἐλαχίστης ῥανίδος, ἥτις οὐδὲ αὐτὴ ἦν ποτε· καὶ προήγαγέν σε ὁ θεὸς εἰς τόνδε τὸν βίον. εἶτα πιστεύεις τὰ ὑπὸ ἀνθρώπων γινόμενα ἀγάλματα θεοὺς εἶναι καὶ ἀρετὰς ποιεῖν. τῷ δὲ ποιήσαντί σε θεῷ ἀπιστεῖς δύνασθαί σε καὶ μεταξὺ ποιῆσαι;

9. Καὶ τὰ μὲν ὀνόματα ὧν φῂς σέβεσθαι θεῶν ὀνόματά ἐστιν νεκρῶν ἀνθρώπων. καὶ τούτων τίνων καὶ ποταπῶν; οὐχὶ Κρόνος μὲν τεκνοφάγος εὑρίσκεται καὶ τὰ ἑαυτοῦ τέκνα ἀναλίσκων; εἰ δὲ καὶ Δία τὸν παῖδα αὐτοῦ εἴποις, κατάμαθε κἀκείνου τὰς πράξεις καὶ τὴν ἀναστροφήν. πρῶτον μὲν ἐν Ἴδῃ ὑπὸ αἰγὸς ἀνετράφη, καὶ ταύτην σφάξας κατὰ τοὺς μύθους καὶ ἐκδείρας ἐποίησεν ἑαυτῷ ἔνδυμα. τὰς δὲ λοιπὰς πράξεις αὐτοῦ, περί τε ἀδελφοκοιτίας καὶ μοιχείας καὶ παιδοφθορίας, ἄμεινον Ὅμηρος καὶ οἱ λοιποὶ ποιηταὶ περὶ αὐτοῦ ἐξηγοῦνται. τί μοι τὸ λοιπὸν καταλέγειν περὶ τῶν υἱῶν αὐτοῦ, Ἡρακλέα μὲν ἑαυτὸν καύσαντα, Διόνυσον δὲ μεθύοντα καὶ μαινόμενον, καὶ Ἀπόλλωνα τὸν Ἀχιλλέα δεδιότα καὶ φεύγοντα καὶ τῆς Δάφνης ἐρῶντα καὶ τὸν Ὑακίνθου μόρον ἀγνοοῦντα, ἢ Ἀφροδίτην τὴν τιτρωσκομένην, καὶ Ἄρεα τὸν βροτολοιγόν, ἔτι δὲ καὶ ἰχῶρα ῥέοντα τούτων τῶν λεγομένων θεῶν;

Καὶ ταῦτα μὲν μέτριον εἰπεῖν, ὅπου γε θεὸς εὑρίσκεται μεμελισμένος ὁ καλούμενος Ὄσιρις, οὗ καὶ κατ' ἔτος γίνονται τελεταὶ ὡς ἀπολλυμένου καὶ εὑρισκομένου καὶ κατὰ μέλος ζητουμένου· οὔτε γὰρ εἰ ἀπόλλυται νοεῖται, οὔτε εἰ εὑρίσκεται δείκνυται. τί δέ μοι λέγειν Ἄττιν ἀποκοπτόμενον ἢ Ἄδωνιν ἐν ὕλῃ ῥεμβόμενον καὶ κυνηγετοῦντα καὶ τιτρωσκόμενον ὑπὸ συός, ἢ Ἀσκληπιὸν κεραυνούμενον, καὶ Σάραπιν τὸν ἀπὸ Σινώπης φυγάδα εἰς Ἀλεξάνδρειαν γεγονότα, ἢ τὴν Σκυθίαν Ἄρτεμιν καὶ αὐτὴν φυγάδα γεγονυῖαν καὶ ἀνδροφόνον καὶ κυνηγέτιν καὶ τοῦ Ἐνδυμίωνος ἐρασθεῖσαν;

Ταῦτα γὰρ οὐχ ἡμεῖς φαμεν, ἀλλὰ οἱ καθ' ὑμᾶς συγγραφεῖς καὶ ποιηταὶ κηρύσσουσιν.

anyone learn unless he first delivers and entrusts himself to the teacher?[2] If, then, the farmer trusts the earth and the sailor the ship and the sick man the physician, do you not want to entrust yourself to God, when you have received so many pledges from him? The first pledge is that he created you, bringing you from non-existence to existence; for if your father and mother once did not exist, certainly you were once nothing. He formed you out of a small moist matter and a tiny drop, which itself previously did not exist. It was God who brought you into this life. Second, you believe that statues made by men are gods and work miracles. Then do you not believe that the God who made you can later make you over again?

Attack on Idolatry

9. The names of the gods you say you worship are the names of dead men. What men were they? What kind? Is not Kronos a child-eater who consumes his own children? And if you should mention his son Zeus, you must learn his deeds and his manner of life. In the first place, he was nourished on Ida by a goat which, according to the myths, he slew and skinned to make himself a garment.[1] As for the rest of his deeds, such as his intercourse with his sister and his adultery and his pederasty, Homer and the other poets have given excellent accounts about him. Why should I go on to list the stories about his sons—Heracles who burned himself up, Dionysus who was drunk and crazy, Apollo who feared Achilles and fled and loved Daphne and was ignorant of the fate of Hyacinthus? What of Aphrodite who was wounded, and Ares the *bane of men* [*Il.* v. 31, 455]? Why mention the *ichor flowing* from these so-called *gods* [*Il.* v. 340]?

These stories are relatively tolerable when compared with that of a dismembered god called Osiris, whose mysteries take place annually on the supposition that he is lost and found and sought for, member by member. Actually it is not known whether he is lost or not, nor is there proof that he is found. Why should I mention the castrated Attis, or Adonis wandering in a wood and hunting and wounded by a boar, or Asclepius struck by lightning, or Sarapis the fugitive from Sinope who came to Alexandria, or the Scythian Artemis who herself was a fugitive as well as a murderess and huntress, in love with Endymion?

It is not we who say these things; your own historians and poets proclaim them.

8. [2] Such analogies were used to prove a similar point in the Platonic Academy; cf. Xenophon, *Mem.* iii. 3. 9; *Cyr.* i. 6. 21; Cicero, *Lucullus* 109; later in Philo, *Abr.* 263, 272; M. Aurelius vi. 55; Origen, *C. Cels.* i. 11, etc.
9. [1] For this rather unusual story cf. A. B. Cook, *Zeus* iii. 1 (Cambridge, 1940), 839 n. 6; and Lactantius, *Div. inst.* i. 21. 39.

10. Τί μοι λοιπὸν καταλέγειν τὸ πλῆθος ὧν σέβονται ζώων Αἰγύπτιοι, ἑρπετῶν τε καὶ κτηνῶν καὶ θηρίων καὶ πετεινῶν καὶ ἐνύδρων νηκτῶν, ἔτι δὲ καὶ ποδόνιπτρα καὶ ἤχους αἰσχύνης; εἰ δὲ καὶ Ἕλληνας εἴποις καὶ τὰ λοιπὰ ἔθνη, σέβονται λίθους καὶ ξύλα καὶ τὴν λοιπὴν ὕλην, ὥς ἔφθημεν εἰρηκέναι, ἀπεικονίσματα νεκρῶν ἀνθρώπων. Φειδίας μὲν γὰρ εὑρίσκεται ἐν Πείσῃ ποιῶν[1] Ἠλείοις τὸν Ὀλύμπιον Δία, καὶ Ἀθηναίοις ἐν ἀκροπόλει τὴν Ἀθηνᾶν.

Πεύσομαι δέ σου κἀγώ, ὦ ἄνθρωπε, πόσοι Ζῆνες εὑρίσκονται· Ζεὺς μὲν γὰρ ἐν πρώτοις προσαγορεύεται Ὀλύμπιος καὶ Ζεὺς Λατεάριος καὶ Ζεὺς Κάσσιος καὶ Ζεὺς Κεραύνιος καὶ Ζεὺς Προπάτωρ καὶ Ζεὺς Παννύχιος καὶ Ζεὺς Πολιοῦχος καὶ Ζεὺς Καπετώλιος. καὶ ὁ μὲν Ζεὺς παῖς Κρόνου, βασιλεὺς Κρητῶν γενόμενος, ἔχει τάφον ἐν Κρήτῃ· οἱ δὲ λοιποὶ ἴσως οὐδὲ ταφῆς κατηξιώθησαν. εἰ δὲ καὶ εἴποις τὴν μητέρα τῶν λεγομένων θεῶν, μή μοι γένοιτο διὰ στόματος τὰς πράξεις αὐτῆς ἐξειπεῖν (ἀθέμιτον γὰρ ἡμῖν τὰ τοιαῦτα καὶ ὀνομάζειν), ἢ τῶν θεραπόντων αὐτῆς τὰς πράξεις ὑφ᾽ ὧν θεραπεύεται, ὁπόσα τε τέλη καὶ εἰσφορὰς παρέχει τῷ βασιλεῖ αὐτή τε καὶ οἱ υἱοὶ αὐτῆς.

Οὐ γάρ εἰσιν θεοί, ἀλλὰ εἴδωλα, καθὼς προειρήκαμεν, ἔργα χειρῶν ἀνθρώπων καὶ δαιμόνια ἀκάθαρτα. γένοιντο δὲ τοιοῦτοι οἱ ποιοῦντες αὐτὰ καὶ οἱ ἐλπίζοντες ἐπ᾽ αὐτοῖς.

11. Τοιγαροῦν μᾶλλον τιμήσω τὸν βασιλέα, οὐ προσκυνῶν αὐτῷ, ἀλλὰ εὐχόμενος ὑπὲρ αὐτοῦ. θεῷ δὲ τῷ ὄντως θεῷ καὶ ἀληθεῖ προσκυνῶ, εἰδὼς ὅτι ὁ βασιλεὺς ὑπ᾽ αὐτοῦ γέγονεν. ἐρεῖς οὖν μοι· "Διὰ τί οὐ προσκυνεῖς τὸν βασιλέα;" ὅτι οὐκ εἰς τὸ προσκυνεῖσθαι γέγονεν, ἀλλὰ εἰς τὸ τιμᾶσθαι τῇ νομίμῳ τιμῇ. θεὸς γὰρ οὐκ ἔστιν, ἀλλὰ ἄνθρωπος, ὑπὸ θεοῦ τεταγμένος, οὐκ εἰς τὸ προσκυνεῖσθαι, ἀλλὰ εἰς τὸ δικαίως κρίνειν. τρόπῳ γάρ τινι παρὰ θεοῦ οἰκονομίαν πεπίστευται· καὶ γὰρ αὐτὸς οὓς ἔχει ὑφ᾽ ἑαυτὸν τεταγμένους οὐ βούλεται βασιλεῖς καλεῖσθαι· τὸ γὰρ βασιλεὺς αὐτοῦ ἐστιν ὄνομα, καὶ οὐκ ἄλλῳ ἐξόν ἐστιν τοῦτο καλεῖσθαι· οὕτως οὐδὲ προσκυνεῖσθαι ἀλλ᾽ ἢ μόνῳ θεῷ.

Ὥστε κατὰ πάντα πλανᾶσαι, ὦ ἄνθρωπε. τὸν δὲ βασιλέα τίμα εὐνοῶν αὐτῷ, ὑποτασσόμενος αὐτῷ, εὐχόμενος ὑπὲρ αὐτοῦ. τοῦτο

10. [1] ποιῶν] Gesner: οἴων V

10. Why should I go on to list the multitude of animals which the Egyptians worship, their reptiles and domestic animals and wild beasts and birds and river fishes, in addition to footbaths and shameful sounds? If you were to mention the Greeks and the other nations, they worship objects of stone and wood and other materials, as we have just said, the images of dead men. For we find Phidias in Pisa making the Olympian Zeus for the people of Elis[1] and the Athena on the Acropolis.

I shall inquire of you, O man, how many kinds of Zeus there are. First there is Zeus called Olympian, and there are Zeus Latiaris and Zeus Kassios and Zeus Keraunios and Zeus Propator and Zeus Pannychios and Zeus Poliouchos and Zeus Capitolinus. Zeus the child of Kronos, who was king of the Cretans, has a tomb on Crete; the rest of them were probably not considered worth burying. And if you should mention the Mother of the so-called gods, far be it from me to relate her deeds with my mouth (for it is not lawful for us even to mention such things), or the deeds by which her servants worship her, or the taxes and tributes she and her sons pay to the emperor.

For they are not gods but *idols*, as we said above, the *works of men's hands* [Ps. 113: 12; 134: 15], unclean *demons* [Ps. 95: 5]. *May those who make them* and set their hope on them *become like them* [Ps. 113: 16; 134: 18]!

Emperor-Worship

11. Accordingly, I will pay honour to the emperor not by worshipping him but by praying for him. I worship the God who is the real and true God, since I know that the emperor was made by him. You will say to me, 'Why do you not worship the emperor?' Because he was made not to be worshipped but to be honoured with legitimate honour. He is not God but a man appointed by God [cf. Rom. 13: 1], not to be worshipped but to judge justly. For in a certain way he has been *entrusted with a stewardship* [1 Cor. 9: 17] from God. He himself has subordinates whom he does not permit to be called emperors, for 'emperor' is his name and it is not right for another to be given this title. Similarly worship must be given to God alone.

You are entirely mistaken, O man. *Honour the emperor* [1 Pet. 2: 17] by wishing him well, by obeying him, by praying for him

---

10. [1] Presumably Theophilus lays emphasis on this statue because a copy of it was in the temple of Apollo at Daphne near Antioch (Ammianus Marcellinus xxii. 13. 1).

γὰρ ποιῶν ποιεῖς τὸ θέλημα τοῦ θεοῦ. λέγει γὰρ ὁ νόμος ὁ τοῦ θεοῦ· "Τίμα υἱὲ θεὸν καὶ βασιλέα, καὶ μηδένι αὐτῶν ἀπειθὴς ᾖς· ἐξαίφνης γὰρ τίσονται τοὺς ἐχθροὺς αὐτῶν."

12. Περὶ δὲ τοῦ σε καταγελᾶν μου, καλοῦντά με χριστιανόν, οὐκ οἶδας ὃ λέγεις. πρῶτον μὲν ὅτι τὸ χριστὸν ἡδὺ καὶ εὔχρηστον καὶ ἀκαταγέλαστόν ἐστιν. ποῖον γὰρ πλοῖον δύναται εὔχρηστον εἶναι καὶ σώζεσθαι, ἐὰν μὴ πρῶτον χρισθῇ; ἢ ποῖος πύργος ἢ οἰκία εὔμορφος καὶ εὔχρηστός ἐστιν, ἐπὰν οὐ κέχρισται; τίς δὲ ἄνθρωπος εἰσελθὼν εἰς τόνδε τὸν βίον ἢ ἀθλῶν οὐ χρίεται ἐλαίῳ; ποῖον δὲ ἔργον ἢ κόσμιον δύναται εὐμορφίαν ἔχειν, ἐὰν μὴ χρισθῇ καὶ στιλβωθῇ; εἶτα ἀὴρ μὲν καὶ πᾶσα ἡ ὑπ' οὐρανὸν τρόπῳ τινὶ χρίεται φωτὶ καὶ πνεύματι. σὺ δὲ οὐ βούλει χρισθῆναι ἔλαιον[1] θεοῦ; τοιγαροῦν ἡμεῖς τούτου εἵνεκεν καλούμεθα χριστιανοί ὅτι χριόμεθα ἔλαιον[2] θεοῦ.

13. Ἀλλὰ καὶ τὸ ἀρνεῖσθαί σε νεκροὺς ἐγείρεσθαι· φῂς γάρ· "Δεῖξόν μοι κἂν ἕνα ἐγερθέντα ἐκ νεκρῶν, ἵνα ἰδὼν πιστεύσω"· πρῶτον μὲν τί μέγα, εἰ θεασάμενος τὸ γεγονὸς πιστεύσῃς; εἶτα πιστεύεις μὲν Ἡρακλέα καύσαντα ἑαυτὸν ζῆν καὶ Ἀσκληπιὸν κεραυνωθέντα ἐγηγέρθαι. τὰ δὲ ὑπὸ τοῦ θεοῦ σοι λεγόμενα ἀπιστεῖς; ἴσως καὶ ἐπιδείξω σοι νεκρὸν ἐγερθέντα καὶ ζῶντα, καὶ τοῦτο ἀπιστήσεις.

Ὁ μὲν οὖν θεός σοι πολλὰ τεκμήρια ἐπιδείκνυσιν εἰς τὸ πιστεύειν αὐτῷ. εἰ γὰρ βούλει, κατανόησον τὴν τῶν καιρῶν καὶ ἡμερῶν καὶ νυκτῶν τελευτήν, πῶς καὶ αὐτὰ τελευτᾷ καὶ ἀνίσταται. τί δὲ καὶ οὐχὶ ἡ τῶν σπερμάτων καὶ καρπῶν γινομένη ἐξανάστασις, καὶ τοῦτο εἰς τὴν χρῆσιν τῶν ἀνθρώπων; εἰ γὰρ τύχοι εἰπεῖν, κόκκος σίτου ἢ τῶν λοιπῶν σπερμάτων, ἐπὰν βληθῇ εἰς τὴν γῆν, πρῶτον ἀποθνήσκει καὶ λύεται, εἶτα ἐγείρεται καὶ γίνεται στάχυς. ἡ δὲ τῶν δένδρων καὶ ἀκροδρύων φύσις, πῶς οὐχὶ κατὰ πρόσταγμα θεοῦ ἐξ ἀφανοῦς καὶ ἀοράτου κατὰ καιροὺς προσφέρουσιν τοὺς καρπούς; ἔτι μὴν ἐνίοτε καὶ στρουθίον ἢ τῶν λοιπῶν πετεινῶν, καταπιὸν σπέρμα μηλέας ἢ συκῆς ἤ τινος ἑτέρου, ἦλθεν ἐπί τινα λόφον πετρώδη ἢ τάφον καὶ ἀφώδευσεν, κἀκεῖνο δραξάμενον ἀνέφυ δένδρον, τό ποτε καταποθὲν καὶ διὰ τοσαύτης θερμασίας διελθόν. ταῦτα δὲ πάντα ἐνεργεῖ

12. [1] ἔλαιον] V²: ἔλαιος V   [2] ἔλαιον] V²: ἔλεος V

[cf. 1 Tim. 2:2], for by so doing you will perform *the will of God* [1 Pet. 2:15]; the law of God says, 'Honour, my son, God and the king, and be disobedient to neither one; for they will suddenly destroy their enemies' [Prov. 24:21 f.].

The Name Christian (continued from c. 1)

12. As for your ridiculing me when you call me a Christian, you do not know what you are saying. In the first place, what is anointed is sweet and useful, not ridiculous. What boat can be useful and seaworthy unless it is first caulked? What tower or house is attractive and useful unless it is whitewashed? What man on entering this life or being an athlete is not anointed with oil? What work of art or ornament can possess attractiveness unless it is greased and polished? Furthermore, the air and everything under heaven is anointed, so to speak, by light and spirit. Do you not want to be anointed with the oil of God? We are actually called Christians just because we are anointed with the oil of God.

Belief in Resurrection (continued from c. 8)

13. But as for your denying that the dead are raised—for you may say, 'Show me even one person raised from the dead, so that by seeing I may believe'—in the first place, what importance would your believing have after you have seen the event? In the second place, you actually believe that Heracles, who burned himself up, is alive and that Asclepius, struck by lightning, was raised. And do you disbelieve what is said to you by God? Even if I were to show you a dead man raised and alive, you might perhaps disbelieve this.

God has given you many indications for believing him. If you will, consider the termination of seasons and days and nights and how they die and rise again. And what of the resurrection of seeds and fruits, occurring for the benefit of mankind? One might mention that a grain of wheat or of other seeds when cast into the earth first dies and is destroyed, then is raised and becomes an ear. And does not the nature of trees and fruits yield seasonable fruits, by God's command, out of what is obscure and invisible? Furthermore, sometimes a sparrow or some other bird has swallowed a seed of an apple or a fig or something else and comes to some rocky hill or tomb and excretes it. Then that seed which had formerly been swallowed and had passed through such heat takes root and grows into a tree. *All these things the Sophia of God works* [1 Cor. 12:11]

ἡ τοῦ θεοῦ σοφία, εἰς τὸ ἐπιδεῖξαι καὶ διὰ τούτων ὅτι δυνατός ἐστιν ὁ θεὸς ποιῆσαι τὴν καθολικὴν ἀνάστασιν ἁπάντων ἀνθρώπων.

Εἰ δὲ καὶ θαυμασιώτερον θέαμα θέλεις θεάσασθαι γινόμενον πρὸς ἀπόδειξιν ἀναστάσεως, οὐ μόνον τῶν ἐπιγείων πραγμάτων ἀλλὰ καὶ τῶν ἐν οὐρανῷ, κατανόησον τὴν ἀνάστασιν τῆς σελήνης τὴν κατὰ μῆνα γενομένην, πῶς φθίνει ἀποθνήσκει ἀνίσταται πάλιν. ἔτι ἄκουσον καὶ ἐν σοὶ αὐτῷ ἔργον ἀναστάσεως γινόμενον, κἂν ἀγνοεῖς, ὦ ἄνθρωπε. ἴσως γάρ ποτε νόσῳ περιπεσὼν ἀπώλεσάς σου τὰς σάρκας καὶ τὴν ἰσχὺν καὶ τὸ εἶδος, ἐλέους δὲ τυχὼν παρὰ θεοῦ καὶ ἰάσεως πάλιν ἀπέλαβές σου τὸ σῶμα καὶ τὸ εἶδος καὶ τὴν ἰσχύν· καὶ ὥσπερ οὐκ ἔγνως ποῦ ἐπορεύθησάν σου αἱ σάρκες ἀφανεῖς γενόμεναι, οὕτως οὐκ ἐπίστασαι οὐδὲ πόθεν ἐγένοντο ἢ πόθεν ἦλθον. ἀλλὰ ἐρεῖς· "'Εκ τροφῶν καὶ χυμῶν ἐξαιματουμένων." καλῶς ἀλλὰ καὶ τοῦτο ἔργον θεοῦ καὶ οὕτω δημιουργήσαντος, καὶ οὐκ ἄλλου τινός.

14. Μὴ οὖν ἀπίστει, ἀλλὰ πίστευε. καὶ γὰρ ἐγὼ ἠπίστουν τοῦτο ἔσεσθαι, ἀλλὰ νῦν κατανοήσας αὐτὰ πιστεύω, ἅμα καὶ ἐπιτυχὼν ἱεραῖς γραφαῖς τῶν ἁγίων προφητῶν, οἳ καὶ προεῖπον διὰ πνεύματος θεοῦ τὰ προγεγονότα[1] ᾧ τρόπῳ γέγονεν καὶ τὰ ἐνεστῶτα τίνι τρόπῳ γίνεται καὶ τὰ ἐπερχόμενα ποίᾳ τάξει ἀπαρτισθήσεται. ἀπόδειξιν οὖν λαβὼν τῶν γινομένων καὶ προαναπεφωνημένων οὐκ ἀπιστῶ, ἀλλὰ πιστεύω πειθαρχῶν θεῷ· ᾧ, εἰ βούλει, καὶ σὺ ὑποτάγηθι πιστεύων αὐτῷ, μὴ νῦν ἀπιστήσας πεισθῇς ἀνιώμενος, τότε ἐν αἰωνίοις τιμωρίαις.

Ὧν τιμωριῶν προειρημένων ὑπὸ τῶν προφητῶν μεταγενέστεροι γενόμενοι οἱ ποιηταὶ καὶ φιλόσοφοι ἔκλεψαν ἐκ τῶν ἁγίων γραφῶν, εἰς τὸ[2] δόγματα αὐτῶν ἀξιόπιστα γενηθῆναι. πλὴν καὶ αὐτοὶ προεῖπον περὶ τῶν κολάσεων τῶν μελλουσῶν ἔσεσθαι ἐπὶ τοὺς ἀσεβεῖς καὶ ἀπίστους, ὅπως ᾖ ἐμμάρτυρα πᾶσιν, πρὸς τὸ μὴ εἰπεῖν τινας ὅτι οὐκ ἠκούσαμεν οὐδὲ ἔγνωμεν.

Εἰ δὲ βούλει, καὶ σὺ ἔντυχε φιλοτίμως ταῖς προφητικαῖς γραφαῖς· καὶ αὐταί σε τρανότερον ὁδηγήσουσιν πρὸς τὸ ἐκφυγεῖν τὰς αἰωνίους κολάσεις καὶ τυχεῖν τῶν αἰωνίων ἀγαθῶν[3] τοῦ θεοῦ. ὁ γὰρ δοὺς στόμα εἰς τὸ λαλεῖν καὶ πλάσας οὓς εἰς τὸ ἀκούειν καὶ

14. [1] προγεγονότα] V²: προγεγραμμένα V   [2] τό] B: τὰ V   [3] ἀγαθῶν] B: καὶ praem. V

in order to demonstrate, even through these, that God is powerful enough to bring about the general resurrection of all men.

If you wish to behold a still more marvellous sight, taking place to provide proof of resurrection not only from matters on earth but also from those in heaven, consider the monthly resurrection of the moon, how it wanes, dies, and rises again. Listen further: an example of resurrection takes place in yourself, even if you are ignorant of it, O man. Perhaps you once fell sick and lost flesh, strength, and appearance; but when you obtained mercy and healing from God, you recovered your body, appearance, and strength. Just as you did not know where your flesh went when it vanished, so you did not know whence it originated when it came back. But you will say: 'From solids and liquids converted into blood.' Certainly! But this too is the work of God, who formed them in this way, not of anyone else.

Christian Faith a Necessity

14. *Do not disbelieve*, then, *but believe* [John 20: 27]. I too did not believe that resurrection would take place, but now that I have considered these matters I believe. At that time I encountered the sacred writings of the holy prophets, who through the Spirit of God foretold past events in the way that they happened, present events in the way they are happening, and future events in the order in which they will be accomplished. Because I obtained proof from the events which took place after being predicted, I *do not disbelieve but believe*, in obedience to God. If you will, you too must obey him and believe him, so that after disbelieving now you will not be persuaded later, punished with eternal tortures.

These tortures were predicted by the prophets, but later poets and philosophers stole them from the holy scriptures in order to make their own teaching seem trustworthy. In any case, however, they too foretold the punishments to come upon the ungodly and the incredulous, so that these punishments might be attested to all and no one might say, 'We did not hear nor did we know' [cf. *Kerygma Petri*, fr. 3].

If you will, you too must reverently read the prophetic writings. They will be your best guides for escaping the eternal punishments and for obtaining the eternal benefits of God. For *he who gave the mouth for speech and formed the ear for hearing and made eyes for vision* [Exod. 4: 11; Ps. 93: 9] will examine everything and will judge

ποιήσας ὀφθαλμοὺς εἰς τὸ ὁρᾶν ἐξετάσει τὰ πάντα καὶ κρινεῖ τὸ δίκαιον, ἀποδιδοὺς ἑκάστῳ κατὰ ἀξίαν τῶν μισθῶν. τοῖς μὲν καθ' ὑπομονὴν διὰ ἔργων ἀγαθῶν ζητοῦσι τὴν ἀφθαρσίαν δωρήσεται ζωὴν αἰώνιον, χαράν, εἰρήνην, ἀνάπαυσιν καὶ πλήθη ἀγαθῶν, ὧν οὔτε ὀφθαλμὸς εἶδεν οὔτε οὖς ἤκουσεν οὔτε ἐπὶ καρδίαν ἀνθρώπου ἀνέβη· τοῖς δὲ ἀπίστοις καὶ καταφρονηταῖς καὶ ἀπειθοῦσι τῇ ἀληθείᾳ, πειθομένοις δὲ τῇ ἀδικίᾳ, ἐπὰν ἐμφύρωνται μοιχείαις καὶ πορνείαις καὶ ἀρσενοκοιτίαις καὶ πλεονεξίαις καὶ ταῖς ἀθεμίτοις εἰδωλολατρείαις, ἔσται ὀργὴ καὶ θύμος, θλίψις καὶ στενοχωρία· καὶ τὸ τέλος τοὺς τοιούτους καθέξει πῦρ αἰώνιον.

Ἐπειδὴ προσέθηκας, ὦ ἑταῖρε, "Δεῖξόν μοι τὸν θεόν σου", οὗτός μου θεός, καὶ συμβουλεύω σοι φοβεῖσθαι αὐτὸν καὶ πιστεύειν αὐτῷ.

justly, *rewarding each one in accordance with what he deserves* [Rom. 2: 6]. *To those who with endurance seek imperishability through good works, he will give eternal life* [Rom. 2: 7], joy, peace, rest, and the totality of good things *which eye has not seen nor ear heard, nor have they entered the heart of man* [1 Cor. 2: 9]. But to the unbelieving, who despise and *disobey the truth but obey unrighteousness* [Rom. 2: 8], when they are full of adulteries and fornications and homosexual acts and greed and *lawless idolatry* [1 Pet. 4: 3], there will come *wrath and anger, tribulation and anguish* [Rom. 2: 8 f.], and finally eternal fire will overtake such men.

Since you made this request, my friend, 'Show me your God', this is my God. I advise you to fear him and believe him.

τὸ β′

1. Ἐπειδὴ πρὸ τούτων τῶν ἡμερῶν ἐγένετο λόγος ἡμῖν, ὦ ἀγαθώτατε Αὐτόλυκε, πυθομένου σου τίς μου ὁ θεὸς καὶ δι' ὀλίγου παρασχόντος σου τὰ ὦτα τῇ ὁμιλίᾳ ἡμῶν,[1] περὶ τῆς θεοσεβείας μου ἐξεθέμην σοι· ἔτι δὲ καὶ ἀποταξάμενοι ἑαυτοῖς μετὰ πλείστης φιλίας ἐπορεύθημεν ἕκαστος εἰς τὸν ἑαυτοῦ οἶκον, καίπερ σκληρῶς τὰ πρῶτά σου ἔχοντος πρὸς ἡμᾶς· οἶδας γὰρ καὶ μέμνησαι ὅτι ὑπέλαβες μωρίαν εἶναι τὸν λόγον ἡμῶν. σοῦ οὖν μετὰ ταῦτα προτρεψαμένου με, κἂν ἰδιώτης ὦ τῷ λόγῳ, πλὴν βούλομαί σοι καὶ νῦν διὰ τοῦδε τοῦ συγγράμματος ἀκριβέστερον ἐπιδεῖξαι τὴν ματαιοπονίαν καὶ ματαίαν θρησκείαν ἐν ᾗ κατέχῃ, ἅμα καὶ δι' ὀλίγων τῶν κατά σε ἱστοριῶν ὧν ἀναγινώσκεις, ἴσως δὲ οὐδέπω γινώσκεις, τὸ ἀληθὲς φανερόν σοι ποιῆσαι.

2. Καὶ γὰρ γελοιόν μοι δοκεῖ λιθοξόους μὲν καὶ πλάστας ἢ ζωγράφους ἢ χωνευτὰς πλάσσειν τε καὶ γράφειν καὶ γλύφειν καὶ χωνεύειν καὶ θεοὺς κατασκευάζειν, οἵ, ἔπαν γένωνται ὑπὸ τῶν τεχνιτῶν, οὐδὲν αὐτοὺς ἡγοῦνται· ὅταν δὲ ἀγορασθῶσιν ὑπό τινων καὶ ἀνατεθῶσιν εἰς ναὸν καλούμενον ἢ οἶκόν τινα, τούτοις οὐ μόνον θύουσιν οἱ ὠνησάμενοι, ἀλλὰ καὶ οἱ ποιήσαντες καὶ πωλήσαντες ἔρχονται μετὰ σπουδῆς καὶ παρατάξεως θυσιῶν τε καὶ σπονδῶν εἰς τὸ προσκυνεῖν αὐτοῖς καὶ ἡγοῦνται θεοὺς αὐτούς, οὐκ εἰδότες ὅτι τοιοῦτοί εἰσιν ὁποῖοι καὶ ὅτε ἐγένοντο ὑπ' αὐτῶν ἤτοι λίθος ἢ χαλκός, ἢ ξύλον ἢ χρῶμα, ἢ καὶ ἑτέρα τις ὕλη.

Τοῦτο δὴ καὶ ὑμῖν συμβέβηκεν τοῖς ἀναγινώσκουσι τὰς ἱστορίας καὶ γενεαλογίας τῶν λεγομένων θεῶν. ὁπόταν γὰρ ἐπιτυγχάνετε ταῖς γενέσεσιν αὐτῶν, ὡς ἀνθρώπους αὐτοὺς νοεῖτε· ὕστερον δὲ θεοὺς προσαγορεύετε καὶ θρησκεύετε αὐτοῖς, οὐκ ἐφιστάνοντες οὐδὲ συνιέντες ὅτι οἵους αὐτοὺς ἀνέγνωτε γεγονέναι τοιοῦτοι καὶ ἐγεννήθησαν.

3. Καὶ τῶν μὲν τότε θεῶν, εἴπερ ἐγεννῶντο, γένεσις πολλὴ ηὑρίσκετο. τὸ δὲ νῦν ποῦ θεῶν γένεσις δείκνυται; εἰ γὰρ τότε ἐγέννων καὶ

---

1. [1] ἡμῶν] Valckenaer: ἡμῖν V: μου Otto

Book II

1. Some time ago we had a discussion, O excellent Autolycus, and when you asked me who my God is and briefly lent your ears to my discourse, I set forth the nature of my religion for you. Furthermore, we parted from each other with great friendliness when each went to his own house, though at first you had been unfavourably disposed toward us; you know and remember that you supposed that our teaching was mere foolishness. Since you later requested it of me, even though I am *unskilled in speaking* [2 Cor. 11:6], I wish to provide for you, through the present treatise, a more accurate proof concerning the pointless labour and pointless religion in which you are confined. I shall use a few of those history books which you read—though perhaps you do not yet understand them—in order to make the truth plain to you.

Absurdities of Idolatry and Mythology

2. To me it seems ridiculous that sculptors, moulders, painters, and smelters should mould, paint, carve, cast, and construct gods. While they are being made by the artisans these men consider them to be nothing at all [cf. 1 Cor. 8:4], but after they are purchased by anyone and set up in a so-called temple or in some house, not only do the buyers sacrifice to them, but those who made and sold them eagerly come to worship them with an array of sacrifices and libations. They regard them as gods, since they do not know that they are just the same as they were when they were made by them—stone or bronze or wood or pigment or some other material.

This is what has happened to you when you read the histories and genealogies of the so-called gods. When you are reading about their births, you think of them as men. Afterwards, however, you call them gods and worship them because you do not recognize or understand that they were generated just in the way that, as you read, they came into existence.

The Gods according to Mythology

3. We find that in the past the generation of the gods was quite prolific (if they were actually generated). But where does any

ἐγεννῶντο, δῆλον ὅτι ἐχρῆν καὶ ἕως τοῦ δεῦρο γίνεσθαι θεοὺς γεννητούς· εἰ δὲ μή γε, ἀσθενὲς τὸ τοιοῦτο νοηθήσεσθαι· ἢ γὰρ ἐγήρασαν, διὸ οὐκ ἔτι γεννῶσιν, ἢ ἀπέθανον καὶ οὐκ ἔτι εἰσίν. εἰ γὰρ ἐγεννῶντο θεοί, ἐχρῆν καὶ ἕως τοῦ δεῦρο γεννᾶσθαι, καθάπερ γὰρ καὶ ἄνθρωποι γεννῶνται· μᾶλλον δὲ καὶ πλείονες θεοὶ ὤφειλον εἶναι τῶν ἀνθρώπων, ὥς φησιν Σίβυλλα·

Εἰ δὲ θεοὶ γεννῶσι καὶ ἀθάνατοί γε μένουσι,
πλείονες ἀνθρώπων γεγεννημένοι ἄν[1] θεοὶ ἦσαν,
οὐδὲ τόπος στῆναι θνητοῖς οὐκ ἄν ποθ' ὑπῆρξεν.

εἰ γὰρ ἀνθρώπων θνητῶν καὶ ὀλιγοχρονίων ὄντων τὰ γεννώμενα τέκνα ἕως τοῦ δεῦρο δείκνυται, καὶ οὐ πέπαυται τὸ μὴ γεννᾶσθαι ἀνθρώπους, διὸ πληθύουσι πόλεις καὶ κῶμαι, ἔτι μὴν καὶ χῶραι κατοικοῦνται, πῶς οὐχὶ μᾶλλον ἐχρῆν θεοὺς τοὺς μὴ ἀποθνήσκοντας κατὰ τοὺς ποιητὰς γεννᾶν καὶ γεννᾶσθαι, καθώς φατε θεῶν γένεσιν γεγενῆσθαι; πρὸς τί δὲ τότε μὲν[2] τὸ ὄρος τὸ καλούμενον Ὄλυμπος ὑπὸ θεῶν κατῳκεῖτο, νυνὶ δὲ ἔρημον τυγχάνει; ἢ τίνος εἵνεκεν τότε μὲν ὁ Ζεὺς ἐν τῇ Ἴδῃ κατῴκει (ἐγινώσκετο οἰκῶν ἐκεῖ κατὰ τὸν Ὅμηρον καὶ τοὺς λοιποὺς ποιητάς) νῦνι δὲ ἀγνοεῖται; διὰ τί δὲ καὶ οὐκ ἦν πανταχόσε, ἀλλὰ ἐν μέρει γῆς εὑρίσκετο; ἢ γὰρ τῶν λοιπῶν ἠμέλει, ἢ ἀδύνατος ἦν τοῦ πανταχόσε εἶναι καὶ τῶν πάντων προνοεῖν. εἰ γὰρ ἦν, εἰ τύχοι εἰπεῖν, ἐν τόπῳ ἀνατολικῷ, οὐκ ἦν ἐν τόπῳ δυτικῷ· εἰ δὲ αὖ πάλιν ἐν τοῖς δυτικοῖς ἦν, οὐκ ἦν ἐν τοῖς ἀνατολικοῖς. Θεοῦ δὲ τοῦ ὑψίστου καὶ παντοκράτορος καὶ τοῦ ὄντως θεοῦ τοῦτό ἐστιν μὴ μόνον τὸ πανταχόσε εἶναι, ἀλλὰ καὶ πάντα ἐφορᾶν καὶ πάντων ἀκούειν, ἔτι[3] μὴν μηδὲ τὸ ἐν τόπῳ χωρεῖσθαι· εἰ δὲ μή γε, μείζων ὁ χωρῶν τόπος αὐτοῦ εὑρεθήσεται· μεῖζον γάρ ἐστιν τὸ χωροῦν τοῦ χωρουμένου· Θεὸς γὰρ οὐ χωρεῖται, ἀλλὰ αὐτός ἐστι τόπος τῶν ὅλων.

Πρὸς τί δὲ καὶ καταλέλοιπεν ὁ Ζεὺς τὴν Ἴδην; πότερον τελευτήσας, ἢ οὐκ ἔτι ἤρεσεν αὐτῷ ἐκεῖνο τὸ ὄρος; ποῦ δὲ καὶ ἐπορεύθη; εἰς οὐρανούς; οὐχί. ἀλλὰ ἐρεῖς εἰς Κρήτην; ναί· ὅπου καὶ τάφος αὐτῷ ἕως τοῦ δεῦρο δείκνυται. πάλιν φήσεις εἰς Πεῖσαν, ὁ κλέων ἕως τοῦ δεῦρο τὰς χεῖρας Φειδίου.

Ἔλθωμεν τοίνυν ἐπὶ τὰ συγγράμματα τῶν φιλοσόφων καὶ ποιητῶν.

3. [1] ἂν] Rzach: οἱ δὲ V: οἱ Fell   [2] τότε μὲν] Otto: μὲν τότε V   [3] ἔτι] Humphry: ὅτι V

generation of the gods come to light now? If they then begot and were begotten, it is obvious that generated gods ought to come into existence up to the present day. Otherwise, such a race must be considered weak: either they have grown old and for this reason no longer generate offspring, or they have died and no longer exist. If the gods were generated, they ought to be generated up to the present day, just as men are generated—or rather, there should be more gods than men, as the Sibyl says [fr. 2 Geffcken]:

> But if gods beget offspring and remain immortal,
> There would be more begotten gods than men,
> Nor would a place exist where mortals could stand.

For if the children generated by men who are mortal and short-lived are brought to light up to the present day, and the generation of men has not ceased, and therefore cities and villages multiply and even the country is inhabited, how much more should the gods (who according to the poets do not die) generate and be generated? (In your view this is how the race of gods came into existence.) Why was the mountain called Olympus formerly inhabited by gods but now is deserted? Why did Zeus then live on Ida (he was known to live there according to Homer and the other poets) when now he is unknown? Why was he not everywhere instead of in one part of the earth? For either he neglected the other parts or else he was unable to be everywhere and provide for everything. If, for example, he was in the east, he was not in the west; if, again, he was in the west, he was not in the east. But it is characteristic of the Most High and Almighty God, who is actually God, not only to be everywhere but to *look upon everything and hear everything* [*Od.* xi. 108], and not to be confined in a place; otherwise, the place containing him would be greater than he is, for what contains is greater than what is contained. God is not contained but is himself the locus of the universe.

Why did Zeus abandon Ida? Did he die, or did that mountain no longer please him? And where did he go? To the heavens? Certainly not. Will you say he went to Crete? Yes! where his tomb can be seen to this very day. Again, you will say he went to Pisa and even now makes the skill of Phidias renowned.

Let us turn, then, to the writings of the philosophers and poets.

4. Ἔνιοι μὲν τῆς στοᾶς ἀρνοῦνται καὶ τὸ ἐξ ὅλου θεὸν εἶναι, ἤ, εἰ καί ἐστιν, μηδενός φασιν φροντίζειν τὸν θεὸν πλὴν ἑαυτοῦ. καὶ ταῦτα μὲν παντελῶς Ἐπικούρου καὶ Χρυσίππου ἡ ἄνοια ἀπεφήνατο. ἕτεροι δέ φασιν αὐτοματισμὸν τῶν πάντων εἶναι, καὶ τὸν κόσμον ἀγένητον καὶ φύσιν ἀΐδιον,[1] καὶ τὸ σύνολον πρόνοιαν μὴ εἶναι θεοῦ ἐτόλμησαν ἐξειπεῖν, ἀλλὰ θεὸν εἶναι μόνον φασὶν τὴν ἑκάστου συνείδησιν. ἄλλοι δ' αὖ τὸ δι' ὅλου κεχωρηκὸς πνεῦμα θεὸν δογματίζουσιν.

Πλάτων δὲ καὶ οἱ τῆς αἱρέσεως αὐτοῦ θεὸν μὲν ὁμολογοῦσιν ἀγένητον καὶ πατέρα καὶ ποιητὴν τῶν ὅλων εἶναι· εἶτα ὑποτίθενται θεὸν καὶ ὕλην ἀγένητον καὶ ταύτην φασὶν συνηκμακέναι τῷ θεῷ. εἰ δὲ θεὸς ἀγένητος καὶ ὕλη ἀγένητος, οὐκ ἔτι ὁ θεὸς ποιητὴς τῶν ὅλων ἐστὶν κατὰ τοὺς Πλατωνικούς, οὐδὲ μὴν μοναρχία θεοῦ δείκνυται, ὅσον τὸ κατ' αὐτούς. ἔτι δὲ καὶ ὥσπερ ὁ θεός, ἀγένητος ὤν, καὶ ἀναλλοίωτός ἐστιν, οὕτως, εἰ καὶ ἡ ὕλη ἀγένητος ἦν, καὶ ἀναλλοίωτος καὶ ἰσόθεος ἦν· τὸ γὰρ γενητὸν τρεπτὸν καὶ ἀλλοιωτόν, τὸ δὲ ἀγένητον ἄτρεπτον καὶ ἀναλλοίωτον.

Τί δὲ μέγα, εἰ ὁ θεὸς ἐξ ὑποκειμένης ὕλης ἐποίει τὸν κόσμον; καὶ γὰρ τεχνίτης ἄνθρωπος, ἐπὰν ὕλην λάβῃ ἀπό τινος, ἐξ αὐτῆς ὅσα βούλεται ποιεῖ. θεοῦ δὲ ἡ δύναμις ἐν τούτῳ φανεροῦται ἵνα ἐξ οὐκ ὄντων ποιῇ ὅσα βούλεται, καθάπερ καὶ τὸ ψυχὴν δοῦναι καὶ κίνησιν οὐχ ἑτέρου τινός ἐστιν ἀλλ' ἢ μόνου θεοῦ. καὶ γὰρ ἄνθρωπος εἰκόνα μὲν ποιεῖ, λόγον δὲ καὶ πνοὴν ἢ αἴσθησιν οὐ δύναται δοῦναι τῷ ὑπ' αὐτοῦ γενομένῳ. θεὸς δὲ τούτου πλεῖον τοῦτο κέκτηται, τὸ ποιεῖν λογικόν, ἔμπνουν, αἰσθητικόν. ὥσπερ οὖν ἐν τούτοις πᾶσιν δυνατώτερός ἐστιν ὁ θεὸς τοῦ ἀνθρώπου, οὕτως καὶ τὸ ἐξ οὐκ ὄντων ποιεῖν καὶ πεποιηκέναι τὰ ὄντα, καὶ ὅσα βούλεται καὶ ὡς[2] βούλεται.

5. Ὥστε ἀσύμφωνός ἐστιν ἡ γνώμη κατὰ τοὺς φιλοσόφους καὶ συγγράφεις. τούτων γάρ ταῦτα ἀποφηναμένων, εὑρίσκεται ὁ ποιητὴς Ὅμηρος ἑτέρᾳ ὑποθέσει εἰσάγων γένεσιν οὐ μόνον κόσμου ἀλλὰ καὶ θεῶν. φησὶν γάρ που·

Ὠκεανόν τε, θεῶν γένεσιν, καὶ μητέρα Τηθύν,
ἐξ οὗ δὴ πάντες ποταμοὶ καὶ πᾶσα θάλασσα.

4. [1] ἀΐδιον] Otto; cf. II. 8. 10: ἰδίαν V   [2] καὶ ὡς] Otto; cf. II. 13. 7: καθὼς V

Philosophical Theology

4. Some of the Stoics absolutely deny the existence of God or assert that if God exists he takes thought for no one but himself. Such views certainly exhibit the folly of Epicurus and Chrysippus alike.[1] Others say that everything happens spontaneously, that the universe is uncreated and that nature is eternal; in general they venture to declare that there is no divine providence but that God is only the individual's conscience [cf. [Menander], *Monostichoi* 81 and 107 Jaekel]. Others, on the contrary, hold that the spirit extended through everything is God [*SVF* ii. 1033].

Plato and his followers acknowledge that God is uncreated, the Father and Maker of the universe;[2] next they assume that uncreated matter is also God, and say that matter was coeval with God [cf. Diels, *Dox.* 567, 13; 588, 17–18]. But if God is uncreated and matter is uncreated, then according to the Platonists God is not the Maker of the universe, and as far as they are concerned the unique sovereignty of God is not demonstrated. Furthermore, as God is immutable because he is uncreated, if matter is uncreated it must also be immutable, and equal to God; for what is created is changeable and mutable, while the uncreated is unchangeable and immutable.

What would be remarkable if God made the world out of preexistent matter? Even a human artisan, when he obtains material from someone, makes whatever he wishes out of it. But the power of God is revealed by his making whatever he wishes out of the non-existent, just as the ability to give life and motion belongs to no one but God alone. For a man makes an image but cannot give reason or breath or sensation to what he makes, while God has this power greater than his: the ability to make a being that is rational, breathing, and capable of sensation. As in all these instances God is more powerful than man, so he is in his making and having made the existent out of the non-existent; he made whatever he wished in whatever way he wished.

The Theology of the Poets

5. The opinions of philosophers are inconsistent with those of other writers. For while the former authors made these statements, we find that the poet Homer relies on a different assumption when he introduces the origin not only of the world but also of the gods. For he says somewhere [*Il.* xiv. 201; xxi. 196]:

> Ocean, origin of the gods, and mother Tethys,
> Whence come all rivers and the whole sea.

---

4. [1] Plutarch (*De Stoic. repugn.* 38, 1052 b) similarly criticizes both Epicurus and Chrysippus.   [2] Cf. Plato, *Tim.* 28 c.

ἃ δὴ λέγων οὐκ ἔτι θεὸν συνιστᾷ. τίς γὰρ οὐκ ἐπίσταται τὸν Ὠκεανὸν ὕδωρ εἶναι; εἰ δὲ ὕδωρ, οὐκ ἄρα θεός. ὁ δὲ θεός, εἰ τῶν ὅλων ποιητής ἐστιν, καθὼς καὶ ἔστιν, ἄρα καὶ τοῦ ὕδατος καὶ τῶν θαλασσῶν κτίστης ἐστίν. Ἡσίοδος δὲ καὶ αὐτὸς οὐ μόνον θεῶν γένεσιν ἐξεῖπεν, ἀλλὰ καὶ αὐτοῦ τοῦ κόσμου. καὶ τὸν μὲν κόσμον γενητὸν εἰπὼν ἠτόνησεν εἰπεῖν ὑφ᾽ οὗ γέγονεν. ἔτι μὴν καὶ θεοὺς ἔφησεν Κρόνον καὶ τὸν ἐξ αὐτοῦ Δία, Ποσειδῶνά τε καὶ Πλούτωνα, καὶ τούτους μεταγενεστέρους εὑρίσκομεν τοῦ κόσμου. ἔτι δὲ καὶ τὸν Κρόνον πολεμεῖσθαι ὑπὸ τοῦ Διὸς τοῦ ἰδίου παιδὸς ἱστορεῖ. οὕτως γάρ φησιν·

Κάρτει νικήσας πατέρα Κρόνον· εὖ δὲ ἕκαστα
ἀθανάτοις διέταξεν ὅμως καὶ ἐπέφραδε τιμάς.

εἶτα ἐπιφέρει λέγων τὰς τοῦ Διὸς θυγατέρας, ἃς καὶ Μούσας προσαγορεύει, ὧν ἱκέτης εὑρίσκεται βουλόμενος μαθεῖν παρ᾽ αὐτῶν τίνι τρόπῳ τὰ πάντα γεγένηται. λέγει γάρ·

Χαίρετε, τέκνα Διός, δότε δ᾽[1] ἱμερόεσσαν ἀοιδήν.
κλείετε δ᾽ ἀθανάτων μακάρων γένος αἰὲν ἐόντων,
οἳ γῆς ἐξεγένοντο καὶ οὐρανοῦ ἀστερόεντος,
νυκτός τε δνοφερῆς, οὕς ἁλμυρὸς ἔτρεφε πόντος.
εἴπατε δ᾽ ὡς τὰ πρῶτα θεοὶ καὶ γαῖα[2] γένοντο,
καὶ ποταμοὶ καὶ πόντος ἀπείριτος, οἴδματι θύων,
ἄστρα τε λαμπετόωντα καὶ οὐρανὸς εὐρὺς[3] ὕπερθεν,
ὥς τ᾽ ἄφενος δάσσαντο καὶ ὡς τιμὰς διέλοντο,
ἠδὲ καὶ ὡς τὰ πρῶτα πολύπτυχον ἔσχον Ὄλυμπον.
ταῦτά μοι ἔσπετε Μοῦσαι Ὀλύμπια δώματ᾽ ἔχουσαι
ἐξ ἀρχῆς, καὶ εἴπατ᾽ ὅ τι πρῶτον γένετ᾽ αὐτῶν.

πῶς δὲ ταῦτα ἠπίσταντο αἱ Μοῦσαι, μεταγενέστεραι οὖσαι τοῦ κόσμου; ἢ πῶς ἠδύναντο διηγήσασθαι τῷ Ἡσιόδῳ, ὅπου δὴ ὁ πατὴρ αὐτῶν οὔπω γεγένηται;

6. Καὶ ὕλην μὲν τρόπῳ τινὶ ὑποτίθεται, καὶ κόσμου ποίησιν, λέγων·

Ἤτοι μὲν πρώτιστα χάος γένετ᾽, αὐτὰρ ἔπειτα
γαῖ᾽ εὐρύστερνος, πάντων ἕδος ἀσφαλὲς αἰεὶ

[1] δότε δ᾽] Hes. Th. 104 (West): δὲ τὸ δ᾽ V   [2] γαῖα] Hes. Th. 108 (West): γε V   [3] εὐρὺς] Hes. Th. 110 (West): om. V

But when he says this he does not establish the fact of God. For who does not understand that Ocean is water? And if water, then not God. If God is the creator of the universe, as he is, he must be the creator of water and the seas as well.

And Hesiod himself made a declaration not only about the origin of the gods but also about that of the world itself; but after calling the world created he lacked the force to say by whom it was created. Furthermore, he mentioned as gods Kronos, his son Zeus, Poseidon, and Pluto, those whom we find to have originated later than the world. Moreover, he describes how war was waged against Kronos by his own son Zeus. For he speaks thus [*Theog.* 73–4]:

> By force having overcome his father Kronos, fairly
> He divided privileges and assigned honours to the immortals.

Then he goes on to mention the daughters of Zeus, whom he further calls 'Muses', and we find him supplicating them in his desire to learn from them how everything originated. For he says [*Theog.* 104–10; 112–15]:

> Hail, children of Zeus! Grant lovely song
> And celebrate the race of the immortals, blessed and eternal,
> Those born of earth and of starry heaven,
> And of dark night, whom the salt sea nourished.
> Tell how at first the gods and earth came to be,
> And the rivers and the boundless sea with raging swell,
> The shining stars and the broad heaven above;
> How they divided the wealth and assumed different honours,
> And how at first they took many-folded Olympus.
> Tell me these things, Muses who have Olympian dwellings,
> From the beginning, and say which of them first came to be.

How did the Muses know these things when they originated later than the world? How could they describe them to Hesiod when their father had not yet been born?

6. In a certain way he assumes the existence of matter and the origin of the world when he says [*Theog.* 116–23, 126–33]:

> First Chaos came to be, and then
> Wide-bosomed earth, ever-sure foundation of all

ἀθανάτων, οἳ ἔχουσι κάρη νιφόεντος Ὀλύμπου,
Τάρταρά τ᾽ ἠερόεντα, μυχὸν χθονὸς εὐρυοδείης,
ἠδ᾽ Ἔρος, ὃς κάλλιστος ἐν ἀθανάτοισι θεοῖσι,
λυσιμελής, πάντων τε θεῶν πάντων τ᾽ ἀνθρώπων
δάμναται ἐν στήθεσσι νόον καὶ ἐπίφρονα βουλήν.
ἐκ Χάεος δ᾽ Ἔρεβός τε μέλαινά τε Νὺξ ἐγένοντο.
Γαῖα δέ τοι πρῶτον μὲν ἐγείνατο ἶσον ἑωυτῇ
Οὐρανὸν ἀστερόενθ᾽, ἵνα μιν περὶ πάντα καλύπτῃ,
ὄφρ᾽ εἴη μακάρεσσι θεοῖς ἕδος ἀσφαλὲς αἰεί·
γείνατο δ᾽ οὔρεα μακρά, θεᾶν χαρίεντας ἐναύλους[1]
Νυμφέων, αἳ ναίουσιν ἀν᾽ οὔρεα βησσήεντα·
ἠδὲ[2] καὶ ἀτρύγετον πέλαγος τέκεν οἴδματι θῦον,
πόντον, ἄτερ φιλότητος ἐφιμέρου· αὐτὰρ ἔπειτα
Οὐρανῷ εὐνηθεῖσα τεκ᾽ Ὠκεανὸν βαθυδίνην.

καὶ ταῦτα εἰπὼν οὐδὲ οὕτως ἐδήλωσεν ὑπὸ τίνος ἐγένοντο. εἰ γὰρ ἐν πρώτοις ἦν χάος, καὶ ὕλη τις προϋπέκειτο ἀγένητος οὖσα, τίς ἄρα ἦν ὁ ταύτην μετασκευάζων καὶ μεταρρυθμίζων καὶ μεταμορφῶν; πότερον αὐτὴ ἑαυτὴν ἡ ὕλη μετεσχημάτιζεν καὶ ἐκόσμει; ὁ γὰρ Ζεὺς μετὰ χρόνον πολὺν γεγένηται, οὐ μόνον τῆς ὕλης ἀλλὰ καὶ τοῦ κόσμου καὶ πλήθους ἀνθρώπων· ἔτι μὴν καὶ ὁ πατὴρ αὐτοῦ Κρόνος. ἢ μᾶλλον ἦν κύριόν τι τὸ ποιῆσαν αὐτήν, λέγω δὲ θεός, ὁ καὶ κατακοσμήσας αὐτήν;

Ἔτι μὴν κατὰ πάντα τρόπον φλυαρῶν εὑρίσκεται καὶ ἐναντία ἑαυτῷ λέγων. εἰπὼν γὰρ γῆν καὶ οὐρανὸν καὶ θάλασσαν ἐξ αὐτῶν τοὺς θεοὺς βούλεται γεγονέναι, καὶ ἐκ τούτων ἀνθρώπους δεινοτάτους τινὰς συγγενεῖς θεῶν καταγγέλλει, Τιτάνων γένος καὶ Κυκλώπων καὶ Γιγάντων πληθύν, τῶν τε κατὰ Αἴγυπτον δαιμόνων, ἢ ματαίων ἀνθρώπων, ὡς[3] μέμνηται Ἀπολλωνίδης, ὁ καὶ Ὡράπιος ἐπικληθείς, ἐν βίβλῳ τῇ ἐπιγραφομένῃ Σεμενουθὶ καὶ ταῖς λοιπαῖς κατ᾽ αὐτὸν ἱστορίαις περί τε τῆς θρησκείας τῆς Αἰγυπτιακῆς καὶ τῶν βασιλέων αὐτῶν.[4]

7. Τί δέ μοι λέγειν τοὺς κατὰ Ἕλληνας μύθους καὶ τὴν ἐν αὐτοῖς ματαιοπονίαν,[1] Πλούτωνα μὲν σκότους βασιλεύοντα, καὶ Ποσειδῶνα

---

6. [1] χαρίεντας ἐναύλους] Hes. Th. 129 (West): χαρίεσσαν ἐν αὐτοῖς V [2] ἠδὲ] Hes. Th. 131 (West): ἢ V [3] ὡς V: ὦν Maran [4] αὐτῶν] Maran: αὐτῶν καὶ τὴν ἐν αὐτοῖς ματαιοπονίαν V; cf. II. 7 n. 1.

7. [1] καὶ τὴν ἐν αὐτοῖς ματαιοπονίαν] Maran transp. ex II. 6 n. 4: om. V

> The immortals, who hold the peaks of snowy Olympus,
> And dim Tartarus, the depth of broad-pathed Earth,
> And Eros, fairest among the immortal gods
> Who unnerves the limbs and overcomes the mind
> And wise counsel of all gods and all men.
> From Chaos came Erebus and black Night.
> And Earth first bore, equal to herself, to cover her everywhere,
> Starry heaven, that there might be an ever-sure abode for the blessed gods;
> And she brought forth long hills, graceful haunts
> Of goddess Nymphs who dwell in woody hills;
> She bore also the fruitless deep with his raging swell,
> Pontus, without sweet union of love; and afterwards
> She lay with Heaven and bore deep-swirling Ocean.[1]

He says this, but he still does not explain by whom they were made. If originally there was chaos, and a certain uncreated matter already subsisted, who was it who reshaped, remodelled, and transformed it?[2] Did matter itself reshape and arrange itself? Zeus came into existence much later, not only after matter but even after the world and great numbers of men, and so did his father Kronos. Was there not instead some sovereign principle that made matter— I mean God, the one who set it in order?

Moreover, we find Hesiod talking absolute nonsense and contradicting himself. For he mentions earth and heaven and sea and wants the gods to have originated from them, and he speaks of certain terrible men as descendants of the gods, a race of Titans and a great number of Cyclopes and Giants [cf. *Theog.* 139, 185, 207]—not to mention the Egyptian demons (or foolish men) recorded by Apollonides surnamed Horapius in his book entitled *Semenouthi*[3] [*FHG* iv. 309] and in the rest of his histories concerning the Egyptian religion and their kings.

Myths and Genealogies

7. Why should I mention the Greek myths and the vain labour in them—Pluto reigning over darkness, and Poseidon submerging

---

6. [1] Translation by H. G. Evelyn-White, slightly altered.

[2] For the argument compare Sext. Emp. *Adv. math.* x. 18–19.

[3] References to 'the hieratic law Semnouthi' on the functions of priests and *pastophori* occur in a first-century papyrus (*Pubblicazioni della Società italiana per la ricerca dei Papiri*, x. 1149); cf. R. Merkelbach in *Zeitschrift für Papyrologie und Epigraphik* ii (1968) 11.

ὑπὸ πόντων δύνοντα καὶ τῇ Μελανίππῃ περιπλεκόμενον καὶ υἱὸν ἀνθρωποβόρον γεννήσαντα, ἢ περὶ τῶν τοῦ Διὸς παίδων ὁπόσα οἱ συγγραφεῖς ἐτραγῴδησαν; καὶ ὅτι οὗτοι ἄνθρωποι καὶ οὐ θεοὶ ἐγεννήθησαν, τὸ γένος αὐτῶν αὐτοὶ καταλέγουσιν.

Ἀριστοφάνης δὲ ὁ κωμικὸς ἐν ταῖς ἐπιγραφομέναις "Ορνισιν, ἐπιχειρήσας περὶ τῆς τοῦ κόσμου ποιήσεως, ἔφη ἐν πρώτοις ᾠὸν γεγενῆσθαι τὴν σύστασιν τοῦ κόσμου, λέγων·

Πρώτιστα τεκὼν μελανόπτερος ᾠόν.[2]

Ἀλλὰ καὶ Σάτυρος ἱστορῶν τοὺς δήμους Ἀλεξανδρέων, ἀρξάμενος ἀπὸ Φιλοπάτορος τοῦ καὶ Πτολεμαίου προσαγορευθέντος, τούτου μηνύει Διόνυσον ἀρχηγέτην γεγονέναι· διὸ καὶ φυλὴν ὁ Πτολεμαῖος πρώτην κατέστησεν. λέγει οὖν ὁ Σάτυρος οὕτως·

"Διονύσου καὶ Ἀλθαίας τῆς Θεστίου γεγενῆσθαι Δηϊάνειραν, τῆς δὲ καὶ Ἡρακλέους τοῦ Διὸς Ὕλλον, τοῦ δὲ Κλεοδαῖον,[3] τοῦ δὲ Ἀριστόμαχον, τοῦ δὲ Τήμενον, τοῦ δὲ Κεῖσον, τοῦ δὲ Μάρωνα, τοῦ δὲ Θέστιον, τοῦ δὲ Ἀκοόν, τοῦ δὲ Ἀριστοδαμίδαν,[4] τοῦ δὲ Καρανόν, τοῦ δὲ Κοινόν, τοῦ δὲ Τυρίμμαν, τοῦ δὲ Περδίκκαν, τοῦ δὲ Φίλιππον, τοῦ δὲ Ἀέροπον, τοῦ δὲ Ἀλκέταν, τοῦ δὲ Ἀμύνταν, τοῦ δὲ Βόκρον, τοῦ δὲ Μελέαγρον, τοῦ δὲ Ἀρσινόην, τῆς δὲ καὶ Λάγου Πτολεμαῖον τὸν καὶ Σωτῆρα, τοῦ δὲ καὶ Βερενίκης[5] Πτολεμαῖον τὸν Φιλάδελφον, τοῦ δὲ καὶ Ἀρσινόης Πτολεμαῖον τὸν Εὐεργέτην, τοῦ δὲ καὶ Βερενίκης τῆς Μάγα[6] τοῦ ἐν Κυρήνῃ βασιλεύσαντος Πτολεμαῖον τὸν Φιλοπάτορα.[7] ἡ μὲν οὖν πρὸς Διόνυσον τοῖς ἐν Ἀλεξανδρείᾳ βασιλεύσασιν συγγένεια οὕτως περιέχει. ὅθεν καὶ ἐν τῇ Διονυσίᾳ φυλῇ δημοί εἰσιν κατακεχωρισμένοι. Ἀλθηὶς ἀπὸ τῆς γενομένης γυναικὸς Διονύσου, θυγατρὸς δὲ Θεστίου, Ἀλθαίας. Δηϊανειρὶς ἀπὸ τῆς θυγατρὸς Διονύσου καὶ Ἀλθαίας, γυναικὸς δὲ Ἡρακλέους. ὅθεν καὶ τὰς προσωνυμίας ἔχουσιν οἱ κατ' αὐτοὺς δῆμοι· Ἀριαδνὶς ἀπὸ τῆς θυγατρὸς Μίνω, γυναικὸς δὲ Διονύσου, παιδὸς πατροφίλης[8] τῆς μιχθείσης Διονύσῳ ἐν μορφῇ †Πρύμνιδι†,[9] Θεστὶς ἀπὸ Θεστίου τοῦ Ἀλθαίας πατρός, Θοαντὶς ἀπὸ Θοαντὸς παιδὸς Διονύσου, Σταφυλὶς ἀπὸ Σταφύλου υἱοῦ Διονύσου, Εὐαινὶς ἀπὸ Εὐνόος υἱοῦ Διονύσου,

7. [2] ᾠόν] Aristoph. Av. 695 (Hall–Geldart): ἠὼς V [3] Κλεοδαῖον] P. Oxy. 2465; cf. Zwicker in RE xi. 673 f.: Κλεοδαῖμον V: Κλεόδημον V[2] [4] Ἀριστοδαμίδαν P. Oxy. 2465: Ἀριστομίδαν V [5] Βερενίκης] Wolf: Βερονίκης V [6] Βερενίκης τῆς Μάγα] Wolf: Βερονίκης τῆς μέγα V [7] Φιλοπάτορα] Maran: Φιλάδελφον V [8] πατροφίλης] Wolf: πατροφίλας V [9] πρύμνιδι V; cf. P. Oxy. 2465, fr. 3, col. ii, l. 14: πρυμνητοῦ Nolte

under the sea and embracing Melanippe and begetting a cannibal son, or the tragic tales composed about the sons of Zeus? Authors describe their genealogies because they were begotten as men, not as gods.

Aristophanes the comic poet said in the work entitled *The Birds*, when he undertook to speak about the creation of the world, that an egg was the original source of the foundation of the world, and he said [*Aves* 695]:[1]

Black-winged laid first an egg.

And Satyrus, describing the demes of the Alexandrians, beginning from Philopator who was also called Ptolemaeus, mentions Dionysus as the founder of his family; for this reason Ptolemaeus established the tribe as the first in rank. Now Satyrus speaks as follows [*FHG* iii. 164–5; *FGrHist* III c 631; P. Oxy. 2465]:

'From Dionysus and Althaea, the daughter of Thestius, was born Deianira; from her and Heracles son of Zeus, Hyllus; from him Cleodaeus; from him Aristomachus; from him Temenus; from him Ceisus; from him Maron; from him Thestius; from him Acous; from him Aristodamidas; from him Caranus; from him Coenus; from him Tyrimmas; from him Perdiccas;[2] from him Philippus, from him Aeropus; from him Alcetas; from him Amyntas; from him Bocrus; from him Meleager; from him Arsinoe; from her and Lagus, Ptolemaeus Soter; from him and Berenice, Ptolemaeus Philadelphus; from him and Arsinoe, Ptolemaeus Euergetes; from him and Berenice, the daughter of Maga formerly king of Cyrene, Ptolemaeus Philopator. This is the relation of the kings in Alexandria to Dionysus. Hence in the Dionysiac tribe the demes are thus assigned: Altheis from the wife of Dionysus and daughter of Thestius, Althaea; Deianeris from the daughter of Dionysus and Althaea, who was wife of Heracles. Hence also the other tribes have their appellations. Ariadnis from the daughter of Minos and wife of Dionysus, a child devoted to her father and one who had intercourse with Dionysus in the form *** Prymnis[3] ***, Thestis from Thestius the father of Althaea, Thoantis from Thoas the child of Dionysus, Staphylis from Staphylus the son of Dionysus, Euaenis

7. [1] Cf. O. Kern, *Orphicorum fragmenta* (Berlin, 1922), fr. 1, p. 80.

[2] *The Oxyrhynchus Papyri*, Part XXVII, ed. E. G. Turner *et al.* (London, 1962), no. 2465, fr. 1, col. ii, line 22, shows that Theophilus accidentally omitted the name of Argaeus at this point.

[3] The text of Theophilus is obviously corrupt and the numerous emendations have not improved it. 'Prymnidi', however, almost certainly refers to the Prymnis who, it is now known, was mentioned by Satyrus (P. Oxy. 2465, fr. 3, col. ii, line 14).

Μαρωνὶς ἀπὸ Μάρωνος υἱοῦ Ἀριάδνης καὶ Διονύσου. οὗτοι γὰρ πάντες υἱοὶ Διονύσου."

Ἀλλὰ καὶ ἕτεραι πολλαὶ ὀνομασίαι γεγόνασιν καί εἰσιν ἕως τοῦ δεῦρο, ἀπὸ Ἡρακλέους Ἡρακλεῖδαι καλούμενοι, καὶ ἀπὸ Ἀπόλλωνος Ἀπολλωνίδαι καὶ Ἀπολλώνιοι, καὶ ἀπὸ Ποσειδῶνος Ποσειδώνιοι, καὶ ἀπὸ Διὸς Δῖοι καὶ Διογέναι.

8. Καὶ τί μοι τὸ λοιπὸν τὸ πλῆθος τῶν τοιούτων ὀνομασιῶν καὶ γενεαλογιῶν καταλέγειν; ὥστε κατὰ πάντα τρόπον ἐμπαίζονται οἱ συγγραφεῖς πάντες καὶ ποιηταὶ καὶ φιλόσοφοι λεγόμενοι, ἔτι μὴν καὶ οἱ προσέχοντες αὐτοῖς. μύθους γὰρ μᾶλλον καὶ μωρίας συνέταξαν περὶ τῶν κατ' αὐτοὺς θεῶν· οὐ γὰρ ἀπέδειξαν αὐτοὺς θεοὺς ἀλλὰ ἀνθρώπους, οὓς μὲν μεθύσους, ἑτέρους δὲ πόρνους καὶ φονεῖς. Ἀλλὰ καὶ περὶ τῆς κοσμογονίας ἀσύμφωνα ἀλλήλοις καὶ φαῦλα ἐξεῖπον. πρῶτον μὲν ὅτι τινὲς ἀγένητον τὸν κόσμον ἀπεφήναντο, καθὼς καὶ ἔμπροσθεν ἐδηλώσαμεν, καὶ οἱ μὲν ἀγένητον αὐτὸν καὶ ἀΐδιον[1] φύσιν φάσκοντες οὐκ ἀκόλουθα εἶπον τοῖς γενητὸν αὐτὸν δογματίσασιν. εἰκασμῷ γὰρ ταῦτα καὶ ἀνθρωπίνῃ ἐννοίᾳ ἐφθέγξαντο, καὶ οὐ κατὰ ἀλήθειαν.

Ἕτεροι δ' αὖ εἶπον πρόνοιαν εἶναι, καὶ τὰ τούτων[2] δόγματα ἀνέλυσαν. Ἄρατος μὲν οὖν φησιν·

Ἐκ Διὸς ἀρχώμεσθα, τὸν οὐδέποτ' ἄνδρες ἐῶμεν
ἄρρητον. μεσταὶ δὲ Διὸς πᾶσαι μὲν ἀγυιαί,
πᾶσαι δ' ἀνθρώπων ἀγοραί, μεστὴ δὲ θάλασσα
καὶ λιμένες· πάντῃ δὲ Διὸς κεχρήμεθα πάντες.
τοῦ γὰρ καὶ γένος ἐσμέν· ὁ δ' ἤπιος ἀνθρώποισιν
δεξιὰ σημαίνει, λαοὺς δ' ἐπὶ ἔργον ἐγείρει
μιμνῄσκων βιότοιο· λέγει δ' ὅτε βῶλος ἀρίστη
βουσί τε καὶ μακέλῃσι, λέγει δ' ὅτε δεξιαὶ ὧραι
καὶ φυτὰ γυρῶσαι καὶ σπέρματα πάντα βαλέσθαι.

τίνι οὖν πιστεύσωμεν, πότερον Ἀράτῳ ἢ Σοφοκλεῖ λέγοντι·

Πρόνοια δ' ἐστὶν οὐδενός,[3]
εἰκῇ κράτιστον[4] ζῆν ὅπως δύναιτό τις;

8. [1] ἀΐδιον] Otto; cf. p. 26 n. 1 : ἰδίαν V   [2] τὰ τούτων] V; praem. ἕτεροι Maran: τὰ ἑαυτῶν Diels   [3] οὐδενός] V; cf. Zeegers-Vander Vorst, pp. 156–7: add. σαφής Soph. Oedip. rex 978 (Pearson)   [4] κράτιστον] Soph. Oedip. rex 979 (Pearson): κρατεῖτο V

from Eunous the son of Dionysus, Maronis from Maron the son of Ariadne and Dionysus; all these were sons of Dionysus.'

And there were many other appellations which continue up to the present time: from Heracles came those who were called Heraclidae, from Apollo Apollonidae and Apollonii, from Poseldon Posidonii, and from Zeus Dii and Diogenae.

The Poets and Providence

8. Why should I continue to list the multitude of such names and genealogies? All the historians and poets and so-called philosophers are deceived in every respect, and so are those who pay attention to them. For they have composed myths and foolishness concerning their gods by showing them to be not gods but men, some of them drunkards, others fornicators and murderers.

Moreover, they made inconsistent and evil statements about the origin of the world. In the first place, some of them declared that the world was uncreated, as we have already explained [II. 4]; and those who said that it was uncreated and that nature is eternal disagreed with those who held that it came into existence. They made these statements by conjecture and by human thought, not in accordance with the truth.

Others, again, said that providence exists, while still others demolished their doctrines. On the one hand, Aratus said [*Phaen.* 1–9]:

Let us take our beginning from Zeus, whom we men never leave Unmentioned; all highways are full of Zeus,
All market-places; full are the sea
And the harbours; everywhere we all have need of Zeus.
For we are his offspring; he is kind and to men
Gives favourable omens, arouses the peoples to work,
Reminding them of the livelihood they must make; he tells when clod is best
For oxen and picks, he tells when hours are favourable
For digging plants and for sowing all seeds.[1]

Whom shall we believe? Aratus, or Sophocles, who says [*Oedip. rex* 978–9]:

There is no evidence of providence;
It is best to live at random, however one can.

---

8. [1] This quotation and most of those following are derived from an anthology underlying those compiled by the fourth-century writers Stobaeus and Orion. The lines from Aratus were quoted by the Jewish apologist Aristobulus (in Eusebius, *Praep. ev.* 13, 12, 6); cf. Stob. i. 1. 4 (I, 23, 12 Wachsmuth).

Ὅμηρος δὲ πάλιν τούτῳ οὐ συνᾴδει. λέγει γάρ·

Ζεὺς δ' ἀρετὴν ἄνδρεσσιν ὀφέλλει τε μινύθει τε.

καὶ Σιμωνίδης·

Οὔτις ἄνευ θεῶν
ἀρετὰν λάβεν, οὐ πόλις, οὐ βρότος·
θεὸς ὁ παμμῆτις, ἀπήμαντον δ' οὐδὲν
ἐστιν ἐν αὐτοῖς.

ὁμοίως καὶ Εὐριπίδης·

Οὐκ ἔστιν οὐδὲν χωρὶς ἀνθρώποις θεοῦ.[5]

καὶ Μένανδρος·

Οὐκ ἄρα φροντίζει τις ἡμῶν ἢ μόνος θεός.[6]

καὶ πάλιν Εὐριπίδης·

Σῶσαι γὰρ ὁπόταν τῷ θεῷ δοκῇ,
πολλὰς προφάσεις δίδωσιν εἰς σωτηρίαν.

καὶ Θέστιος·[7]

Θεοῦ θέλοντος σώζῃ, κἂν ἐπὶ ῥιπὸς πλέῃς.[8]

καὶ τὰ τοιαῦτα μυρία εἰπόντες ἀσύμφωνα ἑαυτοῖς ἐξεῖπον. ὁ γοῦν Σοφοκλῆς ἀπρονοησίαν εἴρων ἐν ἑτέρῳ λέγει·[9]

Θεοῦ δὲ πληγὴν οὐχ ὑπερπηδᾷ βροτός.

Πλὴν καὶ πληθὺν εἰσήγαγον ἢ καὶ μοναρχίαν εἶπον, καὶ πρόνοιαν εἶναι τοῖς λέγουσιν ἀπρονοησίαν τἀναντία εἰρήκασιν. ὅθεν Εὐριπίδης ὁμολογεῖ λέγων·

Σπουδάζομεν δὲ πολλ' ὑπ' ἐλπίδων, μάτην
πόνους ἔχοντες, οὐδὲν εἰδότες.

Καὶ μὴ θέλοντες ὁμολογοῦσιν τὸ ἀληθὲς μὴ ἐπίστασθαι· ὑπὸ δαιμόνων δὲ ἐμπνευσθέντες καὶ ὑπ' αὐτῶν φυσιωθέντες ἃ εἶπον δι' αὐτῶν εἶπον. ἤτοι γὰρ οἱ ποιηταί, Ὅμηρος δὴ καὶ Ἡσίοδος ὥς

8. [5] ἀνθρώποις] V: ἀνθρώπων Orion, Flor. v. 7   θεοῦ] V: θεῶν Orion
[6] φροντίζει τις ἡμῶν ἢ μόνος θεός] V: φρον[τί]ζουσιν ἡμῶν [ο]ἱ [θεοί] Menander, Epitrep. 734 (Körte)   [7] Θέστιος] V: ἐκ τοῦ Θυέστου Orion, Flor. v. 5
[8] σώζῃ] V: om. Orion   πλέῃς] V: πλέοις Orion   [9] εἴρων ἐν ἑτέρῳ λέγει] Einarson: ἐν ἑτέρῳ λέγει V

Homer, on the other hand, disagrees with him, for he says [*Il.* xx. 242]:

> Zeus increases or diminishes virtue in men.[2]

And Simonides [fr. 61 Bergk]:

> No one apart from the gods
> Has acquired virtue, no city, no mortal.
> God is all-contriving, but nothing free from misery
> Is among men.[3]

Similarly also Euripides [fr. 391]:

> Nothing happens to men apart from God.[4]

And Menander [fr. 752; *Epitrepontes* 734]:

> No one takes thought for us but God alone.

And again Euripides [fr. 1089]:

> Whenever a god desires to save,
> He gives many opportunities for safety.

And Thestius [Euripides fr. 397]:

> If God will, you are safe, even if you sail on a mat.[5]

In making countless such statements they contradicted themselves. For Sophocles, who teaches the non-existence of providence, elsewhere says [fr. 876]:

> No mortal escapes the blow of God.[6]

Nevertheless, they introduced a multitude of gods or else spoke of the divine monarchy; to those who said that providence exists they expressed the contrary belief in the non-existence of providence. For this reason Euripides admits [fr. 391] that:

> Our hopes make us endeavour for many things, in vain
> Having labour, knowing nothing.[7]

So unwillingly they admit that they do not know the truth. Inspired by demons and puffed up by them, they said what they said through them. For such poets as Homer and Hesiod, inspired as they say by the Muses, spoke out of imagination and error, not by

---

8. [2] Stob. i. 1. 4 (I, 23, 22); Orion v. 13; cf. Plutarch, *De aud. poet.* 6.
   [3] Stob. i. 1. 10 (I, 24, 14).   [4] Orion v. 7.
   [5] Stob. i. 1. 19 (I, 28, 14); Orion v. 6 (ἐκ τοῦ Θυέστου); cf. [Menander], *Monost.* 349 Jaekel; Plutarch, *De Pyth. orac.* 22; Lucian, *Hermot.* 28 (with schol.); other references in Zeegers-Vander Vorst, i. 151.
   [6] Stob. i. 3. 7 (I, 53, 16); cf. [Menander], *Monost.* 345 Jaekel.
   [7] Orion v. 7.

φασιν ὑπὸ Μουσῶν ἐμπνευσθέντες, φαντασίᾳ καὶ πλάνῃ ἐλάλησαν, καὶ οὐ καθαρῷ πνεύματι ἀλλὰ πλάνῳ. ἐκ τούτου δὲ σαφῶς δείκνυται, εἰ καὶ οἱ δαιμονῶντες ἐνίοτε καὶ μέχρι τοῦ δεῦρο ἐξορκίζονται κατὰ τοῦ ὀνόματος τοῦ ὄντως θεοῦ, καὶ ὁμολογεῖ αὐτὰ τὰ πλάνα πνεύματα εἶναι δαίμονες, οἱ καὶ τότε εἰς ἐκείνους ἐνεργήσαντες, πλὴν ἐνίοτέ τινες τῇ ψυχῇ ἐκνήψαντες ἐξ αὐτῶν εἶπον ἀκόλουθα τοῖς προφήταις, ὅπως εἰς μαρτύριον αὐτοῖς τε καὶ πᾶσιν ἀνθρώποις περί τε θεοῦ μοναρχίας καὶ κρίσεως καὶ τῶν λοιπῶν ὧν ἔφασαν.

9. Οἱ δὲ τοῦ θεοῦ ἄνθρωποι, πνευματοφόροι πνεύματος ἁγίου καὶ προφῆται γενόμενοι, ὑπ' αὐτοῦ τοῦ θεοῦ ἐμπνευσθέντες καὶ σοφισθέντες, ἐγένοντο θεοδίδακτοι καὶ ὅσιοι καὶ δίκαιοι. διὸ καὶ κατηξιώθησαν τὴν ἀντιμισθίαν ταύτην λαβεῖν, ὄργανα θεοῦ γενόμενοι καὶ χωρήσαντες σοφίαν τὴν παρ' αὐτοῦ, δι' ἧς σοφίας εἶπον καὶ τὰ περὶ τῆς κτίσεως τοῦ κόσμου, καὶ τῶν λοιπῶν ἁπάντων. καὶ γὰρ περὶ λοιμῶν καὶ λιμῶν καὶ πολέμων προεῖπον. καὶ οὐχ εἷς ἢ δύο ἀλλὰ πλείονες κατὰ χρόνους καὶ καιροὺς ἐγενήθησαν[1] παρὰ Ἑβραίοις, ἀλλὰ καὶ παρὰ Ἕλλησιν Σίβυλλα καὶ πάντες φίλα ἀλλήλοις καὶ σύμφωνα εἰρήκασιν, τά τε πρὸ αὐτῶν γεγενημένα καὶ τὰ κατ' αὐτοὺς γεγονότα καὶ τὰ καθ' ἡμᾶς νυνὶ τελειούμενα· διὸ καὶ πεπείσμεθα καὶ περὶ τῶν μελλόντων οὕτως ἔσεσθαι, καθὼς καὶ τὰ πρῶτα ἀπήρτισται.

10. Καὶ πρῶτον μὲν συμφώνως ἐδίδαξαν ἡμᾶς, ὅτι ἐξ οὐκ ὄντων τὰ πάντα ἐποίησεν. οὐ γάρ τι τῷ θεῷ συνήκμασεν· ἀλλ' αὐτὸς ἑαυτοῦ τόπος ὢν καὶ ἀνενδεὴς ὢν καὶ ὑπάρχων πρὸ τῶν αἰώνων ἠθέλησεν ἄνθρωπον ποιῆσαι ᾧ γνωσθῇ· τούτῳ οὖν προητοίμασεν τὸν κόσμον. ὁ γὰρ γενητὸς καὶ προσδεής ἐστιν, ὁ δὲ ἀγένητος οὐδένος προσδεῖται.

Ἔχων οὖν ὁ θεὸς τὸν ἑαυτοῦ λόγον ἐνδιάθετον ἐν τοῖς ἰδίοις σπλάγχνοις ἐγέννησεν αὐτὸν μετὰ τῆς ἑαυτοῦ σοφίας ἐξερευξάμενος πρὸ τῶν ὅλων. τοῦτον τὸν λόγον ἔσχεν ὑπουργὸν τῶν ὑπ' αὐτοῦ γεγενημένων, καὶ δι' αὐτοῦ τὰ πάντα πεποίηκεν. οὗτος λέγεται ἀρχή, ὅτι ἄρχει καὶ κυριεύει πάντων τῶν δι' αὐτοῦ δεδημιουργημένων. οὗτος οὖν, ὢν πνεῦμα θεοῦ καὶ ἀρχὴ καὶ σοφία καὶ δύναμις ὑψίστου, κατήρχετο εἰς τοὺς προφήτας καὶ δι'

9. [1] ἐγενήθησαν] Fell: ἐγεννήθησαν V

a pure spirit but by one of error. This is clearly proved by the fact that up to the present day those who are possessed by demons are sometimes exorcized in the name of the real God, and the deceiving spirits themselves confess that they are the demons who were also at work at that time in the poets—except that sometimes some poets, becoming sober in soul and departing from the demons, made statements in agreement with those of the prophets in order to bear witness to themselves and to all men concerning the sole rule of God and the judgement and the other matters they discussed.

Inspiration and Truth in the Prophets

9. The men of God, who were possessed by a holy Spirit and became prophets and were inspired and instructed by God himself, were taught by God and became holy and righteous. For this reason they were judged worthy to receive the reward of becoming instruments of God and containing Wisdom from him. Through Wisdom they spoke about the creation of the world and about everything else; for they also prophesied about pestilences and famines and wars. There were not just one or two of them but more at various times and seasons among the Hebrews, as well as the Sibyl among the Greeks. All of them were consistent with one another and with themselves, and they described events which had previously occurred, events in their own time, and events which are now being fulfilled in our times. For this reason we are persuaded that their predictions of coming events will prove correct, just as the former events took place exactly.

Creation through the Logos

10. In the first place, in complete harmony they taught us that he made everything out of the non-existent. For there was nothing coeval with God; he was his own locus; he lacked nothing; he *existed before the ages* [Ps. 54: 20]. He wished to make man so that he might be known by him; for him, then, he prepared the world. For he who is created has needs, but he who is uncreated lacks nothing.

Therefore God, having his own Logos innate in his own bowels [cf. Ps. 109: 3], generated him together with his own Sophia, *vomiting* him *forth* [Ps. 44. 2] before everything else. He used this Logos as his servant in the things created by him, and through him he made all things [cf. John 1: 3]. He is called Beginning because

αὐτῶν ἐλάλει τὰ περὶ τῆς ποιήσεως τοῦ κόσμου καὶ τῶν λοιπῶν ἁπάντων. οὐ γὰρ ἦσαν οἱ προφῆται ὅτε ὁ κόσμος ἐγίνετο, ἀλλ' ἡ σοφία ἡ τοῦ θεοῦ ἡ ἐν αὐτῷ οὖσα[1] καὶ ὁ λόγος ὁ ἅγιος αὐτοῦ ὁ ἀεὶ συμπαρὼν αὐτῷ. διὸ δὴ καὶ διὰ Σολομῶνος προφήτου οὕτως λέγει· "Ἡνίκα δ' ἡτοίμασεν τὸν οὐρανόν, συμπαρήμην αὐτῷ, καὶ ὡς ἰσχυρὰ ἐποίει τὰ θεμέλια τῆς γῆς, ἤμην παρ' αὐτῷ ἁρμόζουσα." Μωσῆς δὲ ὁ καὶ Σολομῶνος πρὸ πολλῶν ἐτῶν γενόμενος, μᾶλλον δὲ ὁ λόγος ὁ τοῦ θεοῦ ὡς δι' ὀργάνου δι' αὐτοῦ φησιν· "Ἐν ἀρχῇ ἐποίησεν ὁ θεὸς τὸν οὐρανὸν καὶ τὴν γῆν." πρῶτον ἀρχὴν καὶ ποίησιν ὠνόμασεν, εἶθ' οὕτως τὸν θεὸν συνέστησεν· οὐ γὰρ ἀργῶς χρὴ καὶ ἐπὶ κενῷ θεὸν ὀνομάζειν. προῄδει γὰρ ἡ θεία σοφία μέλλειν φλυαρεῖν τινας καὶ πληθὺν θεῶν ὀνομάζειν τῶν οὐκ ὄντων. ὅπως οὖν ὁ τῷ ὄντι θεὸς διὰ ἔργων νοηθῇ, καὶ ὅτι ἐν τῷ λόγῳ αὐτοῦ ὁ θεὸς πεποίηκεν τὸν οὐρανὸν καὶ τὴν γῆν καὶ τὰ ἐν αὐτοῖς, ἔφη· "Ἐν ἀρχῇ ἐποίησεν ὁ θεὸς τὸν οὐρανὸν καὶ τὴν γῆν." εἶτα εἰπὼν τὴν ποίησιν αὐτῶν δηλοῖ ἡμῖν· "Ἡ δὲ γῆ ἦν ἀόρατος καὶ ἀκατασκεύαστος καὶ σκότος ἐπάνω τῆς ἀβύσσου, καὶ πνεῦμα θεοῦ ἐπεφέρετο ἐπάνω τοῦ ὕδατος."

Ταῦτα ἐν πρώτοις διδάσκει ἡ θεία γραφή, τρόπῳ τινὶ ὕλην γενητήν, ὑπὸ τοῦ θεοῦ γεγονυῖαν, ἀφ' ἧς πεποίηκεν καὶ δεδημιούργηκεν ὁ θεὸς τὸν κόσμον.

11. Ἀρχὴ δὲ τῆς ποιήσεως φῶς ἐστιν, ἐπειδὴ τὰ κοσμούμενα τὸ φῶς φανεροῖ. διὸ λέγει· "Καὶ εἶπεν ὁ θεός· Γενηθήτω φῶς. καὶ ἐγένετο φῶς. καὶ ἴδεν ὁ θεὸς τὸ φῶς ὅτι καλόν."[1] δηλονότι καλὸν ἀνθρώπῳ γεγονός.

"Καὶ διεχώρισεν ἀνὰ μέσον τοῦ φωτὸς καὶ ἀνὰ μέσον τοῦ σκότους. καὶ ἐκάλεσεν ὁ θεὸς τὸ φῶς ἡμέραν, καὶ τὸ σκότος ἐκάλεσε νύκτα. καὶ ἐγένετο ἑσπέρα καὶ ἐγένετο πρωΐ, ἡμέρα μία. καὶ εἶπεν ὁ θεός· Γενηθήτω στερέωμα ἐν μέσῳ τοῦ ὕδατος, καὶ ἔστω διαχωρίζον ἀνὰ μέσον ὕδατος καὶ ὕδατος. καὶ ἐγένετο οὕτως. καὶ ἐποίησεν ὁ θεὸς τὸ στερέωμα, καὶ διεχώρισεν ἀνὰ μέσον τοῦ ὕδατος ὃ ἦν ὑποκάτω τοῦ στερεώματος, καὶ ἀνὰ μέσον τοῦ ὕδατος τοῦ ἐπάνω τοῦ στερεώματος.

---

10. [1] ἡ τοῦ θεοῦ ἡ ἐν αὐτῷ οὖσα] Nautin: ἡ ἐν αὐτῷ οὖσα ἡ τοῦ θεοῦ V
11. [1] καὶ ἐγένετο φῶς. καὶ ἴδεν ὁ θεὸς τὸ φῶς ὅτι καλόν.] Fell; cf. Gen. 1:3: om. V

he leads and dominates everything fashioned through him. It was he, *Spirit of God* [Gen. 1 : 2] and *Beginning* [Gen. 1 : 1] and *Sophia* [Prov. 8 : 22] and *Power of the Most High* [Luke 1 : 35], who came down into the prophets and spoke through them about the creation of the world and all the rest [cf. II. 9]. For the prophets did not exist when the world came into existence; there were the Sophia of God which is in him and his holy Logos who is always present with him. For this reason he speaks thus through Solomon the prophet: 'When he prepared the heaven I was with him, and when he made strong the foundations of the earth I was with him, binding them fast' [Prov. 8 : 27–9]. And Moses, who lived many years before Solomon—or rather, the Logos of God speaking through him as an instrument—says: 'In the Beginning God made heaven and earth' [Gen. 1 : 1]. First he mentioned Beginning and creation, and only then did he introduce God, for it is not right to mention God idly and in vain [cf. Exod. 20 : 7]. For the divine Sophia knew in advance that some persons were going to speak nonsense and make mention of a multitude of non-existent gods. Therefore, in order for the real God to be known through his works, and to show that by his Logos God made heaven and earth and what is in them, he said: 'In the Beginning God made heaven and earth.' Then after mentioning their creation he gives us an explanation: 'And the earth was invisible and formless, and darkness was above the abyss, and the Spirit of God was borne above the water' [Gen. 1 : 2].

These are the first teachings which the divine scripture gives. It indicates that the matter from which God made and fashioned the world was in a way created, having been made by God.

The Text of Genesis

11. Light is the beginning of the creation, since the light reveals the things being set in order. Therefore it says [Gen. 1 : 3–2 : 3]: 'And God said, Let there be light. And there was light, and God saw the light, that it was good.' Made good, that is to say, for man.

'And he divided between the light and the darkness. And God called the light Day and the darkness he called Night. And it was evening and it was morning, day one. And God said, Let there be a firmament in the midst of the water, and let it be dividing between water and water. And it happened thus. And God made the firmament, and he divided between the water which was beneath the firmament and the water which was above the firmament. And

καὶ ἐκάλεσεν ὁ θεὸς τὸ στερέωμα οὐρανόν· καὶ ἴδεν ὁ θεὸς ὅτι καλόν. καὶ ἐγένετο ἑσπέρα καὶ ἐγένετο πρωΐ, ἡμέρα δευτέρα. καὶ εἶπεν ὁ θεός· Συναχθήτω τὸ ὕδωρ τὸ ὑποκάτω τοῦ οὐρανοῦ εἰς συναγωγὴν μίαν, καὶ ὀφθήτω ἡ ξηρά. καὶ ἐγένετο οὕτως. καὶ συνήχθη τὸ ὕδωρ εἰς τὰς συναγωγὰς αὐτῶν, καὶ ὤφθη ἡ ξηρά. καὶ ἐκάλεσεν ὁ θεὸς τὴν ξηρὰν γῆν, καὶ τὰ συστήματα τῶν ὑδάτων ἐκάλεσεν θαλάσσας. καὶ ἴδεν ὁ θεὸς ὅτι καλόν. καὶ εἶπεν ὁ θεός· Βλαστησάτω ἡ γῆ βοτάνην χόρτου σπεῖρον σπέρμα κατὰ γένος καὶ καθ᾽ ὁμοιότητα, καὶ ξύλον κάρπιμον ποιοῦν κάρπον, οὗ τὸ σπέρμα αὐτοῦ ἐν αὐτῷ εἰς ὁμοιότητα. καὶ ἐγένετο οὕτως. καὶ ἐξήνεγκεν ἡ γῆ βοτάνην χόρτου σπεῖρον σπέρμα κατὰ γένος, καὶ ξύλον κάρπιμον ποιοῦν κάρπον, οὗ τὸ σπέρμα ἐν αὐτῷ κατὰ γένος ἐπὶ τῆς γῆς. καὶ ἴδεν ὁ θεὸς ὅτι καλόν. καὶ ἐγένετο ἑσπέρα καὶ ἐγένετο πρωΐ, ἡμέρα τρίτη. καὶ εἶπεν ὁ θεός· Γενηθήτωσαν φωστῆρες ἐν τῷ στερεώματι τοῦ οὐρανοῦ, εἰς φαῦσιν ἐπὶ τῆς γῆς καὶ διαχωρίζειν ἀνὰ μέσον τῆς ἡμέρας καὶ ἀνὰ μέσον τῆς νυκτός, καὶ ἔστωσαν εἰς σημεῖα καὶ εἰς καιροὺς καὶ εἰς ἡμέρας καὶ εἰς ἐνιαυτούς, καὶ ἔστωσαν εἰς φαῦσιν ἐν τῷ στερεώματι τοῦ οὐρανοῦ φαίνειν ἐπὶ τῆς γῆς. καὶ ἐγένετο οὕτως. καὶ ἐποίησεν ὁ θεὸς τοὺς δύο φωστῆρας τοὺς μεγάλους, τὸν φωστῆρα τὸν μέγαν εἰς ἀρχὰς τῆς ἡμέρας, καὶ τὸν φωστῆρα τὸν ἐλάσσω εἰς ἀρχὰς τῆς νυκτός, καὶ τοὺς ἀστέρας. καὶ ἔθετο αὐτοὺς ὁ θεὸς ἐν τῷ στερεώματι τοῦ οὐρανοῦ, ὥστε φαίνειν ἐπὶ τῆς γῆς, καὶ ἄρχειν τῆς ἡμέρας καὶ τῆς νυκτός, καὶ διαχωρίζειν ἀνὰ μέσον τοῦ φωτὸς καὶ ἀνὰ μέσον τοῦ σκότους. καὶ ἴδεν ὁ θεὸς ὅτι καλόν. καὶ ἐγένετο ἑσπέρα καὶ ἐγένετο πρωΐ, ἡμέρα τετάρτη. καὶ εἶπεν ὁ θεός· Ἐξαγαγέτω τὰ ὕδατα ἑρπετὰ ψυχῶν ζωσῶν καὶ πετεινὰ πετόμενα ἐπὶ τῆς γῆς κατὰ τὸ στερέωμα τοῦ οὐρανοῦ. καὶ ἐγένετο οὕτως. καὶ ἐποίησεν ὁ θεὸς τὰ κήτη τὰ μεγάλα καὶ πᾶσαν ψυχὴν ζώων ἑρπετῶν, ἃ ἐξήγαγεν τὰ ὕδατα κατὰ γένη αὐτῶν, καὶ πᾶν πετεινὸν πτερωτὸν κατὰ γένος. καὶ ἴδεν ὁ θεὸς ὅτι καλά. καὶ εὐλόγησεν αὐτὰ ὁ θεὸς λέγων· Αὐξάνεσθε καὶ πληθύνεσθε, καὶ πληρώσατε τὰ ὕδατα τῆς θαλάσσης, καὶ τὰ πετεινὰ πληθυνέτω ἐπὶ τῆς γῆς. καὶ ἐγένετο ἑσπέρα καὶ ἐγένετο πρωΐ, ἡμέρα πέμπτη. καὶ εἶπεν ὁ θεός· Ἐξαγαγέτω ἡ γῆ ψυχὴν ζῶσαν κατὰ γένος, τετράποδα καὶ ἑρπετὰ καὶ θηρία τῆς γῆς κατὰ γένος. καὶ ἐγένετο οὕτως. καὶ ἐποίησεν ὁ θεὸς τὰ θηρία τῆς γῆς κατὰ γένος καὶ τὰ κτήνη κατὰ γένος, καὶ πάντα τὰ ἑρπετὰ τῆς γῆς. καὶ ἴδεν ὁ θεὸς ὅτι καλόν. καὶ

God called the firmament Heaven; and God saw that it was good. And it was evening and it was morning, the second day. And God said, Let the water beneath the firmament be gathered into one assembly, and let the dry land appear. And it happened thus. And the water was gathered into their assemblies and the dry land appeared. And God called the dry land Earth, and the bodies of waters he called Seas. And God saw that it was good. And God said, Let the earth bloom with edible grasses that scatter seeds after their kind and likeness, and fruit-bearing trees that produce fruit, and have their seeds in them after their likeness. And it happened thus. And the earth brought forth edible grasses that scatter seeds after their kind, and fruit-bearing trees that produce fruit in them after their likeness, on the earth. And God saw that it was good. And it was evening and it was morning, the third day. And God said, Let luminaries appear in the firmament of heaven, to give light on the earth and to divide between the day and the night, and let them be for signs and for seasons and days and for years, and let them be for lighting in the firmament of heaven, to shine on the earth. And it happened thus. And God made the two great luminaries, the great luminary to rule the day and the lesser luminary to rule the night, and the stars; and God set them in the firmament of heaven to shine on the earth and to rule the day and the night and to divide between the light and the darkness. And God saw that it was good. And it was evening and it was morning, the fourth day. And God said, Let the waters bring forth reptiles of living souls, and birds flying over the earth throughout the firmament of heaven. And it happened thus. And God made the great sea animals and every soul of reptile animals which the waters brought forth after their kinds and every winged bird after its kind. And God saw that they were good. And God blessed them, saying, Increase and multiply, and fill the waters of the sea, and let the birds multiply on the earth. And it was evening and it was morning, the fifth day. And God said, Let the earth bring forth living soul after its kind, and quadrupeds and reptiles and beasts of the earth after their kind. And it happened thus. And God made the beasts of the earth after their kind, and the flocks after their kind, and all the reptiles of the earth. And God saw that it was

εἶπεν ὁ θεός· Ποιήσωμεν ἄνθρωπον κατ' εἰκόνα ἡμετέραν καὶ καθ' ὁμοίωσιν, καὶ ἀρχέτωσαν τῶν ἰχθύων τῆς θαλάσσης καὶ τῶν πετεινῶν τοῦ οὐρανοῦ καὶ τῶν κτηνῶν καὶ πάσης τῆς γῆς καὶ πάντων τῶν ἑρπετῶν τῶν ἑρπόντων ἐπὶ τῆς γῆς. καὶ ἐποίησεν ὁ θεὸς τὸν ἄνθρωπον, κατ' εἰκόνα θεοῦ ἐποίησεν αὐτόν, ἄρσεν καὶ θῆλυ ἐποίησεν αὐτούς. καὶ εὐλόγησεν αὐτοὺς ὁ θεὸς λέγων· Αὐξάνεσθε καὶ πληθύνεσθε, καὶ πληρώσατε τὴν γῆν, καὶ κατακυριεύσατε αὐτῆς, καὶ ἄρχετε τῶν ἰχθύων τῆς θαλάσσης καὶ τῶν πετεινῶν τοῦ οὐρανοῦ καὶ πάντων τῶν κτηνῶν καὶ πάσης τῆς γῆς καὶ πάντων τῶν ἑρπετῶν τῶν ἑρπόντων ἐπὶ τῆς γῆς. καὶ εἶπεν ὁ θεός· Ἰδοὺ δέδωκα ὑμῖν πᾶν χόρτον σπόριμον σπεῖρον σπέρμα, ὅ ἐστιν ἐπάνω πάσης τῆς γῆς καὶ πᾶν ξύλον, ὃ ἔχει ἐν αὐτῷ καρπὸν σπέρματος σπορίμου, ὑμῖν ἔσται εἰς βρῶσιν, καὶ πᾶσιν τοῖς θηρίοις τῆς γῆς καὶ πᾶσιν τοῖς πετεινοῖς τοῦ οὐρανοῦ καὶ παντὶ ἑρπετῷ ἕρποντι ἐπὶ τῆς γῆς, ὃ ἔχει ἐν αὐτῷ πνοὴν ζωῆς, πάντα χόρτον χλωρὸν εἰς βρῶσιν. καὶ ἐγένετο οὕτως. καὶ ἴδεν ὁ θεὸς πάντα ὅσα ἐποίησεν, καὶ ἰδοὺ καλὰ λίαν. καὶ ἐγένετο ἑσπέρα καὶ ἐγένετο πρωΐ, ἡμέρα ἕκτη. καὶ συνετελέσθησαν ὁ οὐρανὸς καὶ ἡ γῆ καὶ πᾶς ὁ κόσμος αὐτῶν. καὶ συνετέλεσεν ὁ θεὸς ἐν τῇ ἡμέρᾳ τῇ ἕκτῃ τὰ ἔργα αὐτοῦ ἃ ἐποίησεν, καὶ κατέπαυσεν ἐν τῇ ἡμέρᾳ τῇ ἑβδόμῃ ἀπὸ πάντων τῶν ἔργων αὐτοῦ ὧν ἐποίησεν. καὶ εὐλόγησεν ὁ θεὸς τὴν ἡμέραν τὴν ἑβδόμην, καὶ ἡγίασεν αὐτήν, ὅτι ἐν αὐτῇ κατέπαυσεν ἀπὸ πάντων τῶν ἔργων αὐτοῦ ὧν ἤρξατο ὁ θεὸς ποιῆσαι."

12. Τῆς μὲν οὖν ἑξαημέρου οὐδεὶς ἀνθρώπων δυνατὸς κατ' ἀξίαν τὴν ἐξήγησιν καὶ τὴν οἰκονομίαν πᾶσαν ἐξειπεῖν, οὐδὲ εἰ μυρία στόματα ἔχοι καὶ μυρίας γλώσσας· ἀλλ' οὐδὲ εἰ μυρίοις ἔτεσιν βιώσει τις ἐπιδημῶν ἐν τῷδε τῷ βίῳ, οὐδὲ οὕτως ἔσται ἱκανὸς πρὸς ταῦτα ἀξίως τι εἰπεῖν, διὰ τὸ ὑπερβάλλον μέγεθος καὶ τὸν[1] πλοῦτον τῆς σοφίας τοῦ θεοῦ τῆς οὔσης ἐν ταύτῃ τῇ προγεγραμμένῃ ἑξαημέρῳ.

Πολλοὶ μὲν οὖν τῶν συγγραφέων ἐμιμήσαντο καὶ ἠθέλησαν περὶ τούτων διήγησιν ποιήσασθαι, καίτοι λαβόντες ἐντεῦθεν τὰς ἀφορμάς, ἤτοι περὶ κόσμου κτίσεως ἢ περὶ φύσεως ἀνθρώπου, καὶ οὐδὲ τὸ τυχὸν ἔναυσμα ἄξιόν τι τῆς ἀληθείας ἐξεῖπον. δοκεῖ δὲ τὰ ὑπὸ τῶν

12. [1] τὸν] V²: om. V

good. And God said, Let us make man after our image and after likeness, and let them rule over the fishes of the sea and the birds of the heaven and the flocks and all the earth and all the reptiles which creep on the earth. And God made man, after the image of God he made him, male and female he made them. And God blessed them, saying, Increase and multiply, and fill the earth, and dominate it, and rule over the fishes of the sea and the birds of the heaven and all the flocks and all the earth and all the reptiles which creep on the earth. And God said, Behold, I have given you every edible plant that scatters productive seeds and is upon the whole earth and every tree that has in it the fruit of productive seed; it shall be food for you and for all the beasts of the earth and all the birds of the heaven and every reptile creeping on the earth, which has in it the breath of life, every green herb for food. And it happened thus. And God saw everything which he had made, and behold, it was very good. And it was evening and it was morning, the sixth day. And the heaven and the earth and their whole order were completed. And God completed on the sixth day his works which he made, and he rested on the seventh day from all his works which he made. And God blessed the seventh day and sanctified it, because on it he rested from all his works which God began to make.'

The Six Days' Work of Creation

12. No man can adequately set forth the whole exegesis and plan of the Hexaëmeros (six days' work), even if he were to have ten thousand mouths and ten thousand tongues.[1] Not even if he were to live ten thousand years, continuing in this life, would he be competent to say anything adequately in regard to these matters, because of the *surpassing greatness* [Eph. 1: 19] and *riches of the Wisdom of God* [Rom. 11: 33] to be found in this Hexaëmeros quoted above.

To be sure, many writers have imitated it and have desired to compose a narrative about these matters, but, although they derived their starting-point from it in dealing with the creation of the world or the nature of man, what they said did not contain even a slight spark worthy of the truth. What has been said by philosophers,

12. [1] Cf. *Il.* ii. 489; E. Norden, *Aeneis Buch VI* (Leipzig, 1903), 286; A. Höfler, *Der Sarapishymnus des Aelios Aristides* (Stuttgart, 1935), 45.

φιλοσόφων ἢ συγγραφέων καὶ ποιητῶν εἰρημένα ἀξιόπιστα μὲν εἶναι, παρὰ τὸ φράσει κεκαλλιωπίσθαι· μωρὸς δὲ καὶ κενὸς ὁ λόγος αὐτῶν δείκνυται, ὅτι πολλὴ μὲν πληθὺς τῆς φλυαρίας αὐτῶν ἐστιν, τὸ τυχὸν δὲ τῆς ἀληθείας ἐν αὐτοῖς οὐχ εὑρίσκεται. καὶ γὰρ εἴ τι δοκεῖ ἀληθὲς δι' αὐτῶν ἐκπεφωνῆσθαι, σύγκρασιν ἔχει τῇ πλάνῃ. καθάπερ φάρμακόν τι δηλητήριον συγκραθὲν μέλιτι ἢ οἴνῳ ἢ ἑτέρῳ τινὶ τὸ πᾶν ποιεῖ βλαβερὸν καὶ ἄχρηστον, οὕτως καὶ ἡ ἐν αὐτοῖς πολυλογία εὑρίσκεται ματαιοπονία καὶ βλάβη μᾶλλον τοῖς πειθομένοις αὐτῇ. ἔτι μὴν καὶ περὶ τῆς ἑβδόμης ἡμέρας, ἣν πάντες μὲν ἄνθρωποι ὀνομάζουσιν, οἱ δὲ πλείους ἀγνοοῦσιν· ὅτι παρ' Ἑβραίοις ὃ καλεῖται σάββατον ἑλληνιστὶ ἑρμηνεύεται ἑβδομάς, ἥτις εἰς πᾶν γένος ἀνθρώπων ὀνομάζεται μέν, δι' ἣν δὲ αἰτίαν καλοῦσιν αὐτὴν οὐκ ἐπίστανται.

Τὸ δὲ εἰπεῖν Ἡσίοδον τὸν ποιητὴν ἐκ Χάους γεγενῆσθαι Ἔρεβος καὶ τὴν Γῆν καὶ Ἔρωτα κυριεύοντα τῶν κατ' αὐτόν τε θεῶν καὶ ἀνθρώπων, μάταιον καὶ ψυχρὸν τὸ ῥῆμα αὐτοῦ καὶ ἀλλότριον πάσης ἀληθείας δείκνυται· θεὸν γὰρ οὐ χρὴ ὑφ' ἡδονῆς νικᾶσθαι, ὅπου γε καὶ οἱ σώφρονες ἄνθρωποι ἀπέχονται πάσης αἰσχρᾶς ἡδονῆς καὶ ἐπιθυμίας κακῆς.

13. Ἀλλὰ καὶ τὸ ἐκ τῶν ἐπιγείων κάτωθεν ἄρξασθαι λέγειν[1] τὴν ποίησιν τῶν γεγενημένων ἀνθρώπινον καὶ ταπεινὸν καὶ πάνυ ἀσθενὲς τὸ ἐννόημα αὐτοῦ ὡς πρὸς θεόν ἐστιν. ἄνθρωπος γὰρ κάτω ὢν ἄρχεται ἐκ τῆς γῆς οἰκοδομεῖν, καὶ οὐ πρὸς τάξιν δύναται καὶ τὴν ὀροφὴν ποιῆσαι ἐὰν μὴ τὸν θεμέλιον ὑπόθηται. θεοῦ δὲ τὸ δυνατὸν ἐν τούτῳ δείκνυται ἵνα πρῶτον μὲν ἐξ οὐκ ὄντων ποιῇ τὰ γινόμενα, καὶ ὡς[2] βούλεται. τὰ γὰρ παρὰ ἀνθρώποις ἀδύνατα δυνατά ἐστιν παρὰ θεῷ. διὸ καὶ ὁ προφήτης πρῶτον εἴρηκεν τὴν ποίησιν τοῦ οὐρανοῦ γεγενῆσθαι τρόπον[3] ἐπέχοντα ὀροφῆς, λέγων· "Ἐν ἀρχῇ ἐποίησεν ὁ θεὸς τὸν οὐρανόν", τουτέστιν διὰ τῆς ἀρχῆς γεγενῆσθαι τὸν οὐρανόν, καθὼς ἔφθημεν δεδηλωκέναι.

Γῆν δὲ λέγει δυνάμει ἔδαφος καὶ θεμέλιον, ἄβυσσον δὲ τὴν πληθὺν τῶν ὑδάτων, καὶ σκότος διὰ τὸ τὸν οὐρανὸν γεγονότα ὑπὸ τοῦ θεοῦ ἐσκεπακέναι καθαπερεὶ πῶμα τὰ ὕδατα σὺν τῇ γῇ, πνεῦμα δὲ

13. [1] λέγειν] Nautin: καὶ praem. V [2] καὶ ὡς] Otto; cf. II. 4. 26: καθὼς V
[3] τρόπον] V: τύπον Nautin

historians, and poets is thought to be trustworthy because of its embellished style, but what they say is proved foolish and pointless by the abundance of their nonsense and the absence of even the slightest measure of the truth in their writings. Even if something true seems to have been proclaimed by them, it is mixed with error. Just as some deadly poison when mixed with honey or wine or anything else makes the whole harmful and useless, so their loquacity is found to be pointless labour and causes harm to those who are persuaded by it. This is true as regards the seventh day—a term which all men use, though most do not understand it; what the Hebrews call Sabbath is rendered 'hebdomad' in Greek. This name is in use among all nations of men, though they do not understand why they give it this name.

And as for Hesiod's statement that from Chaos were created Erebus and Earth and Eros, which rules over gods (as he considers them) and men [II. 6], his discourse is futile and frigid and entirely alien to the truth. A god must not be overcome by pleasure when temperate men abstain from all shameful pleasure and evil lust.

How God Made Heaven and Earth

13. Furthermore, as for Hesiod's notion of describing the creation by starting from beneath, with what is on earth, it is merely human and mean and, indeed, quite feeble in relation to God. For man who is below begins to build from the ground and cannot put on the roof in due course unless he has laid the foundation. But what God is able to do is shown by this, that he first makes existent things out of the non-existent just as he wills. For *things impossible with men are possible with God* [Luke 18: 27]. For this reason the prophet began by speaking of the creation of the heaven, which was fashioned like a roof, and he said, 'In the beginning God made heaven' [Gen. 1: 1]. That is to say that through the Beginning heaven was created, as we have just explained [II. 10].

What he calls 'earth' is equivalent to a base and foundation. 'Abyss' is the 'multitude of the waters'. 'Darkness' is mentioned because the heaven created by God was like a lid covering the

τὸ ἐπιφερόμενον ἐπάνω τοῦ ὕδατος ὃ ἔδωκεν ὁ θεὸς εἰς ζωογόνησιν τῇ κτίσει, καθάπερ ἀνθρώπῳ ψυχήν, τῷ λεπτῷ τὸ λεπτὸν συγκεράσας (τὸ γὰρ πνεῦμα λεπτὸν καὶ τὸ ὕδωρ λεπτόν), ὅπως τὸ μὲν πνεῦμα τρέφῃ τὸ ὕδωρ, τὸ δὲ ὕδωρ σὺν τῷ πνεύματι τρέφῃ τὴν κτίσιν διϊκνούμενον πανταχόσε. ἓν μὲν τὸ πνεῦμα φωτὸς τόπον[4] ἐπέχον ἐμεσίτευεν τοῦ ὕδατος καὶ τοῦ οὐρανοῦ, ἵνα τρόπῳ τινὶ μὴ κοινωνῇ τὸ σκότος τῷ οὐρανῷ ἐγγυτέρῳ ὄντι τοῦ θεοῦ, πρὸ τοῦ εἰπεῖν τὸν θεόν· "Γενηθήτω φῶς." ὥσπερ οὖν καμάρα ὁ οὐρανὸς ὢν συνεῖχε τὴν ὕλην βώλῳ ἐοικυῖαν. καὶ γὰρ εἴρηκεν περὶ τοῦ οὐρανοῦ ἕτερος προφήτης ὀνόματι Ἡσαΐας, λέγων· "Θεὸς οὗτος ὁ ποιήσας τὸν οὐρανὸν ὡς καμάραν καὶ διατείνας ὡς σκηνὴν κατοικεῖσθαι."

Ἡ διάταξις οὖν τοῦ θεοῦ, τοῦτό ἐστιν ὁ λόγος αὐτοῦ, φαίνων ὥσπερ λύχνος ἐν οἰκήματι συνεχομένῳ, ἐφώτισεν τὴν ὑπ' οὐρανόν, χωρὶς μὲν τοῦ κόσμου ποιήσας. καὶ τὸ μὲν φῶς ὁ θεὸς ἐκάλεσεν ἡμέραν, τὸ δὲ σκότος νύκτα· ἐπεί τοί γε ἄνθρωπος οὐκ ἂν ᾔδει καλεῖν τὸ φῶς ἡμέραν ἢ τὸ σκότος νύκτα, ἀλλ' οὐδὲ μὲν τὰ λοιπά, εἰ μὴ τὴν ὀνομασίαν εἰλήφει ἀπὸ τοῦ ποιήσαντος αὐτὰ θεοῦ.

Τῇ μὲν οὖν πρώτῃ ὑποθέσει τῆς ἱστορίας, καὶ γενέσεως τοῦ κόσμου, εἴρηκεν ἡ ἁγία γραφὴ οὐ περὶ τούτου τοῦ στερεώματος ἀλλὰ περὶ ἑτέρου οὐρανοῦ τοῦ ἀοράτου ἡμῖν ὄντος, μεθ' ὃν οὗτος ὁ ὁρατὸς[5] ἡμῖν οὐρανὸς κέκληται στερέωμα, ἐφ' ᾧ ἀνείληπται τὸ ἥμισυ τοῦ ὕδατος, ὅπως ᾖ τῇ ἀνθρωπότητι εἰς ὑετοὺς καὶ ὄμβρους καὶ δρόσους. τὸ δὲ ἥμισυ ὕδατος ὑπελείφθη ἐν τῇ γῇ εἰς ποταμοὺς καὶ πηγὰς καὶ θαλάσσας. ἔτι οὖν συνέχοντος τοῦ ὕδατος τὴν γῆν, μάλιστα κοίλους τόπους, ἐποίησεν ὁ θεὸς διὰ τοῦ λόγου αὐτοῦ τὸ ὕδωρ συναχθῆναι εἰς συναγωγὴν μίαν, καὶ ὁρατὴν γενηθῆναι τὴν ξηράν, πρότερον γεγονυῖαν αὐτὴν ἀόρατον. ὁρατὴ οὖν ἡ γῆ γενομένη ἔτι ὑπῆρχεν ἀκατασκεύαστος. κατεσκεύασεν οὖν αὐτὴν καὶ κατεκόσμησεν ὁ θεὸς διὰ παντοδαπῶν χλοῶν καὶ σπερμάτων καὶ φυτῶν.

14. Σκόπει τὸ λοιπὸν τὴν ἐν τούτοις ποικιλίαν καὶ διάφορον καλλονὴν καὶ πληθύν, καὶ ὅτι δι' αὐτῶν δείκνυται ἡ ἀνάστασις, εἰς δεῖγμα τῆς μελλούσης ἔσεσθαι ἀναστάσεως ἁπάντων ἀνθρώπων.

13. [4] τόπον] Maran: τύπον V   [5] ὁρατὸς] Clauser: ἀόρατος V

waters with the earth. The 'spirit borne over the water' was the one given by God to give life to the creation, like the soul in man, when he mingled tenuous elements together (for the spirit is tenuous and the water is tenuous), so that the spirit might nourish the water and the water with the spirit might nourish the creation by penetrating it from all sides. The unique spirit occupied the place of light and was situated between the water and the heaven so that, so to speak, the darkness might not communicate with the heaven, which was nearer to God, before God said: 'Let there be light.' Like a vaulted ceiling, then, the heaven surrounded matter, which was like a lump. For another prophet, Isaiah by name, has spoken about the heaven, saying: 'This is God, who made the heaven like a vaulted ceiling and stretched it out like a tent to live in' [Isa. 40: 22].

Therefore the Command of God, his Logos, shining like a lamp in a closed room, illuminated the region under the heaven, making light separately from the world. 'And God called the light day and the darkness night', since man certainly would not have known how to call the light day or the darkness night, or the names of anything else, unless he had received their appellation from the God who made them.

In this preliminary statement in the narrative of the creation of the world, the holy scripture spoke not about this firmament but about another heaven which is invisible to us. Afterwards this heaven visible to us is called 'firmament'. On it was raised up half of the water so that it might serve mankind for rains and showers and dews. The other half of the water was left on the earth for rivers and springs and seas. While the water still surrounded the earth, especially the low-lying places, God by his Logos made the water come together into one assembly and made visible the dry land which was previously invisible. Though the earth became visible it was still unfurnished; then God formed it and adorned it with all sorts of herbs and seeds and plants.

14. Further, consider their variety and their remarkable beauty and numbers, and the fact that through them the resurrection is signified, for a proof of the future resurrection of all men [1. 13]. For

Τίς γὰρ κατανοήσας οὐ θαυμάσει ἐκ συκῆς κεγχραμίδος γίνεσθαι συκῆν, ἢ τῶν λοιπῶν σπερμάτων ἐλαχίστων φύειν παμμεγέθη δένδρα;

Τὸν δὲ κόσμον ἐν ὁμοιώματι ἡμῖν λέγομεν εἶναι τῆς θαλάσσης. ὥσπερ γὰρ θάλασσα, εἰ μὴ εἶχεν τὴν τῶν ποταμῶν καὶ πηγῶν ἐπίρρυσιν καὶ ἐπιχορηγίαν εἰς τροφήν, διὰ τὴν ἁλμυρότητα αὐτῆς πάλαι ἂν ἐκπεφρυγμένη ἦν, οὕτως καὶ ὁ κόσμος, εἰ μὴ ἐσχήκει τὸν τοῦ θεοῦ νόμον καὶ τοὺς προφήτας ῥέοντας καὶ πηγάζοντας τὴν γλυκύτητα καὶ εὐσπλαγχνίαν καὶ δικαιοσύνην καὶ διδαχὴν τῶν ἁγίων ἐντολῶν τοῦ θεοῦ, διὰ τὴν κακίαν καὶ ἁμαρτίαν τὴν πληθύουσαν ἐν αὐτῷ ἤδη ἂν ἐκλελοίπει.

Καὶ καθάπερ ἐν θαλάσσῃ νῆσοί εἰσιν αἱ μὲν οἰκηταὶ καὶ ἔνυδροι καὶ καρποφόροι, ἔχουσαι ὅρμους καὶ λιμένας πρὸς τὸ τοὺς χειμαζομένους ἔχειν ἐν αὐτοῖς καταφυγάς, οὕτως δέδωκεν ὁ θεὸς τῷ κόσμῳ κυμαινομένῳ καὶ χειμαζομένῳ ὑπὸ τῶν ἁμαρτημάτων τὰς συναγωγάς, λεγομένας δὲ ἐκκλησίας ἁγίας, ἐν αἷς καθάπερ λιμέσιν εὐόρμοις ἐν νήσοις αἱ διδασκαλίαι τῆς ἀληθείας εἰσίν, πρὸς ἃς καταφεύγουσιν οἱ θέλοντες σώζεσθαι, ἐρασταὶ γινόμενοι τῆς ἀληθείας καὶ βουλόμενοι ἐκφυγεῖν τὴν ὀργὴν καὶ κρίσιν τοῦ θεοῦ. καὶ ὥσπερ αὖ νῆσοί εἰσιν ἕτεραι πετρώδεις καὶ ἄνυδροι καὶ ἄκαρποι καὶ θηριώδεις καὶ ἀοίκητοι ἐπὶ βλάβῃ τῶν πλεόντων καὶ χειμαζομένων, ἐν αἷς περιπείρεται τὰ πλοῖα καὶ ἐξαπόλλυνται ἐν αὐταῖς οἱ κατερχόμενοι, οὕτως εἰσὶν αἱ διδασκαλίαι τῆς πλάνης, λέγω δὲ τῶν αἱρέσεων, αἳ ἐξαπολλύουσιν τοὺς προσιόντας αὐταῖς. οὐ γὰρ ὁδηγοῦνται ὑπὸ τοῦ λόγου τῆς ἀληθείας, ἀλλὰ καθάπερ πειρᾶται, ἐπὰν πληρώσωσιν τὰς ναῦς, ἐπὶ τοὺς προειρημένους τόπους περιπείρουσιν ὅπως ἐξαπολέσωσιν αὐτάς, οὕτως συμβαίνει καὶ τοῖς πλανωμένοις ἀπὸ τῆς ἀληθείας ἐξαπόλλυσθαι ὑπὸ τῆς πλάνης.

15. Τετάρτῃ ἡμέρᾳ ἐγένοντο οἱ φωστῆρες. ἐπειδὴ ὁ θεὸς προγνώστης ὢν ἠπίστατο τὰς φλυαρίας τῶν ματαίων φιλοσόφων, ὅτι ἤμελλον λέγειν ἀπὸ τῶν στοιχείων εἶναι τὰ ἐπὶ τῆς γῆς φυόμενα, πρὸς τὸ ἀθετεῖν τὸν θεόν· ἵν' οὖν τὸ ἀληθὲς δειχθῇ, προγενέστερα γέγονεν τὰ φυτὰ καὶ τὰ σπέρματα τῶν στοιχείων· τὰ γὰρ μεταγενέστερα οὐ δύναται ποιεῖν τὰ αὐτῶν προγενέστερα. ταῦτα δὲ δεῖγμα καὶ τύπον

what person who considers it will not marvel that a fig tree comes into existence from a fig seed, or that very great trees grow from other tiny seeds [cf. Matt. 13: 32]?

The Meaning of the Sea

And we say that for us the world is in the likeness of the sea. For just as the sea, if it did not have the flow of rivers and springs as a supply of nourishment, would long ago have been parched because of its saltiness, so also the world, if it had not had the law of God and the prophets flowing and gushing forth with sweetness and compassion [cf. 1 Clem. 14: 3] and righteousness and the teaching of God's holy commandments, would already have failed because of the evil and sin abounding in it.

And as in the sea there are some islands which are habitable and well-watered and fertile, and have anchorages and havens so that those who are tossed by storms can take refuge in them, so God gave the world, which is agitated and tossed by sins, certain assemblies called holy churches, in which as in havens with good mooring-places are the teachings of truth. In these will take refuge those who wish to be saved, when they are lovers of truth and want to escape the wrath and judgement of God. And as, again, there are other islands which are rocky and waterless and barren, full of wild beasts and uninhabitable, harmful to those who sail and are tossed by storms, islands on which ships are impaled and those who land perish, so also are the teachings of error—I mean of the heresies—which destroy those who approach them. For they are not guided by the word of truth, but just as pirates, when they have filled ships, run them on the places mentioned above, in order to destroy them, so it happens that those who stray from the truth are destroyed by error.

The Fourth Day of Creation

15. On the fourth day the luminaries came into existence. Since God has foreknowledge, he understood the nonsense of the foolish philosophers who were going to say that the things produced on earth come from the stars,[1] so that they might set God aside [1 Thess. 4 : 8]. In order therefore that the truth might be demonstrated, plants and seeds came into existence before the stars. For what comes into existence later cannot cause what is prior to it.[2] And these things contain a pattern and type of a great mystery.

---

15. [1] Philo (*Opif.* 45–6) similarly criticizes the view that the sun is the source of all physical life and growth; cf. K. Reinhardt, *Poseidonios* (Munich, 1921), 205–7; M. Pohlenz, *Die Stoa* (Göttingen, 1948), 223–4.

[2] A philosophical commonplace; cf. Sext. Emp. *Pyrrh. hyp.* iii. 25.

ἐπέχει μεγάλου μυστηρίου. ὁ γὰρ ἥλιος ἐν τύπῳ θεοῦ ἐστιν, ἡ δὲ σελήνη ἀνθρώπου. καὶ ὥσπερ ὁ ἥλιος πολὺ διαφέρει τῆς σελήνης δυνάμει καὶ δόξῃ, οὕτως πολὺ διαφέρει ὁ θεὸς τῆς ἀνθρωπότητος καὶ καθάπερ ὁ ἥλιος πλήρης πάντοτε διαμένει μὴ ἐλάσσων γινόμενος, οὕτως πάντοτε ὁ θεὸς τέλειος διαμένει, πλήρης ὢν πάσης δυνάμεως καὶ συνέσεως καὶ σοφίας καὶ ἀθανασίας καὶ πάντων τῶν ἀγαθῶν· ἡ δὲ σελήνη κατὰ μῆνα φθίνει καὶ δυνάμει ἀποθνήσκει, ἐν τύπῳ οὖσα ἀνθρώπου, ἔπειτα ἀναγεννᾶται καὶ αὔξει εἰς δεῖγμα τῆς μελλούσης ἔσεσθαι ἀναστάσεως.

Ὡσαύτως καὶ αἱ τρεῖς ἡμέραι πρὸ[1] τῶν φωστήρων γεγονυῖαι τύποι εἰσὶν τῆς τριάδος, τοῦ θεοῦ καὶ τοῦ λόγου αὐτοῦ καὶ τῆς σοφίας αὐτοῦ. τετάρτῳ δὲ τόπῳ[2] ἐστὶν ἄνθρωπος ὁ προσδεὴς τοῦ φωτός, ἵνα ᾖ θεός, λόγος, σοφία, ἄνθρωπος. διὰ τοῦτο καὶ τετάρτῃ ἡμέρᾳ ἐγενήθησαν φωστῆρες.

Ἡ δὲ τῶν ἄστρων θέσις οἰκονομίαν καὶ τάξιν ἔχει τῶν δικαίων καὶ εὐσεβῶν καὶ τηρούντων τὸν νόμον καὶ τὰς ἐντολὰς τοῦ θεοῦ. οἱ γὰρ ἐπιφανεῖς ἀστέρες καὶ λαμπροί εἰσιν εἰς μίμησιν τῶν προφητῶν· διὰ τοῦτο καὶ μένουσιν ἀκλινεῖς, μὴ μεταβαίνοντες τόπον[3] ἐκ τόπου. οἱ δὲ ἑτέραν ἔχοντες τάξιν τῆς λαμπρότητος τύποι εἰσὶν τοῦ λαοῦ τῶν δικαίων. οἱ δ' αὖ μεταβαίνοντες καὶ φεύγοντες τόπον[4] ἐκ τόπου, οἱ καὶ πλάνητες καλούμενοι, καὶ αὐτοὶ τύπος τυγχάνουσιν τῶν ἀφισταμένων ἀνθρώπων ἀπὸ τοῦ θεοῦ, καταλιπόντων τὸν νόμον καὶ τὰ προστάγματα αὐτοῦ.

16. Τῇ δὲ πέμπτῃ ἡμέρᾳ τὰ ἐκ τῶν ὑδάτων ἐγενήθη ζῷα, δι' ὧν καὶ ἐν τούτοις δείκνυται ἡ πολυποίκιλος σοφία τοῦ θεοῦ. τίς γὰρ δύναιτ' ἂν τὴν ἐν αὐτοῖς πληθὺν καὶ γονὴν παμποίκιλον ἐξαριθμῆσαι; ἔτι μὴν καὶ εὐλογήθη ὑπὸ τοῦ θεοῦ τὰ ἐκ τῶν ὑδάτων γενόμενα, ὅπως ᾖ καὶ τοῦτο εἰς δεῖγμα τοῦ μέλλειν λαμβάνειν τοὺς ἀνθρώπους μετάνοιαν καὶ ἄφεσιν ἁμαρτιῶν διὰ ὕδατος καὶ λουτροῦ παλιγγενεσίας πάντας τοὺς προσιόντας τῇ ἀληθείᾳ καὶ ἀναγεννωμένους καὶ λαμβάνοντας εὐλογίαν παρὰ τοῦ θεοῦ.

Ἀλλὰ καὶ τὰ κήτη καὶ τὰ πετεινὰ τὰ σαρκοβόρα ἐν ὁμοιώματι τυγχάνει τῶν πλεονεκτῶν καὶ παραβατῶν. ὥσπερ γὰρ ἐκ μιᾶς

15. [1] πρὸ] Wolf: om. V [2] τόπῳ] Maran: τύπῳ V [3] τόπον] V: praem. εἰς Gesner [4] τόπον] V: praem. εἰς Fell

For the sun exists as a type of God and the moon as a type of man. As the sun greatly surpasses the moon in power and brightness, so God greatly surpasses mankind; and just as the sun always remains full and does not wane, so God always remains perfect and is full of all power, intelligence, wisdom, immortality, and all good things. But the moon wanes every month and virtually dies, for it exists as a type of man; then it is reborn and waxes as a pattern of the future resurrection [1. 13].

Similarly the three days prior to the luminaries are types of the triad[3] of God and his Logos and his Sophia. In the fourth place is man, who is in need of light—so that there might be God, Logos, Sophia, Man. For this reason the luminaries came into existence on the fourth day.

The disposition of the stars corresponds to the arrangement and rank of the righteous and godly men who keep the law and the commandments of God. For the stars which are clearly visible and radiant exist in imitation of the prophets; for this reason they remain unswerving, not passing over to one position from another. Those which possess a secondary degree of radiance are types of the people of the righteous [cf. Isa. 60: 21]. On the other hand, those which pass over and flee from one position to another and are called 'planets' are a type of the men who depart from God, abandoning his law and ordinances.

The Fifth Day of Creation

16. On the fifth day were created the animals from the waters; through these, as in them, is demonstrated *the manifold wisdom of God* [Eph. 3 : 10]. For who could enumerate their numbers and their varied progeny? Furthermore, those created from the waters were blessed by God so that this might serve as a pattern of men's future reception of repentance and remission of sins through water and a *bath of regeneration* [Tit. 3: 5], in the case of all who approach the truth and are reborn and receive a blessing from God.

But also the great fish and the carnivorous birds are in the likeness of greedy men and transgressors. For as marine animals and

15. [3] This 'triad' is not precisely the Trinity, since in Theophilus' mind man can be added to it.

φύσεως ὄντα τὰ ἔνυδρα καὶ τὰ πετεινά, ἔνια μὲν μένει ἐν¹ τῷ κατὰ φύσιν μὴ ἀδικοῦντα τὰ ἑαυτῶν ἀσθενέστερα, ἀλλὰ τηρεῖ νόμον τοῦ θεοῦ καὶ ἀπὸ τῶν σπερμάτων τῆς γῆς ἐσθίει, ἔνια δὲ ἐξ αὐτῶν παραβαίνει τὸν νόμον τοῦ θεοῦ σαρκοβοροῦντα, καὶ² ἀδικεῖ τὰ ἑαυτῶν ἀσθενέστερα, οὕτως καὶ οἱ δίκαιοι φυλάσσοντες τὸν νόμον τοῦ θεοῦ οὐδένα δάκνουσιν ἢ ἀδικοῦσιν, ὁσίως καὶ δικαίως ζῶντες, οἱ δὲ ἅρπαγες καὶ φονεῖς καὶ ἄθεοι ἐοίκασιν κήτεσιν καὶ θηρίοις καὶ πετεινοῖς τοῖς σαρκοβόροις· δυνάμει γὰρ καταπίνουσιν τοὺς ἀσθενεστέρους ἑαυτῶν. Ἡ μὲν οὖν τῶν ἐνύδρων καὶ ἑρπετῶν γονή, μετεσχηκυῖα τῆς εὐλογίας τοῦ θεοῦ, οὐδὲν ἴδιον πάνυ κέκτηται.

17. Ἕκτῃ δὲ ἡμέρᾳ ὁ θεὸς ποιήσας τὰ τετράποδα καὶ τὰ θηρία καὶ ἑρπετὰ τὰ χερσαῖα τὴν πρὸς αὐτὰ εὐλογίαν παρασιωπᾷ, τηρῶν τῷ ἀνθρώπῳ τὴν εὐλογίαν, ὃν ἤμελλεν ἐν τῇ ἕκτῃ ἡμέρᾳ ποιεῖν.

Ἅμα καὶ εἰς τύπον ἐγένοντο τά τε τετράποδα καὶ θηρία ἐνίων ἀνθρώπων τῶν τὸν θεὸν ἀγνοούντων καὶ ἀσεβούντων καὶ τὰ ἐπίγεια φρονούντων καὶ μὴ μετανοούντων. οἱ γὰρ ἐπιστρέφοντες ἀπὸ τῶν ἀνομιῶν καὶ δικαίως ζῶντες ὥσπερ πετεινὰ ἀνίπτανται τῇ ψυχῇ, τὰ ἄνω φρονοῦντες καὶ εὐαρεστοῦντες τῷ θελήματι τοῦ θεοῦ. οἱ δὲ τὸν θεὸν ἀγνοοῦντες καὶ ἀσεβοῦντες ὅμοιοί εἰσιν ὀρνέοις τὰ πτερὰ μὲν ἔχουσιν, μὴ δυναμένοις δὲ ἀνίπτασθαι καὶ τὰ ἄνω τρέχειν τῆς θειότητος. οὕτως καὶ οἱ τοιοῦτοι ἄνθρωποι μὲν λέγονται, τὰ δὲ χαμαιφερῆ καὶ τὰ ἐπίγεια φρονοῦσιν, καταβαρούμενοι ὑπὸ τῶν ἁμαρτιῶν.

Θηρία δὲ ὠνόμασται τὰ ζῷα ἀπὸ τοῦ θηρεύεσθαι,¹ οὐχ ὡς κακὰ ἀρχῆθεν γεγενημένα ἢ ἰοβόλα, οὐ γάρ τι κακὸν ἀρχῆθεν γέγονεν ἀπὸ θεοῦ ἀλλὰ τὰ πάντα καλὰ καὶ καλὰ λίαν, ἡ δὲ ἁμαρτία ἡ περὶ τὸν ἄνθρωπον κεκάκωκεν αὐτά· τοῦ γὰρ ἀνθρώπου παραβάντος καὶ αὐτὰ συμπαρέβη. ὥσπερ γὰρ δεσπότης οἰκίας ἐὰν αὐτὸς εὖ πράσσῃ, ἀναγκαίως καὶ οἱ οἰκέται εὐτάκτως ζῶσιν, ἐὰν δὲ ὁ κύριος ἁμαρτάνῃ, καὶ οἱ δοῦλοι συναμαρτάνουσιν, τῷ αὐτῷ τρόπῳ γέγονεν καὶ τὰ περὶ τὸν ἄνθρωπον κύριον ὄντα ἁμαρτῆσαι, καὶ τὰ δοῦλα συνήμαρτεν. ὁπόταν οὖν πάλιν ὁ ἄνθρωπος ἀναδράμῃ εἰς τὸ κατὰ φύσιν μηκέτι κακοποιῶν, κἀκεῖνα ἀποκατασταθήσεται εἰς τὴν ἀρχῆθεν ἡμερότητα.

16. ¹ ἐν] Wolf: om. V   ² καὶ] Wolf: om. V
17. ¹ θηρεύεσθαι] V: θηριοῦσθαι Otto

birds are of one nature, and some remain in their natural state, not harming those weaker than themselves but keeping the law of God and eating seeds from the earth, but some of them transgress the law of God, eating flesh and harming those weaker than themselves, so also the righteous who keep the law of God do not bite or harm anyone but live in holiness and justice, but robbers and murderers and the godless are like great fish and wild animals and carnivorous birds. They virtually consume those weaker than themselves.

Although the progeny of marine animals and reptiles shared in the blessing of God, it acquired no special characteristic of its own.[1]

The Sixth Day of Creation

17. On the sixth day, after making the quadrupeds and the wild animals and the land reptiles, God omits mention of a blessing for them, reserving the blessing for man, whom he was going to make on the sixth day.

The quadrupeds and wild animals were a type of those men who are ignorant of God and sin against him and *mind earthly things* [Phil. 3: 19] and do not repent. For those who repent of their iniquities and live righteously [cf. Ezek. 18: 21–3] take flight in soul like birds, *minding things above* [Col. 3: 2] and taking pleasure in the will of God. But those who are ignorant of God and sin against him are like birds which have wings but are unable to fly and to run the upward course to the divine nature. Thus those of this sort are called men, but *mind* low and *earthly things* and are weighed down by sins.

Wild animals (*thēria*) are so called from their being hunted (*thēreuesthai*). They were not originally created evil or poisonous, for nothing was originally created evil by God; everything was good and *very good* [Gen. 1: 31]. The sin of man made them evil, for when man transgressed they transgressed with him. If the master of a house does well, his servants necessarily live properly; if the master sins, his slaves sin with him. Just so, it turned out that man, the master, sinned and the slaves sinned with him. Whenever man again returns to his natural state and so no longer does evil, they too will be restored to their original tameness [cf. Isa. 11 : 6–9].

---

16. [1] In other words, like man it remained able to disobey God.

18. Τὰ δὲ περὶ τῆς τοῦ ἀνθρώπου ποιήσεως, ἀνέκφραστός ἐστιν ὡς πρὸς ἄνθρωπον ἡ κατ' αὐτὸν δημιουργία, καίπερ σύντομον ἔχει ἡ θεία γραφὴ τὴν κατ' αὐτὸν ἐκφώνησιν. ἐν τῷ γὰρ εἰπεῖν τὸν θεόν· "Ποιήσωμεν ἄνθρωπον κατ' εἰκόνα καὶ καθ' ὁμοίωσιν τὴν ἡμετέραν", πρῶτον μηνύει τὸ ἀξίωμα τοῦ ἀνθρώπου. πάντα γὰρ λόγῳ ποιήσας ὁ θεὸς καὶ τὰ πάντα πάρεργα ἡγησάμενος μόνον ἰδίων[1] ἔργον χειρῶν ἄξιον ἡγεῖται τὴν ποίησιν τοῦ ἀνθρώπου. ἔτι μὴν καὶ ὡς[2] βοηθείας χρῄζων ὁ θεὸς εὑρίσκεται λέγων· "Ποιήσωμεν ἄνθρωπον κατ' εἰκόνα καὶ καθ' ὁμοίωσιν." οὐκ ἄλλῳ δέ τινι εἴρηκεν· "Ποιήσωμεν", ἀλλ' ἢ τῷ ἑαυτοῦ λόγῳ καὶ τῇ ἑαυτοῦ σοφίᾳ. ποιήσας δὲ αὐτὸν καὶ εὐλογήσας εἰς τὸ αὐξάνεσθαι καὶ πληρῶσαι τὴν γῆν ὑπέταξεν αὐτῷ ὑποχείρια καὶ ὑπόδουλα τὰ πάντα, προσέταξεν δὲ καὶ ἔχειν τὴν δίαιταν αὐτὸν ἀρχῆθεν ἀπὸ τῶν καρπῶν τῆς γῆς καὶ τῶν σπερμάτων καὶ χλοῶν καὶ ἀκροδρύων, ἅμα καὶ συνδίαιτα κελεύσας εἶναι τὰ ζῶα τῷ ἀνθρώπῳ εἰς τὸ καὶ αὐτὰ ἐσθίειν ἀπὸ τῶν σπερμάτων ἁπάντων τῆς γῆς.

19. Οὕτως συντελέσας ὁ θεὸς τὸν οὐρανὸν καὶ τὴν γῆν καὶ τὴν θάλασσαν καὶ πάντα ὅσα ἐν αὐτοῖς ἐν τῇ ἕκτῃ ἡμέρᾳ κατέπαυσεν ἐν τῇ ἑβδόμῃ ἡμέρᾳ ἀπὸ πάντων τῶν ἔργων αὐτοῦ ὧν ἐποίησεν. εἶθ' οὕτως ἀνακεφαλαιοῦται λέγουσα ἡ ἁγία γραφή· "Αὕτη βίβλος γενέσεως οὐρανοῦ καὶ τῆς γῆς, ὅτε ἐγένετο ἡμέρᾳ ᾗ ἐποίησεν ὁ θεὸς τὸν οὐρανὸν καὶ τὴν γῆν, καὶ πᾶν χλωρὸν ἀγροῦ πρὸ τοῦ γενέσθαι, καὶ πάντα χόρτον ἀγροῦ πρὸ τοῦ ἀνατεῖλαι· οὐ γὰρ ἔβρεξεν ὁ θεὸς ἐπὶ τὴν γῆν, καὶ ἄνθρωπος οὐκ ἦν ἐργάζεσθαι τὴν γῆν." διὰ τούτου ἐμήνυσεν ἡμῖν ὅτι καὶ ἡ γῆ πᾶσα κατ' ἐκεῖνο καιροῦ ἐποτίζετο ὑπὸ πηγῆς θείας, καὶ οὐκ εἶχεν χρείαν ἐργάζεσθαι αὐτὴν ἄνθρωπον, ἀλλὰ τὰ πάντα αὐτοματισμῷ ἀνέφυεν ἡ γῆ κατὰ τὴν ἐντολὴν τοῦ θεοῦ, πρὸς τὸ μὴ κοπιᾶν ἐργαζόμενον τὸν ἄνθρωπον.

Ὅπως δὲ καὶ ἡ πλάσις δειχθῇ, πρὸς τὸ μὴ δοκεῖν εἶναι ζήτημα ἐν ἀνθρώποις ἀνεύρετον, ἐπειδὴ εἴρητο ὑπὸ τοῦ θεοῦ· " Ποιήσωμεν ἄνθρωπον" καὶ οὔπω ἡ πλάσις[1] αὐτοῦ πεφανέρωται, διδάσκει ἡμᾶς ἡ γραφὴ λέγουσα· "Πηγὴ δὲ ἀνέβαινεν ἐκ τῆς γῆς καὶ ἐπότιζεν πᾶν τὸ πρόσωπον τῆς γῆς, καὶ ἔπλασεν ὁ θεὸς τὸν ἄνθρωπον χοῦν

18. [1] ἰδίων] Gesner: ἀΐδιον V (cf. II. 4. 5)   [2] ὡς] V: praem. οὐχ Loofs
19. [1] πλάσις] Grant; cf. l. 13 and II. 23. 2: ποίησις V

The Creation of Man

18. As for the creation of man, his fashioning cannot be expressed by man, yet the divine scripture contains a summary mention of it. When God said, 'Let us make man after our image and likeness' [Gen. 1: 26], he first reveals the dignity of man. For after making everything else by a word, God considered all this as incidental; he regarded the making of man as the only work worthy of his own hands. Furthermore, God is found saying 'Let us make man after the image and likeness' as if he needed assistance;[1] but he said 'Let us make' to none other than his own Logos and his own Sophia. When he had made him and had blessed him so that he would increase and fill the earth, he subordinated all other beings to him as subjects and slaves. He also commanded that from the beginning man should have a diet derived from the fruits of the earth and seeds and herbs and fruit trees, and that animals were to have the same diet as man so that they too would eat of all the seeds of the earth.

The Seventh Day

19. Thus God, after completing heaven and earth and everything in them on the sixth day, rested on the seventh day from all the works he had made. Then the holy scripture thus provides a summary: 'This is the book of the creation of heaven and earth, when they were made on the day when God made heaven and earth, and every plant of the field before it came into existence, and every herb of the field before it arose; for God had not yet rained on the earth, and there was no man to till the earth' [Gen. 2: 4–5]. Hereby it reveals to us that at that time the whole earth was watered by a divine spring, and it had no need for a man to till it. The earth brought forth everything spontaneously in accordance with the commandment of God, so that man would not grow weary from labour.

And so that the formation of man might also be indicated—so that there might not seem to be an insoluble problem among men, since 'Let us make man' had been spoken by God but man's formation had not yet been manifested—the scripture teaches us, saying: 'A spring went up from the earth and watered all the face of the earth, and God formed man, dust from the earth, and breathed the breath of life into his face, and man became a living

---

18. [1] The exegesis of Gen. 1: 3 posed problems; cf. Tatian in Clement, *Ecl. proph.* xxxviii. 1 and Origen, *De orat.* xxiv. 5 (*Contra Celsum* vi. 51).

ἀπὸ τῆς γῆς, καὶ ἐνεφύσησεν εἰς τὸ πρόσωπον αὐτοῦ πνοὴν ζωῆς, καὶ ἐγένετο ὁ ἄνθρωπος εἰς ψυχὴν ζῶσαν." ὅθεν καὶ ἀθάνατος ἡ ψυχὴ ὠνόμασται παρὰ τοῖς πλείοσι. μετὰ δὲ τὸ πλάσαι τὸν ἄνθρωπον ὁ θεὸς ἐξελέξατο αὐτῷ χωρίον ἐν τοῖς τόποις τοῖς ἀνατολικοῖς, διάφορον φωτί, διαυγὲς ἀέρι λαμπροτέρῳ, φυτοῖς παγκάλοις, ἐν ᾧ ἔθετο τὸν ἄνθρωπον.

20. Τὰ δὲ ῥητὰ τῆς ἱστορίας τῆς ἱερᾶς ἡ γραφὴ οὕτως περιέχει·

"Καὶ ἐφύτευσεν ὁ θεὸς τὸν παράδεισον ἐν Ἐδὲμ κατὰ ἀνατολὰς καὶ ἔθετο ἐκεῖ τὸν ἄνθρωπον ὃν ἔπλασεν. καὶ ἐξανέτειλεν ὁ θεὸς ⟨ἔτι⟩[1] ἐκ τῆς γῆς πᾶν ξύλον, ὡραῖον εἰς ὅρασιν καὶ καλὸν εἰς βρῶσιν, καὶ τὸ ξύλον τῆς ζωῆς ἐν μέσῳ τοῦ παραδείσου καὶ τὸ ξύλον τοῦ εἰδέναι γνωστὸν καλοῦ καὶ πονηροῦ. ποταμὸς δὲ ἐκπορεύεται ἐξ Ἐδὲμ ποτίζειν τὸν παράδεισον· ἐκεῖθεν ἀφορίζεται εἰς τέσσαρας ἀρχάς. ὄνομα τῷ ἑνὶ Φεισών· οὗτος ὁ κυκλῶν πᾶσαν τὴν γῆν Εὐιλάτ· ἐκεῖ οὖν ἐστιν τὸ χρυσίον. τὸ δὲ χρυσίον τῆς γῆς ἐκείνης καλὸν κἀκεῖ ἐστιν ὁ ἄνθραξ καὶ ὁ λίθος ὁ πράσινος. καὶ ὄνομα τῷ ποταμῷ τῷ δευτέρῳ Γεών· οὗτος κυκλοῖ πᾶσαν τὴν γῆν Αἰθιοπίας. καὶ ὁ ποταμὸς ὁ τρίτος Τίγρις· οὗτος ὁ πορευόμενος κατέναντι Ἀσσυρίων. ὁ δὲ ποταμὸς ὁ τέταρτος Εὐφράτης. καὶ ἔλαβεν κύριος ὁ θεὸς τὸν ἄνθρωπον ὃν ἔπλασεν, καὶ ἔθετο αὐτὸν ἐν τῷ παραδείσῳ ἐργάζεσθαι αὐτὸν καὶ φυλάσσειν. καὶ ἐνετείλατο ὁ θεὸς τῷ Ἀδάμ, λέγων· Ἀπὸ παντὸς ξύλου τοῦ ἐν τῷ παραδείσῳ βρώσει φαγεῖ· ἀπὸ δὲ τοῦ ξύλου τοῦ γινώσκειν καλὸν καὶ πονηρὸν οὐ φάγεσθε[2] ἀπ' αὐτοῦ· ᾗ δ' ἂν ἡμέρᾳ φάγησθε[3] ἀπ' αὐτοῦ θανάτῳ ἀποθανεῖσθε. καὶ εἶπεν κύριος ὁ θεός· Οὐ καλὸν εἶναι τὸν ἄνθρωπον μόνον· ποιήσωμεν αὐτῷ βοηθὸν κατ' αὐτόν. καὶ ἔπλασεν ὁ θεὸς ἔτι ἐκ τῆς γῆς πάντα τὰ θηρία τοῦ ἀγροῦ καὶ πάντα τὰ πετεινὰ τοῦ οὐρανοῦ, καὶ ἤγαγεν αὐτὰ πρὸς τὸν Ἀδάμ. καὶ πᾶν ὃ ἂν ἐκάλεσεν αὐτὰ Ἀδάμ, ψυχὴν ζῶσαν, τοῦτο ὄνομα αὐτοῦ. καὶ ἐκάλεσεν Ἀδὰμ ὀνόματα πᾶσι τοῖς κτήνεσιν καὶ πᾶσι τοῖς πετεινοῖς τοῦ οὐρανοῦ καὶ πᾶσι τοῖς θηρίοις τοῦ ἀγροῦ· τῷ δὲ Ἀδὰμ οὐχ εὑρέθη βοηθὸς ὅμοιος αὐτῷ. καὶ ἐπέβαλεν ὁ θεὸς ἔκστασιν ἐπὶ τὸν Ἀδὰμ καὶ ὕπνωσιν καὶ ἔλαβεν μίαν τῶν πλευρῶν αὐτοῦ καὶ ἀνεπλήρωσεν σάρκα ἀντ' αὐτῆς. καὶ ᾠκοδόμησεν κύριος ὁ θεὸς τὴν πλευράν, ἣν ἔλαβεν ἀπὸ τοῦ Ἀδάμ, εἰς

20. [1] ἔτι] Grant; cf. II. 24. 1 : om. V [2] φάγεσθε] LXX : φάγησθε V
[3] φάγησθε] LXX : φάγεσθε V

soul' [Gen. 2:6-7]. This is why the soul is called immortal by most people. After forming man, God chose a place for him in the eastern regions, excellent for its light, brilliant with brighter air, most beautiful with its plants.[1] In this he placed man.

The History of Man and Paradise

20. The scripture thus contains the words of the sacred history [Gen. 2:8-3:19]:

'And God planted paradise in Eden to the east and there set the man whom he had made. And God further raised up out of the earth every tree beautiful to see and good to eat, and the tree of life in the middle of paradise, and the tree of knowing good and evil. And a river goes out of Eden to water paradise; from there it is separated into four branches. The name of the first is Phison; this is the one which encircles the whole land of Euilat; there, there is gold. The gold of that land is good, and there too there is the ruby and the emerald. And the name of the second is Geon; this encircles the whole land of Ethiopia. And the third river is Tigris; this goes out toward the Assyrians. The fourth river is Euphrates. And the Lord God took the man whom he had formed and set him in paradise to work it and guard it. And God commanded Adam, saying, From every tree in paradise you may eat food; but from the tree of knowing good and evil you may not eat from it; on the day you eat from it you will die in death. And the Lord God said, It is not good for the man to be alone: let us make a helper for him like him. And God further formed from the earth all the beasts of the field and all the birds of the heaven and brought them to Adam. And whatever Adam called them, a living soul, this became its name. And Adam called by name all the flocks and all the birds of the heaven and all the beasts of the field; but for Adam there was not found a helper like him. And God cast a trance over Adam, and he slept; and he took one of his ribs and filled up

---

19. [1] Cf. the Ethiopic *Apocalypse of Peter*, c. 15; G. Quispel and R. M. Grant, 'Note on the Petrine Apocrypha', *Vigiliae Christianae*, vi (1952), 31-2.

γυναῖκα, καὶ ἤγαγεν αὐτὴν πρὸς τὸν Ἀδάμ. καὶ εἶπεν Ἀδάμ· Τοῦτο νῦν ὀστοῦν ἐκ τῶν ὀστῶν μου καὶ σὰρξ ἐκ τῆς σαρκός μου· αὕτη κληθήσεται γυνή, ὅτι ἐκ τοῦ ἀνδρὸς αὐτῆς ἐλήφθη αὐτή. ἕνεκεν τούτου καταλείψει ἄνθρωπος τὸν πατέρα καὶ τὴν μητέρα αὐτοῦ καὶ προσκολληθήσεται πρὸς τὴν γυναῖκα αὐτοῦ καὶ ἔσονται οἱ δύο εἰς σάρκα μίαν. καὶ ἦσαν οἱ δύο γυμνοί, ὅ τε Ἀδὰμ καὶ ἡ γυνὴ αὐτοῦ, καὶ οὐκ ᾐσχύνοντο.

21. " Ὁ δὲ ὄφις ἦν φρονιμώτερος πάντων τῶν θηρίων τῶν ἐπὶ τῆς γῆς, ὧν ἐποίησεν κύριος ὁ θεός. καὶ εἶπεν ὁ ὄφις τῇ γυναικί· Τί ὅτι εἶπεν ὁ θεός· Οὐ μὴ φάγητε ἀπὸ παντὸς ξύλου τοῦ παραδείσου; καὶ εἶπεν ἡ γυνὴ τῷ ὄφει· Ἀπὸ παντὸς ξύλου τοῦ παραδείσου φαγόμεθα, ἀπὸ δὲ καρποῦ τοῦ ξύλου, ὅ ἐστιν ἐν μέσῳ τοῦ παραδείσου, εἶπεν ὁ θεός· Οὐ μὴ φάγησθε[1] ἀπ' αὐτοῦ οὐδὲ μὴ ἅψησθε αὐτοῦ, ἵνα μὴ ἀποθάνητε. καὶ εἶπεν ὁ ὄφις τῇ γυναικί· Οὐ θανάτῳ ἀποθανεῖσθε· ᾔδει γὰρ ὁ θεὸς ὅτι ἐν ᾗ ἂν ἡμέρᾳ φάγητε ἀπ' αὐτοῦ διανοιχθήσονται ὑμῶν οἱ ὀφθαλμοί, καὶ ἔσεσθε ὡς θεοί, γινώσκοντες καλὸν καὶ πονηρόν. καὶ ἴδεν ἡ γυνὴ ὅτι καλὸν τὸ ξύλον εἰς βρῶσιν, καὶ ὅτι ἀρεστὸν τοῖς ὀφθαλμοῖς ἰδεῖν καὶ ὡραῖόν ἐστιν τοῦ κατανοῆσαι καὶ λαβοῦσα τοῦ καρποῦ αὐτοῦ ἔφαγεν καὶ ἔδωκεν καὶ τῷ ἀνδρί αὐτῆς μεθ' ἑαυτῆς, καὶ ἔφαγον. καὶ διηνοίχθησαν οἱ ὀφθαλμοὶ τῶν δύο καὶ ἔγνωσαν ὅτι γυμνοὶ ἦσαν, καὶ ἔρραψαν φύλλα συκῆς καὶ ἐποίησαν ἑαυτοῖς περιζώματα. καὶ ἤκουσαν τῆς φωνῆς κυρίου τοῦ θεοῦ, περιπατοῦντος ἐν τῷ παραδείσῳ τὸ δειλινόν, καὶ ἐκρύβησαν ὅ τε Ἀδὰμ καὶ ἡ γυνὴ αὐτοῦ ἀπὸ προσώπου τοῦ θεοῦ ἐν μέσῳ τοῦ ξύλου τοῦ παραδείσου. καὶ ἐκάλεσεν κύριος ὁ θεὸς τὸν Ἀδὰμ καὶ εἶπεν αὐτῷ· Ποῦ εἶ ⟨Ἀδάμ⟩;[2] καὶ εἶπεν αὐτῷ· Τὴν φωνήν σου ἤκουσα ἐν τῷ παραδείσῳ, καὶ ἐφοβήθην ὅτι γυμνός εἰμι καὶ ἐκρύβην. καὶ εἶπεν αὐτῷ· Τίς ἀνήγγειλέ σοι ὅτι γυμνὸς εἶ, εἰ μὴ ἀπὸ τοῦ ξύλου, οὗ ἐνετειλάμην σοι τούτου μόνου μὴ φαγεῖν, ἀπ' αὐτοῦ ἔφαγες; καὶ εἶπεν Ἀδάμ· Ἡ γυνή, ἣν ἔδωκάς μοι, αὐτή μοι ἔδωκεν ἀπὸ τοῦ ξύλου, καὶ ἔφαγον. καὶ εἶπεν ὁ θεὸς τῇ γυναικί· Τί τοῦτο ἐποίησας; καὶ εἶπεν ἡ γυνή· Ὁ ὄφις ἠπάτησέν με καὶ ἔφαγον. καὶ εἶπεν κύριος ὁ θεὸς τῷ ὄφει· Ὅτι ἐποίησας τοῦτο, ἐπικατάρατος σὺ ἀπὸ πάντων τῶν θηρίων τῶν ἐπὶ τῆς γῆς, ἐπὶ τῷ στήθει καὶ τῇ κοιλίᾳ

21. [1] φάγησθε] Humphry; cf. LXX: φάγεσθε V
[2] Ἀδάμ] Grant; cf. II. 26. 14: om. V

flesh in its place. And the Lord God fashioned the rib which he had taken from Adam into a woman, and he led her to Adam. And Adam said, This now is bone out of my bones and flesh out of my flesh; she will be called woman because she was taken from her man. For this reason a man will leave his father and mother and will unite with his wife, and the two will be one flesh. And the two were naked, Adam and his wife, and they were not ashamed.

21. 'The serpent was the wisest of all the beasts on the earth which the Lord God had made. And the serpent said to the woman, Why did God say, You may not eat from every tree of paradise? And the woman said to the serpent, From every tree of paradise we shall eat, but from the fruit of the tree which is in the middle of paradise, God said, Do not eat from it or touch it, lest you die. And the serpent said to the woman, You will not die in death, for God knew that on the day you eat of it your eyes will be opened and you will be like gods, knowing good and evil. And the woman saw that the tree was good to eat and that it was pleasing to the eyes to see and beautiful to consider; and taking its fruit she ate and gave also to her husband with her, and they ate. And the eyes of both were opened and they knew that they were naked, and they sewed together fig leaves and made themselves girdles. And they heard the voice of the Lord God, who was walking in paradise at evening, and Adam and his wife hid from the face of God in the midst of the trees of paradise. And the Lord God called Adam and said to him, Where are you, Adam? And he said to him, I heard your voice in paradise and I was afraid because I am naked, and I hid. And he said to him, Who told you that you are naked, unless you ate from the tree of which alone I told you not to eat? And Adam said, The woman whom you gave me, she gave it from the tree and I ate. And God said to the woman, Why did you do this? And the woman said, The serpent deceived me, and I ate. And the Lord God said to the serpent, Because you did this, you are

σου πορεύσῃ καὶ γῆν φαγῇ πάσας τὰς ἡμέρας τῆς ζωῆς σου. καὶ ἔχθραν ποιήσω ἀνὰ μέσον σου καὶ ἀνὰ μέσον τῆς γυναικὸς καὶ ἀνὰ μέσον τοῦ σπέρματός σου καὶ τοῦ σπέρματος αὐτῆς· αὐτός σου τηρήσει τὴν κεφαλήν, καὶ σὺ αὐτοῦ τηρήσεις τὴν πτέρναν. καὶ τῇ γυναικὶ εἶπεν· Πληθύνων πληθυνῶ τὰς λύπας σου καὶ τὸν στεναγμόν σου· ἐν λύπῃ τέξῃ τέκνα, καὶ πρὸς τὸν ἄνδρα σου ἡ ἀποστροφή σου, καὶ αὐτός σου κυριεύσει. τῷ δὲ Ἀδὰμ εἶπεν· Ὅτι ἤκουσας τῆς φωνῆς τῆς γυναικός σου καὶ ἔφαγες ἀπὸ τοῦ ξύλου οὗ ἐνετειλάμην σοι μόνου τούτου μὴ φαγεῖν, ἀπ' αὐτοῦ ἔφαγες, ἐπικατάρατος ἡ γῆ ἐν τοῖς ἔργοις σου· ἐν λύπῃ φαγῇ αὐτὴν πάσας τὰς ἡμέρας τῆς ζωῆς σου, ἀκάνθας καὶ τριβόλους ἀνατελεῖ σοι, καὶ φαγῇ τὸν χόρτον τοῦ ἀγροῦ σου. ἐν ἱδρῶτι τοῦ προσώπου σου φαγῇ τὸν ἄρτον σου ἕως τοῦ ἀποστρέψαι σε εἰς τὴν γῆν ἐξ ἧς ἐλήφθης ὅτι γῆ εἶ καὶ εἰς γῆν ἀπελεύσῃ."

Τῆς μὲν οὖν ἱστορίας τοῦ ἀνθρώπου καὶ τοῦ παραδείσου τὰ ῥητὰ τῆς ἁγίας γραφῆς οὕτως περιέχει.

22. Ἐρεῖς οὖν μοι· "Σὺ φῂς τὸν θεὸν ἐν τόπῳ μὴ δεῖν χωρεῖσθαι, καὶ πῶς νῦν λέγεις αὐτὸν ἐν τῷ παραδείσῳ περιπατεῖν;" Ἄκουε ὅ φημι. ὁ μὲν θεὸς καὶ πατὴρ τῶν ὅλων ἀχώρητός ἐστιν καὶ ἐν τόπῳ οὐχ εὑρίσκεται· οὐ γάρ ἐστιν τόπος τῆς καταπαύσεως αὐτοῦ. ὁ δὲ λόγος αὐτοῦ, δι' οὗ τὰ πάντα πεποίηκεν, δύναμις ὢν καὶ σοφία αὐτοῦ, ἀναλαμβάνων τὸ πρόσωπον τοῦ πατρὸς καὶ κυρίου τῶν ὅλων, οὗτος παρεγένετο εἰς τὸν παράδεισον ἐν προσώπῳ τοῦ θεοῦ καὶ ὡμίλει τῷ Ἀδάμ. καὶ γὰρ αὐτὴ ἡ θεία γραφὴ διδάσκει ἡμᾶς τὸν Ἀδὰμ λέγοντα τῆς φωνῆς ἀκηκοέναι. φωνὴ δὲ τί ἄλλο ἐστὶν ἀλλ' ἢ ὁ λόγος ὁ τοῦ θεοῦ, ὅς ἐστιν καὶ υἱὸς αὐτοῦ; οὐχ ὡς οἱ ποιηταὶ καὶ μυθογράφοι λέγουσιν υἱοὺς θεῶν ἐκ συνουσίας γεννωμένους, ἀλλὰ ὡς ἀλήθεια διηγεῖται τὸν λόγον τὸν ὄντα διὰ παντὸς ἐνδιάθετον ἐν καρδίᾳ θεοῦ. πρὸ γάρ τι γίνεσθαι τοῦτον εἶχεν σύμβουλον, ἑαυτοῦ νοῦν καὶ φρόνησιν ὄντα. ὁπότε δὲ ἠθέλησεν ὁ θεὸς ποιῆσαι ὅσα ἐβουλεύσατο, τοῦτον τὸν λόγον ἐγέννησεν προφορικόν, πρωτότοκον πάσης κτίσεως, οὐ κενωθεὶς αὐτὸς τοῦ λόγου, ἀλλὰ λόγον γεννήσας καὶ τῷ λόγῳ αὐτοῦ διὰ παντὸς ὁμιλῶν. ὅθεν διδάσκουσιν ἡμᾶς αἱ ἅγιαι γραφαὶ καὶ πάντες οἱ πνευματοφόροι, ἐξ ὧν Ἰωάννης λέγει· "Ἐν ἀρχῇ ἦν ὁ λόγος, καὶ ὁ λόγος ἦν πρὸς τὸν θεόν·" δεικνὺς ὅτι ἐν πρώτοις μόνος ἦν ὁ θεὸς καὶ ἐν αὐτῷ ὁ λόγος.

accursed from all the beasts which are on the earth; you shall go on your chest and belly, and you shall eat dirt all the days of your life. And I will make enmity between you and the woman and between your seed and her seed; he will look out for your head and you will look out for his heel. And to the woman he said, Multiplying I will multiply your sorrows and your groaning; in sorrow you shall bring forth offspring, and your turning shall be to your husband, and he shall dominate you. And to Adam he said, Because you heard the voice of your wife and ate from the tree from which alone I commanded you not to eat, from this you ate, the earth is accursed by your works; in sorrow you shall eat it all the days of your life; it will bring forth thorns and thistles for you, and you shall eat the herb of your field. By the sweat of your face you shall eat your bread until you return to the earth from which you were taken; for you are earth and to earth you will return.'

Such are the words of the holy scripture which contain the history of man and paradise.

How God 'Walked' in Paradise

22. You will ask me, 'You say that God must not be confined in a place; how then do you say that he walks in paradise?' Hear my reply. Indeed the God and Father of the universe is unconfined and is not present in a place, for *there is no place of his rest* [Isa. 66: 1]. But his Logos, through whom he made all things, who is his *Power and Wisdom* [1 Cor. 1: 24], assuming the role of the Father and Lord of the universe, was present in paradise in the role of God and conversed with Adam. For the divine scripture itself teaches us that Adam said that he 'heard the voice'. What is the 'voice' but the Logos of God, who is also his Son?—not as the poets and mythographers describe sons of gods begotten of sexual union, but as the truth describes the Logos, always innate in the heart of God. For before anything came into existence he had this as his Counsellor, his own Mind and Intelligence. When God wished to make what he had planned to make, he generated this Logos, making him external, as the *firstborn of all creation* [Col. 1: 15]. He did not deprive himself of the Logos but generated the Logos and constantly converses with his Logos. Hence the holy scriptures and all those inspired by the Spirit teach us, and one of them, John, says, 'In the beginning was the Logos, and the Logos was with God' [John 1: 1]. He shows that originally God was alone and the Logos was in him.

ἔπειτα λέγει· "Καὶ θεὸς ἦν ὁ λόγος· πάντα δι' αὐτοῦ ἐγένετο, καὶ χωρὶς αὐτοῦ ἐγένετο οὐδέν." θεὸς οὖν ὢν ὁ λόγος καὶ ἐκ θεοῦ πεφυκώς, ὁπόταν βούληται ὁ πατήρ τῶν ὅλων, πέμπει αὐτὸν εἴς τινα τόπον, ὃς παραγινόμενος καὶ ἀκούεται καὶ ὁρᾶται, πεμπόμενος ὑπ' αὐτοῦ καὶ ἐν τόπῳ εὑρίσκεται.

23. Τὸν οὖν ἄνθρωπον ὁ θεὸς πεποίηκεν ἐν τῇ ἕκτῃ ἡμέρᾳ, τὴν δὲ πλάσιν αὐτοῦ πεφανέρωκεν μετὰ τὴν ἑβδόμην ἡμέραν, ὁπότε καὶ τὸν παράδεισον πεποίηκεν, εἰς τὸ ἐν κρείσσονι τόπῳ καὶ χωρίῳ διαφόρῳ αὐτὸν εἶναι. καὶ ὅτι ταῦτά ἐστιν ἀληθῆ, αὐτὸ τὸ ἔργον δείκνυσιν. πῶς γὰρ οὐκ ἔστιν κατανοῆσαι τὴν μὲν ὠδῖνα, ἣν πάσχουσιν ἐν τῷ τοκετῷ αἱ γυναῖκες, καὶ μετὰ τοῦτο λήθην τοῦ πόνου ποιοῦνται, ὅπως πληρωθῇ ὁ τοῦ θεοῦ λόγος εἰς τὸ αὐξάνεσθαι καὶ πληθύνεσθαι τὸ γένος τῶν ἀνθρώπων; τί δ' οὐχὶ καὶ τὴν τοῦ ὄφεως κατάκρισιν, πῶς στυγητὸς τυγχάνει ἕρπων ἐπὶ τῇ κοιλίᾳ καὶ ἐσθίων γῆν, ὅπως καὶ τοῦτο ᾖ εἰς ἀπόδειξιν ἡμῖν τῶν προειρημένων;

24. Ἐξανατείλας οὖν ὁ θεὸς ἐκ τῆς γῆς ἔτι πᾶν ξύλον, ὡραῖον εἰς ὅρασιν καὶ καλὸν εἰς βρῶσιν. ἐν γὰρ πρώτοις μόνα ἦν τὰ ἐν τῇ τρίτῃ ἡμέρᾳ γεγενημένα, φυτὰ καὶ σπέρματα καὶ χλόαι· τὰ δὲ ἐν τῷ παραδείσῳ ἐγενήθη διαφόρῳ καλλονῇ καὶ ὡραιότητι, ὅπου γε καὶ φυτεία ὠνόμασται ὑπὸ θεοῦ πεφυτευμένη. καὶ τὰ μὲν λοιπὰ φυτὰ ὅμοια καὶ ὁ κόσμος ἔσχηκεν· τὰ δὲ δύο ξύλα, τὸ τῆς ζωῆς καὶ τὸ τῆς γνώσεως, οὐκ ἔσχηκεν ἑτέρα γῆ ἀλλ' ἢ ἐν μόνῳ τῷ παραδείσῳ. ὅτι δὲ καὶ ὁ παράδεισος γῆ ἐστιν καὶ ἐπὶ τῆς γῆς πεφύτευται, ἡ γραφὴ λέγει· "Καὶ ἐφύτευσεν ὁ θεὸς παράδεισον ἐν Ἐδὲμ κατὰ ἀνατολάς, καὶ ἔθετο ἐκεῖ τὸν ἄνθρωπον· καὶ ἐξανέτειλεν ὁ θεὸς ἔτι ἀπὸ τῆς γῆς πᾶν ξύλον ὡραῖον εἰς ὅρασιν καὶ καλὸν εἰς βρῶσιν." τὸ οὖν ἔτι ἐκ τῆς γῆς καὶ κατὰ ἀνατολὰς σαφῶς διδάσκει ἡμᾶς ἡ θεία γραφὴ τὸν παράδεισον ὑπὸ τοῦτον τὸν οὐρανόν, ὑφ' ὃν καὶ ἀνατολαὶ καὶ γῆ εἰσιν. Ἐδὲμ δὲ ἑβραϊστὶ τὸ εἰρημένον ἑρμηνεύεται τρυφή.

Ποταμὸν δὲ σεσήμακεν ἐκπορεύεσθαι ἐξ Ἐδὲμ ποτίζειν τὸν παράδεισον, κἀκεῖθεν διαχωρίζεσθαι εἰς τέσσαρας ἀρχάς· ὧν δύο οἱ καλούμενοι Φεισὼν καὶ Γεὼν ποτίζουσιν τὰ ἀνατολικὰ μέρη, μάλιστα ὁ Γεών, ὁ κυκλῶν πᾶσαν γῆν Αἰθιοπίας, ὅν φασιν ἐν τῇ

Then he says, 'And the Logos was God; everything was made through him, and apart from him nothing was made' [John 1 : 1-3]. Since the Logos is God and derived his nature from God, whenever the Father of the universe wills to do so he sends him into some place where he is present and is heard and seen. He is sent by God and is present in a place.

Proof of the Truth of Genesis
23. God made man on the sixth day but revealed his formation after the seventh day, when he also made paradise so that man might be in a better place and a finer location. Facts prove the truth of these statements. How can one fail to be aware of the pangs which women suffer in childbirth [cf. Gen. 3 : 16]? Afterwards they forget the pain so that God's word may be fulfilled, prescribing the increase and multiplication of the human race [cf. Gen. 1 : 28]. Or the condemnation of the serpent, which is hateful, creeping on its belly and eating dirt [cf. Gen. 3 : 14], so that this too may demonstrate to us the truth of what has been said?

Man's Life in Paradise
24. God then caused to come up from the earth every tree which was beautiful to see and good to eat, for originally there were only the plants, seeds, and herbs produced on the third day. The vegetation in paradise possessed greater goodness and beauty, since paradise is called a 'plantation planted by God'.[1] The other plants there were like those in the world, but the two trees of life and knowledge are found in no other land than in paradise alone. To show that paradise is of earth and was planted on the earth, the scripture says: 'And God planted paradise in Eden to the east, and he set man there; and God also caused to come up from the earth every tree which was beautiful to see and good to eat.' By the expressions 'also from the earth' and 'to the east' the divine scripture clearly teaches us that paradise is under this very heaven under which are the east and the earth. The Hebrew word Eden means 'delight'.

The scripture indicated that a river flows out of Eden to water paradise, and that from there it is divided into four sources. Two called Phison and Geon water the eastern regions, especially Geon, which encircles the whole land of Ethiopia and is a river which they say appears in Egypt, where it is called the Nile. The other two

---

24. [1] Cf. *Didascalia apostolorum* i. 1 (*Const. apost.* i. praef., pp. 2-3 Funk).

Αἰγύπτῳ ἀποφαίνεσθαι τὸν καλούμενον Νεῖλον. οἱ δὲ ἄλλοι δύο ποταμοὶ φανερῶς γινώσκονται παρ' ἡμῖν, οἱ καλούμενοι Τίγρις καὶ Εὐφράτης· οὗτοι γὰρ γειτνιῶσιν ἕως τῶν ἡμετέρων κλιμάτων.

Θεὶς δὲ ὁ θεὸς τὸν ἄνθρωπον, καθὼς προειρήκαμεν, ἐν τῷ παραδείσῳ εἰς τὸ ἐργάζεσθαι καὶ φυλάσσειν αὐτόν, ἐνετείλατο αὐτῷ ἀπὸ πάντων τῶν καρπῶν ἐσθίειν, δηλονότι καὶ ἀπὸ τοῦ τῆς ζωῆς, μόνον δὲ ἐκ τοῦ ξύλου τῆς γνώσεως ἐνετείλατο αὐτῷ μὴ γεύσασθαι. μετέθηκεν δὲ αὐτὸν ὁ θεὸς ἐκ τῆς γῆς, ἐξ ἧς ἐγεγόνει, εἰς τὸν παράδεισον, διδοὺς αὐτῷ ἀφορμὴν προκοπῆς, ὅπως αὐξάνων καὶ τέλειος γενόμενος, ἔτι δὲ καὶ θεὸς ἀναδειχθείς, οὕτως καὶ εἰς οὐρανὸν ἀναβῇ (μέσος γὰρ ὁ ἄνθρωπος ἐγεγόνει, οὔτε θνητὸς ὁλοσχερῶς οὔτε ἀθάνατος τὸ καθόλου, δεκτικὸς δὲ ἑκατέρων· οὕτως καὶ τὸ χωρίον ὁ παράδεισος, ὡς πρὸς καλλονήν, μέσος τοῦ κόσμου καὶ τοῦ οὐρανοῦ γεγένηται), ἔχων ἀϊδιότητα. τὸ δὲ εἰπεῖν ἐργάζεσθαι οὐκ ἄλλην τινὰ ἐργασίαν δηλοῖ ἀλλ' ἢ τὸ φυλάσσειν τὴν ἐντολὴν τοῦ θεοῦ, ὅπως μὴ παρακούσας ἀπολέσῃ ἑαυτόν, καθὼς καὶ ἀπώλεσεν διὰ ἁμαρτίας.

25. Τὸ μὲν ξύλον τὸ τῆς γνώσεως αὐτὸ μὲν καλὸν καὶ ὁ καρπὸς αὐτοῦ καλός. οὐ γάρ, ὥς οἴονταί τινες, θάνατον εἶχεν τὸ ξύλον, ἀλλ' ἡ παρακοή. οὐ γάρ τι ἕτερον ἦν ἐν τῷ καρπῷ ἢ μόνον γνῶσις. ἡ δὲ γνῶσις καλή, ἐπὰν αὐτῇ οἰκείως τις χρήσηται. τῇ δὲ οὔσῃ ἡλικίᾳ ὅδε Ἀδὰμ ἔτη νήπιος ἦν· διὸ οὔπω ἠδύνατο τὴν γνῶσιν κατ' ἀξίαν χωρεῖν. καὶ γὰρ νῦν ἐπὰν γενηθῇ παιδίον, οὐκ ἤδη δύναται ἄρτον ἐσθίειν, ἀλλὰ πρῶτον γάλακτι ἀνατρέφεται, ἔπειτα κατὰ πρόσβασιν τῆς ἡλικίας καὶ ἐπὶ τὴν στερεὰν τροφὴν ἔρχεται. οὕτως ἂν γεγόνει καὶ τῷ Ἀδάμ. διὸ οὐχ ὡς φθονῶν αὐτῷ ὁ θεός, ὥς οἴονταί τινες, ἐκέλευσεν μὴ ἐσθίειν ἀπὸ τῆς γνώσεως. ἔτι μὴν καὶ ἐβούλετο δοκιμάσαι αὐτόν, εἰ ὑπήκοος γίνεται τῇ ἐντολῇ αὐτοῦ. ἅμα δὲ καὶ ἐπὶ πλείονα χρόνον ἐβούλετο ἁπλοῦν καὶ ἀκέραιον διαμεῖναι τὸν ἄνθρωπον νηπιάζοντα. τοῦτο γὰρ ὅσιόν ἐστιν, οὐ μόνον παρὰ θεῷ ἀλλὰ καὶ παρὰ ἀνθρώποις, τὸ ἐν ἁπλότητι καὶ ἀκακίᾳ ὑποτάσσεσθαι τοῖς γονεῦσιν. εἰ δὲ χρὴ τὰ τέκνα τοῖς γονεῦσιν ὑποτάσσεσθαι, πόσῳ μᾶλλον τῷ θεῷ καὶ πατρὶ τῶν ὅλων; ἔτι μὴν καὶ ἄσχημόν ἐστιν τὰ παιδία τὰ νήπια ὑπὲρ ἡλικίαν φρονεῖν. καθάπερ γὰρ τῇ ἡλικίᾳ τις πρὸς τάξιν αὔξει, οὕτως καὶ ἐν τῷ φρονεῖν. ἄλλως τε

rivers are well known to us (they are called the Tigris and the Euphrates) because they are on the edge of our own regions.

When God set man, as we have already said [II. 19], in paradise to work it and guard it, he commanded him to eat of all the fruits, obviously including those of the tree of life; he commanded him not to taste of the tree of knowledge alone. God transferred him out of the earth from which he was made into paradise, giving him an opportunity for progress so that by growing and becoming mature, and furthermore having been declared a god, he might also ascend into heaven (for man was created in an intermediate state, neither entirely mortal nor entirely immortal, but capable of either state; similarly the place paradise—as regards beauty—was created intermediate between the world and heaven), possessing immortality The expression 'to work' implies no other task than keeping the commandment of God, lest by disobedience he destroy himself, as he did through sin.[2]

The Problem of the Tree of Knowledge

25. The tree of knowledge was good and its fruit was good. For the tree did not contain death, as some suppose;[1] this was the result of disobedience. For there was nothing in the fruit but knowledge, and knowledge is good if one uses it properly. In his actual age, Adam was as old as an infant; therefore he was not yet able to acquire knowledge properly. For at the present time when a child is born it cannot eat bread at once, but first it is fed with milk and then, with increasing age, it comes to solid food. So it would have been with Adam. Therefore God was not jealous, as some suppose,[2] in ordering him not to eat of knowledge. Furthermore, he wanted to test him, to see whether he would be obedient to his command. At the same time he wanted the man to remain simple and sincere for a longer time, remaining in infancy. For this is a holy duty not only before God but before men, to obey one's parents in simplicity and without malice. And if children must obey their parents, how much more must they obey the God and Father of the universe! Furthermore, it is shameful for infant children to have thoughts beyond their years; for as one grows in age in an orderly fashion, so one grows in ability to think. Again, when a law commands

---

24. [2] Theophilus may be answering the criticisms of Marcionites: by requiring Adam to work God was showing his own weakness; cf. A. von Harnack, *Marcion: das Evangelium vom fremden Gott* (ed. 2, Leipzig, 1924), 271*.

25. [1] This point was discussed in the *Syllogisms* of the Marcionite Apelles; cf. Ambrose, *De paradiso* vi. 35; Harnack, op. cit., 414*.

[2] This point was also made by Apelles; cf. Ambrose, op. cit., vi. 30; Harnack, op. cit., 414*–15*.

ἐπὰν νόμος κελεύσῃ ἀπέχεσθαι ἀπό τινος καὶ μὴ ὑπακούῃ τις, δῆλον ὅτι οὐχ ὁ νόμος κόλασιν παρέχει, ἀλλὰ ἡ ἀπείθεια καὶ ἡ παρακοή. καὶ γὰρ πατὴρ ἰδίῳ τέκνῳ ἐνίοτε προστάσσει ἀπέχεσθαί τινων, καὶ ἐπὰν οὐχ ὑπακούῃ τῇ πατρικῇ ἐντολῇ, δέρεται καὶ ἐπιτιμίας τυγχάνει διὰ τὴν παρακοήν· καὶ οὐκ ἤδη αὐτὰ τὰ πράγματα πληγαί εἰσιν, ἀλλ' ἡ παρακοὴ τῷ ἀπειθοῦντι ὕβρεις περιποιεῖται. Οὕτως καὶ τῷ πρωτοπλάστῳ ἡ παρακοὴ περιεποιήσατο ἐκβληθῆναι αὐτὸν ἐκ τοῦ παραδείσου· οὐ μέντοι γε ὡς κακοῦ τι ἔχοντος τοῦ ξύλου τῆς γνώσεως, διὰ δὲ τῆς παρακοῆς ὁ ἄνθρωπος ἐξήντλησεν πόνον, ὀδύνην, λύπην, καὶ τὸ τέλος ὑπὸ θάνατον ἔπεσεν.

26. Καὶ τοῦτο δὲ ὁ θεὸς μεγάλην εὐεργεσίαν παρέσχεν τῷ ἀνθρώπῳ, τὸ μὴ διαμεῖναι αὐτὸν εἰς τὸν αἰῶνα ἐν ἁμαρτίᾳ ὄντα. ἀλλὰ τρόπῳ τινὶ ἐν ὁμοιώματι ἐξορισμοῦ ἐξέβαλλεν αὐτὸν ἐκ τοῦ παραδείσου, ὅπως διὰ τῆς ἐπιτιμίας τακτῷ ἀποτίσας χρόνῳ τὴν ἁμαρτίαν καὶ παιδευθεὶς ἐξ ὑστέρου ἀνακληθῇ. διὸ καὶ πλασθέντος τοῦ ἀνθρώπου ἐν τῷ κόσμῳ τούτῳ μυστηριωδῶς ἐν τῇ Γενέσει γέγραπται, ὡς δὶς αὐτοῦ ἐν τῷ παραδείσῳ τεθέντος· ἵνα τὸ μὲν ἅπαξ ᾖ πεπληρωμένον ὅτε[1] ἐτέθη, τὸ δὲ δεύτερον μέλλῃ πληροῦσθαι μετὰ τὴν ἀνάστασιν καὶ κρίσιν. οὐ μὴν ἀλλὰ καὶ καθάπερ σκεῦός τι, ἐπὰν πλασθὲν αἰτίαν τινὰ σχῇ, ἀναχωνεύεται ἢ ἀναπλάσσεται εἰς τὸ γενέσθαι καινὸν καὶ ὁλόκληρον, οὕτως γίνεται καὶ τῷ ἀνθρώπῳ διὰ θανάτου· δυνάμει γὰρ τέθραυσται ἵνα ἐν τῇ ἀναστάσει ὑγιὴς εὑρεθῇ, λέγω δὲ ἄσπιλος καὶ δίκαιος καὶ ἀθάνατος.

Τὸ δὲ καλέσαι καὶ εἰπεῖν τὸν θεόν· "Ποῦ εἶ Ἀδάμ;" οὐχ ὡς ἀγνοῶν τοῦτο ἐποίει ὁ θεός, ἀλλὰ μακρόθυμος ὢν ἀφορμὴν ἐδίδου αὐτῷ μετανοίας καὶ ἐξομολογήσεως.

27. Ἀλλὰ φήσει οὖν τις ἡμῖν· "Θνητὸς φύσει ἐγένετο ὁ ἄνθρωπος;" οὐδαμῶς. "Τί οὖν ἀθάνατος;" οὐδὲ τοῦτό φαμεν. Ἀλλὰ ἐρεῖ τις· "Οὐδὲν οὖν ἐγένετο;" οὐδὲ τοῦτο λέγομεν.[1] οὔτε οὖν φύσει θνητὸς ἐγένετο οὔτε ἀθάνατος. εἰ γὰρ ἀθάνατον αὐτὸν ἀπ' ἀρχῆς πεποιήκει,

26. [1] ὅτε] Maran: ποτὲ V   27. [1] λέγομεν] Wolf: ἐγὼ μὲν V

abstinence from something and someone does not obey, it is not the law which results in punishment but the disobedience and the transgression. For a father sometimes orders his own child to abstain from certain things, and when the child does not obey the paternal command he is beaten and receives chastisement because of his disobedience.[3] The commands themselves are not the blows; the disobedience results in beatings for the disobedient one. So also for the first-formed man, his disobedience resulted in his expulsion from paradise. It was not that the tree of knowledge contained anything evil, but that through disobedience man acquired pain, suffering, and sorrow, and finally fell victim to death.

Why Man was Cast out of Paradise

26. And in so doing, God conferred a great benefit upon man. He did not let him remain for ever in a state of sin but, so to speak, with a kind of banishment he cast him out of paradise, so that through this punishment he might expiate his sin in a fixed period of time and after chastisement might later be recalled. For this reason, when man was formed in this world it is described mysteriously in Genesis as if he had been placed in paradise twice [Gen. 2: 8, 15]; the first description was fulfilled when he was placed there, and the second is going to be fulfilled after the resurrection and judgement. Again, just as when some vessel has been fashioned and has some fault, and is resmelted or refashioned so that it becomes new and perfect, so it happens to man through death; for he has virtually been shattered so that in the resurrection he may be found sound, I mean spotless and righteous and immortal.

God's calling and saying, 'Where are you, Adam?' [Gen. 3: 9]—God did this not as if he were ignorant but because he was patient and gave him an occasion for repentance and confession.[1]

Was Man Mortal or Immortal?

27. But someone will say to us, 'Was man created mortal by nature?' Not at all. 'Was he then created immortal?' We do not say this either. But someone will say, 'Was he then created as nothing at all?'[1] We do not say this. In fact, man was neither

---

25. [3] Apelles argued that a child had no guilt; cf. Ambrose, op. cit., vi. 31; Harnack, op. cit., 414*.

26. [1] Questions about God's goodness and knowledge were raised in the *Syllogisms* of the Marcionite Apelles; cf. Ambrose, *De paradiso* viii. 38, 40, 41; Harnack, op. cit., 415*-16*.

27. [1] This is probably one of the 'syllogisms' directed against the Old Testament by the Marcionite Apelles; cf. Ambrose, *De paradiso* v. 28 and vi. 35; Harnack, op. cit., 413*-14*.

θεὸν αὐτὸν πεποιήκει· πάλιν εἰ θνητὸν αὐτὸν πεποιήκει, ἐδόκει ἂν ὁ θεὸς αἴτιος εἶναι τοῦ θανάτου αὐτοῦ. οὔτε οὖν ἀθάνατον αὐτὸν ἐποίησεν οὔτε μὴν θνητόν, ἀλλά, καθὼς ἐπάνω προειρήκαμεν, δεκτικὸν ἀμφοτέρων, ἵνα εἰ[2] ῥέψῃ ἐπὶ τὰ τῆς ἀθανασίας τηρήσας τὴν ἐντολὴν τοῦ θεοῦ, μισθὸν κομίσηται παρ' αὐτοῦ τὴν ἀθανασίαν καὶ γένηται θεός, εἰ δ' αὖ τραπῇ ἐπὶ τὰ τοῦ θανάτου πράγματα παρακούσας τοῦ θεοῦ, αὐτὸς ἑαυτῷ αἴτιος ᾖ τοῦ θανάτου. ἐλεύθερον γὰρ καὶ αὐτεξούσιον ἐποίησεν ὁ θεὸς τὸν ἄνθρωπον. ὃ οὖν ἑαυτῷ περιεποιήσατο δι' ἀμελείας καὶ παρακοῆς, τοῦτο ὁ θεὸς αὐτῷ νυνὶ δωρεῖται διὰ ἰδίας φιλανθρωπίας καὶ ἐλεημοσύνης, ὑπακούοντος αὐτῷ τοῦ ἀνθρώπου. καθάπερ γὰρ παρακούσας ὁ[3] ἄνθρωπος θάνατον ἑαυτῷ ἐπεσπάσατο, οὕτως ὑπακούσας τῷ θελήματι τοῦ θεοῦ ὁ βουλόμενος δύναται περιποιήσασθαι ἑαυτῷ τὴν αἰώνιον ζωήν. ἔδωκεν γὰρ ὁ θεὸς ἡμῖν νόμον καὶ ἐντολὰς ἁγίας, ἃς πᾶς ὁ ποιήσας δύναται σωθῆναι καὶ τῆς ἀναστάσεως τυχὼν κληρονομῆσαι τὴν ἀφθαρσίαν.

28. Ἐκβληθεὶς δὲ Ἀδὰμ ἐκ τοῦ παραδείσου, οὕτως ἔγνω Εὔαν τὴν γυναῖκα αὐτοῦ, ἣν ὁ θεὸς ἐποίησεν αὐτῷ εἰς γυναῖκα ἐκ τῆς πλευρᾶς αὐτοῦ. καὶ τοῦτο δὲ οὐχ ὡς μὴ δυνάμενος κατ' ἰδίαν πλάσαι τὴν γυναῖκα αὐτοῦ, ἀλλὰ προηπίστατο ὁ θεὸς ὅτι ἤμελλον οἱ ἄνθρωποι πληθὺν θεῶν ὀνομάζειν. προγνώστης οὖν ὢν καὶ εἰδὼς ὅτι ἡ πλάνη ἤμελλεν διὰ τοῦ ὄφεως ὀνομάζειν πληθὺν θεῶν τῶν οὐκ ὄντων (ἑνὸς γὰρ ὄντος θεοῦ, ἔκτοτε ἤδη ἐμελέτα ἡ πλάνη πληθὺν θεῶν ὑποσπείρειν καὶ λέγειν· " Ἔσεσθε ὡς θεοί"), μήπως οὖν ὑπολημφθῇ ὡς ὅτι ὅδε μὲν ὁ θεὸς ἐποίησεν τὸν ἄνδρα, ἕτερος δὲ τὴν γυναῖκα, διὰ τοῦτο ἐποίησεν[1] τοὺς δύο ἄμφω· οὐ μὴν ἀλλὰ καὶ ⟨ἔπλασεν τὸν ἄνδρα μόνον ἐκ γῆς ἵνα⟩[2] διὰ τούτου δειχθῇ τὸ μυστήριον τῆς μοναρχίας τῆς κατὰ τὸν θεόν, ἅμα δ' ἐποίησεν ὁ θεὸς τὴν γυναῖκα αὐτοῦ[3] ⟨ἐκ τῆς πλευρᾶς αὐτοῦ⟩[4] ἵνα πλείων ᾖ ἡ εὔνοια εἰς αὐτήν.[5]

Πρὸς μὲν οὖν τὴν Εὔαν ὁ Ἀδὰμ εἰπών· "Τοῦτο νῦν ὀστοῦν ἐκ τῶν ὀστῶν μου καὶ σὰρξ ἐκ τῆς σαρκός μου", ἔτι καὶ ἐπροφήτευσεν λέγων· "Τούτου ἕνεκεν καταλείψει ἄνθρωπος τὸν πατέρα αὐτοῦ καὶ

27. [2] εἰ] Maran: om. V [3] ὁ] Otto: om. V
28. [1] ἐποίησεν] Nautin: praem. οὖν V: praem. οὐκ Maran [2] ⟨ἔπλασεν–ἵνα⟩] Nautin: ἵνα Otto: om. V [3] αὐτοῦ] καὶ ἔσονται οἱ δύο εἰς cum p. 72. 2-4 σάρκα–πάντων καὶ V: om. Wolf [4] ⟨ἐκ τῆς πλευρᾶς αὐτοῦ⟩] Nautin
[5] αὐτήν] Fell: αὐτούς V

mortal nor immortal by nature. For if God had made him immortal from the beginning, he would have made him God. Again, if he had made him mortal, it would seem that God was responsible for his death. God therefore made him neither immortal nor mortal but, as we have said before [II. 24], capable of both. If he were to turn to the life of immortality by keeping the commandment of God [cf. Matt. 19: 17], he would win immortality as a reward from him and would become a god; but if he turned to deeds of death, disobeying God, he would be responsible for his own death. What man acquired for himself through his neglect and disobedience, God now freely bestows upon him through love and mercy, when man obeys him.[2] For as by disobedience man gained death for himself, so by obedience [cf. Rom. 5: 18–19] to the will of God whoever will can obtain eternal life for himself. For God gave us a law and holy commandments; everyone who performs them can be saved [cf. Matt. 19: 25] and, attaining to the resurrection [cf. Heb. 11: 35], can *inherit imperishability* [1 Cor. 15: 50].[3]

The Creation of Eve

28. It was when Adam had been cast out of paradise that he knew his wife Eve, whom God had made out of his side to be his wife. God made her in this way not because he was unable to make the woman separately but because he knew that men were going to give names to a multitude of gods. Since God possessed foreknowledge and knew that error, through the serpent, was going to refer to a multitude of non-existent gods—for although God is one, error was already undertaking to implant a multitude of gods and say, 'You shall be like gods' [Gen. 3: 5]—so that no one would suppose that one god made man and another made woman, he made the two together. Moreover, he formed only man from the earth so that thus the mystery of the divine unity might be demonstrated. At the same time, God made woman by taking her from his side so that man's love for her might be greater.

Adam said to Eve, 'This is now bone from my bones and flesh from my flesh', and in addition he prophesied, saying, 'For this reason a man will leave his father and mother and will cleave to his

---

27. [2] Theophilus means that man earned death but God gives life. W. Jaeger (*Nemesios von Emesa*, Berlin, 1914, 141) traces the 'Hebrew' doctrine that man was neither mortal nor immortal back to Philo (*Opif.* 135), but Nemesius' statement about it may be based on Theophilus.

[3] For Theophilus' view cf. 2 Baruch 54: 14–19 and P. Bogaert, *Apocalypse de Baruch* (Paris, 1969), i. 405–9; ii. 104–5.

τὴν μητέρα καὶ προσκολληθήσεται πρὸς τὴν γυναῖκα αὐτοῦ, καὶ ἔσονται οἱ δύο εἰς σάρκα μίαν"· ὃ δὴ καὶ αὐτὸ δείκνυται τελειούμενον ἐν ἡμῖν αὐτοῖς. τίς γὰρ ὁ νομίμως γαμῶν οὐ καταφρονεῖ μητρὸς καὶ πατρὸς καὶ πάσης συγγενείας καὶ πάντων τῶν οἰκείων, προσκολλώμενος καὶ ἑνούμενος τῇ ἑαυτοῦ γυναικί, εὐνοῶν μᾶλλον αὐτῇ; διὸ καὶ μέχρι θανάτου πολλάκις ὑπεύθυνοι γίνονταί τινες διὰ τὰς ἑαυτῶν γαμετάς.

Ταύτην τὴν Εὔαν, διὰ τὸ ἀρχῆθεν πλανηθῆναι ὑπὸ τοῦ ὄφεως καὶ ἀρχηγὸν ἁμαρτίας γεγονέναι, ὁ κακοποιὸς δαίμων, ὁ καὶ σατὰν καλούμενος, ὁ τότε διὰ τοῦ ὄφεως λαλήσας αὐτῇ, ἕως καὶ τοῦ δεῦρο ἐνεργῶν ἐν τοῖς ἐνθουσιαζομένοις ὑπ' αὐτοῦ ἀνθρώποις, Εὐὰν ἐκκαλεῖται. δαίμων δὲ καὶ δράκων καλεῖται διὰ τὸ ἀποδεδρακέναι αὐτὸν ἀπὸ τοῦ θεοῦ· ἄγγελος γὰρ ἦν ἐν πρώτοις. καὶ τὰ μὲν περὶ τούτου πολὺς ὁ λόγος· διὸ τανῦν παραπέμπομαι τὴν περὶ αὐτῶν διήγησιν· καὶ γὰρ ἐν ἑτέροις ἡμῖν γεγένηται ὁ περὶ αὐτοῦ λόγος.

29. Ἐν τῷ οὖν γνῶναι τὸν Ἀδὰμ τὴν γυναῖκα αὐτοῦ Εὔαν συλλαβοῦσα ἔτεκεν υἱόν, ᾧ τοὔνομα Κάϊν. καὶ εἶπεν· " Ἐκτησάμην ἄνθρωπον διὰ τοῦ θεοῦ." καὶ προσέθετο ἔτι τεκεῖν δεύτερον, ᾧ ὄνομα Ἄβελ. ἤρξατο ποιμὴν εἶναι προβάτων· Κάϊν δὲ εἰργάζετο τὴν γῆν. τὰ μὲν οὖν κατ' αὐτοὺς πλείω ἔχει τὴν ἱστορίαν, οὐ μὴν ἀλλὰ καὶ τὴν οἰκονομίαν τῆς ἐξηγήσεως· διὸ τὰ τῆς ἱστορίας τοὺς φιλομαθεῖς δύναται ἀκριβέστερον διδάξαι αὐτὴ ἡ βίβλος ἥτις ἐπιγράφεται Γένεσις κόσμου.

Ὁπότε οὖν ἐθεάσατο ὁ σατανᾶς οὐ μόνον τὸν Ἀδὰμ καὶ τὴν γυναῖκα αὐτοῦ ζῶντας, ἀλλὰ καὶ τέκνα πεποιηκότας, ἐφ' ὧν οὐκ ἴσχυσεν θανατῶσαι αὐτοὺς φθόνῳ φερόμενος, ἡνίκα ἑώρα τὸν Ἄβελ εὐαρεστοῦντα τῷ θεῷ, ἐνεργήσας εἰς τὸν ἀδελφὸν αὐτοῦ τὸν καλούμενον Κάϊν ἐποίησεν ἀποκτεῖναι τὸν ἀδελφὸν αὐτοῦ τὸν Ἄβελ. καὶ οὕτως ἀρχὴ θανάτου ἐγένετο εἰς τόνδε τὸν κόσμον ὁδοιπορεῖν ἕως τοῦ δεῦρο ἐπὶ πᾶν γένος ἀνθρώπων.

Ὁ δὲ θεὸς ἐλεήμων ὢν καὶ βουλόμενος ἀφορμὴν μετανοίας καὶ ἐξομολογήσεως παρασχεῖν τῷ Κάϊν, καθάπερ καὶ τῷ Ἀδάμ, εἶπεν· "Ποῦ Ἄβελ ὁ ἀδελφός σου;" ὁ δὲ Κάϊν ἀπεκρίθη ἀπειθῶς τῷ θεῷ εἰπών· "Οὐ γινώσκω· μὴ φύλαξ εἰμὶ τοῦ ἀδελφοῦ μου;" οὕτως ὀργισθεὶς αὐτῷ ὁ θεὸς ἔφη· "Τί ἐποίησας τοῦτο;

wife, and the two shall be one flesh' [Gen. 2: 23–4]. This is actually fulfilled among us. For what man who marries lawfully does not disregard his mother and father and his whole family and all his relatives, while he cleaves to his own wife and unites with her, loving her more than them? For this reason husbands have often suffered even death for the sake of their wives.

The maleficent demon, also called Satan, who then spoke to Eve through the serpent and is still at work in those men who are possessed by him, addressed her as 'Eve' because she was at first deceived by the serpent and became the pioneer of sin.[1] He is called 'demon' and 'dragon' [cf. Rev. 12: 9] because he escaped [*apodedrakenai*] from God;[2] he was originally an angel. There is much to say about him, but for the present I am passing over the account of these matters; the statement about him has been given to us elsewhere.

Cain and Abel

29. When *Adam knew Eve his wife she conceived and bore* a son whose name was *Cain. And she said, 'I have acquired a man through God.' And she bore* another son, whose name was *Abel*. He proceeded to become a *shepherd of sheep*, while *Cain tilled the ground* [Gen. 4: 1–2]. There is a fuller narrative about these sons, in addition to an exegetical treatment; those who love learning can obtain a most accurate narrative from the book itself which is entitled *Genesis of the World*.[1]

When Satan saw that Adam and his wife not only were alive but had produced offspring, he was overcome by envy because he was not strong enough to put them to death; and because he saw Abel pleasing God, he worked upon his brother called Cain and made him kill his brother Abel. And so the beginning of death came into this world, to reach the whole race of men to this very day.

But God, who is merciful and desired to provide for Cain, as he had for Adam, an opportunity for repentance and confession, said: 'Where is your brother Abel?' [Gen. 4: 9]. But Cain, who did not trust God, answered: 'I do not know; am I my brother's keeper?' So God became angry with him and said: 'Why did you do this?

---

28. [1] Theophilus is trying to identify the name 'Eve' with the Bacchic cry 'Euan'.

[2] *Drakōn* from *drakein*, Porphyry, *De abst.* iii. 8; Adrasteia from *apodidraskein*, *SVF* ii. 528.

29. [1] Possibly, but not certainly, the book of Genesis.

φωνὴ αἵματος τοῦ ἀδελφοῦ σου βοᾷ πρός με ἐκ τῆς γῆς. καὶ νῦν ἐπικατάρατος σὺ ἀπὸ τῆς γῆς, ἣ ἔχανεν δέξασθαι τὸ αἷμα τοῦ ἀδελφοῦ σου ἐκ χειρός σου· στένων καὶ τρέμων ἔσῃ ἐπὶ τῆς γῆς." διὸ ἔκτοτε φοβηθεῖσα ἡ γῆ οὐκέτι ἀνθρώπου αἷμα παραδέχεται, ἀλλ' οὐδέ τινος ζώου· ᾗ φανερὸν ὅτι οὐκ ἔστιν αὐτὴ αἰτία, ἀλλ' ὁ παραβὰς ἄνθρωπος.

30. Ὁ οὖν Κάϊν καὶ αὐτὸς ἔσχεν υἱὸν ᾧ ὄνομα Ἐνώχ. καὶ ᾠκοδόμησεν πόλιν, ἣν ἐπωνόμασεν ἐπὶ τῷ ὀνόματι τοῦ υἱοῦ αὐτοῦ Ἐνώχ. ἀπὸ τότε ἀρχὴ ἐγένετο τοῦ οἰκοδομεῖσθαι πόλεις, καὶ τοῦτο πρὸ κατακλυσμοῦ, οὐχ ὡς Ὅμηρος ψεύδεται λέγων·

Οὐ γάρ πω πεπόλιστο πόλις μερόπων ἀνθρώπων.

Τῷ δὲ Ἐνὼχ ἐγενήθη υἱὸς ὀνόματι Γαϊδάδ· ἐγέννησεν τὸν καλούμενον Μεήλ, καὶ Μεὴλ τὸν Μαθουσάλα, καὶ Μαθουσάλα[1] τὸν Λάμεχ. ὁ δὲ Λάμεχ ἔλαβεν ἑαυτῷ δύο γυναῖκας, αἷς ὀνόματα Ἀδᾶ καὶ Σελᾶ. ἔκτοτε ἀρχὴ ἐγένετο τῆς πολυμιξίας, ἀλλὰ καὶ τῆς μουσικῆς. τῷ γὰρ Λάμεχ ἐγένοντο τρεῖς υἱοί, Ὠβήλ, Ἰουβάλ, Θοβέλ. καὶ ὁ μὲν Ὠβὴλ, ἐγένετο ἀνὴρ ἐν σκηναῖς κτηνοτροφῶν, Ἰουβὰλ δέ ἐστιν ὁ καταδείξας ψαλτήριον καὶ κιθάραν, Θοβὲλ δὲ ἐγένετο σφυροκόπος χαλκεὺς χαλκοῦ καὶ σιδήρου. ἕως μὲν οὖν τούτου ἔσχεν τὸν κατάλογον τὸ σπέρμα τοῦ Κάϊν· καὶ τὸ λοιπὸν εἰς λήθην αὐτοῦ γέγονεν τὸ σπέρμα τῆς γενεαλογίας, διὰ τὸ ἀδελφοκτονῆσαι αὐτὸν τὸν ἀδελφόν.

Εἰς τὸν τόπον δὲ τοῦ Ἄβελ ἔδωκεν ὁ θεὸς συλλαβεῖν τὴν Εὔαν καὶ τεκεῖν υἱόν, ὃς κέκληται Σήθ· ἀφ' οὗ τὸ λοιπὸν γένος τῶν ἀνθρώπων ὁδεύει μέχρι τοῦ δεῦρο. τοῖς δὲ βουλομένοις καὶ φιλομαθέσιν καὶ περὶ πασῶν τῶν γενεῶν εὔκολόν ἐστιν ἐπιδεῖξαι διὰ τῶν ἁγίων γραφῶν. καὶ γὰρ ἐκ μέρους ἡμῖν γεγένηται ἤδη λόγος ἐν ἑτέρῳ λόγῳ, ὡς ἐπάνω προειρήκαμεν, τῆς γενεαλογίας ἡ τάξις ἐν τῇ πρώτῃ βίβλῳ τῇ περὶ ἱστοριῶν.

Ταῦτα δὲ πάντα ἡμᾶς διδάσκει τὸ πνεῦμα τὸ ἅγιον, τὸ διὰ Μωσέως καὶ τῶν λοιπῶν προφητῶν, ὥστε τὰ καθ' ἡμᾶς τοὺς θεοσεβεῖς ἀρχαιότερα γράμματα τυγχάνει, οὐ μὴν ἀλλὰ καὶ ἀληθέστερα πάντων συγγραφέων καὶ ποιητῶν δείκνυται ὄντα. ἀλλὰ μὴν

30. [1] καὶ Μαθουσάλα] Gesner: om. V

The voice of your brother's blood cries out to me from the earth. And now you are accursed from the earth, which opened to receive your brother's blood from your hand; you shall be groaning and trembling on the earth' [cf. Gen. 4: 9–14]. Therefore since then the fearful earth no longer receives blood, either human or animal. From this it is clear that it is not responsible; man who transgressed is responsible.

The Descendants of Cain and Seth

30. Then Cain himself had a son, whose name was Enoch. And he built a city which he called by the name of his son Enoch [Gen. 4: 17]. At that time came the beginning of the construction of cities, before the deluge and not as Homer falsely says: 'For a city of mortal men had not yet been built' [*Il.* xx. 217]. *Enoch had a son named Gaidad, who begot one called Meél; Meél begot Mathousala,* and *Mathousala Lamech. Lamech took for himself two wives,* whose names were *Ada* and *Sela*. At that time came the beginning of polygamy as well as that of music. For Lamech had three sons, Obel, Jubal, and Thobel. Obel was *a herdsman living in tents*; *Jubal is the one who invented the psaltery and the lyre*; and *Thobel was a hammerer and smith in bronze and iron* [Gen. 4: 18–22]. Up to this point the seed of Cain has a genealogy, but henceforth the seed of his genealogy passed into oblivion because of his fratricide.

To replace Abel, God allowed Eve to conceive and bear a son, who was called Seth; from him the rest of the human race is derived up to the present day. For those who desire and love learning, it is easy to make a description of all the generations from the holy scriptures. And there already exists for us a partial account elsewhere, as we said above [II. 29],—the order of the genealogy in the first book, which is on history.

All these things are taught us by the Holy Spirit which spoke through Moses and the other prophets; so that the books which belong to us, the worshippers of God, are proved to be writings not only more ancient but also more true than all historians and poets.

καὶ τὰ περὶ τῆς μουσικῆς ἐφλυάρησάν τινες εὑρετὴν Ἀπόλλωνα γεγενῆσθαι, ἄλλοι δὲ 'Ορφέα ἀπὸ τῆς τῶν ὀρνέων ἡδυφωνίας φασὶν ἐξευρηκέναι τὴν μουσικήν. κενὸς δὲ καὶ μάταιος ὁ λόγος αὐτῶν δείκνυται· μετὰ γὰρ πολλὰ ἔτη τοῦ κατακλυσμοῦ οὗτοι ἐγένοντο. τὰ δὲ περὶ τοῦ Νῶε, ὃς κέκληται ὑπὸ ἐνίων Δευκαλίων, ἐν τῇ βίβλῳ ᾗ προειρήκαμεν ἡ διήγησις ἡμῖν γεγένηται ᾗ, εἰ βούλει, καὶ σὺ δύνασαι ἐντυχεῖν.

31. Μετὰ τὸν κατακλυσμὸν ἀρχὴ πάλιν ἐγένετο πόλεων καὶ βασιλέων τὸν τρόπον τοῦτον. πρώτη πόλις Βαβυλών, καὶ 'Ορὲχ καὶ Ἀρχὰθ καὶ Χαλανὴ ἐν τῇ γῇ Σενναάρ. καὶ βασιλεὺς ἐγένετο αὐτῶν ὀνόματι Νεβρώθ. ἐκ τούτων ἐξῆλθεν ὀνόματι Ἀσσούρ· ὅθεν καὶ Ἀσσύριοι προσαγορεύονται. Νεβρὼθ δὲ ᾠκοδόμησεν πόλεις τὴν Νινευὴ καὶ τὴν Ῥοβοὼμ καὶ τὴν Καλὰκ καὶ τὴν Δασὲν ἀνὰ μέσον Νινευὴ καὶ ἀνὰ μέσον Καλάκ. ἡ δὲ Νινευὴ ἐγενήθη ἐν πρώτοις πόλις μεγάλη. ἕτερος δὲ υἱὸς τοῦ Σὴμ υἱοῦ[1] τοῦ Νῶε ὀνόματι Μεστραεὶν ἐγέννησεν τοὺς Λουδουεὶμ καὶ τοὺς καλουμένους Ἐνεμιγεὶμ καὶ τοὺς Λαβιεὶμ καὶ τοὺς Νεφθαλεὶμ καὶ τοὺς Πατροσωνιεὶμ καὶ τοὺς Χασλωνιείμ, ὅθεν ἐξῆλθεν Φυλιστιείμ.

Τῶν μὲν οὖν τριῶν υἱῶν τοῦ Νῶε καὶ τῆς συντελείας αὐτῶν καὶ γενεαλογίας, ἐγένετο ἡμῖν ὁ κατάλογος ἐν ἐπιτομῇ ἐν ᾗ προειρήκαμεν βίβλῳ. καὶ νῦν δὲ τὰ παραλελειμμένα ἐπιμνησθησόμεθα περί τε πόλεων καὶ βασιλέων, τῶν τε γεγενημένων ὁπότε ἦν χεῖλος ἓν καὶ μία γλῶσσα. πρὸ τοῦ τὰς διαλέκτους μερισθῆναι αὗται αἱ προγεγραμμέναι ἐγενήθησαν πόλεις. ἐν δὲ τῷ μέλλειν αὐτοὺς διαμερίζεσθαι, συμβούλιον ἐποίησαν γνώμῃ ἰδίᾳ, καὶ οὐ διὰ θεοῦ, οἰκοδομῆσαι πόλιν καὶ πύργον, οὗ ἡ ἄκρα φθάσῃ εἰς τὸν οὐρανὸν ἀφικέσθαι, ὅπως ποιήσωσιν ἑαυτοῖς ὄνομα δόξης. ἐπειδὴ οὖν παρὰ προαίρεσιν θεοῦ βαρὺ ἔργον ἐτόλμησαν ποιῆσαι, κατέβαλεν αὐτῶν ὁ θεὸς τὴν πόλιν καὶ τὸν πύργον κατέστρωσεν. ἔκτοτε ἐνήλλαξεν τὰς γλώσσας τῶν ἀνθρώπων, δοὺς ἑκάστῳ διάφορον διάλεκτον. Σίβυλλα μὲν οὕτως σεσήμακεν, καταγγέλλουσα ὀργὴν τῷ κόσμῳ μέλλειν ἔρχεσθαι.

31. [1] υἱοῦ] Gesner: υἱὸς V

We may also mention that some writers have spoken nonsense concerning music; they have said that Apollo was its inventor or that Orpheus found music from the sweet song of birds (ὀρνέων-φωνία).[1] Their statement is proved empty and vain by the fact that these persons lived many years after the deluge. And the story of Noah, by some called Deucalion, has already been explained for us in the book which we mentioned before; if you will, you too can read it.

Cities after the Deluge

31. After the deluge there was a new *beginning* of cities and kings which took place in the following way. The first city was *Babylon, then Orech and Archath and Chalane in the land of Sennaar.* There was a king of these named Nebroth. From these *came forth* a certain *Assour,* from whom the Assyrians took their name. Nebroth built the cities of *Nineveh and Roboom and Kalak and Dasen, between Nineveh and Kalak.* Nineveh was an especially *great city.* Another son of Sem son of Noah, named *Mestraein,* begot the *Loudoueim and the* so-called *Enemigeim and the Labieim and the Nephthaleim and the Patrosonieim and the Chaslonieim, from whom the Phylistieim came forth* [Gen. 10: 10–14].

As for the three sons of Noah and their relationships and their genealogies, we have a brief catalogue in the book previously mentioned [II. 30]. Now, however, we shall mention the remaining facts about cities and kings and about the events which occurred when *there was one lip and one tongue* [Gen. 11: 1]. Before the division of languages the previously mentioned cities were in existence. But when men were about to be divided they took counsel with their own judgement, not with God, *to build a city and a tower whose top might reach heaven* [Gen. 11: 4] so that they might *make* a glorious *name* for themselves. Since, then, they undertook a burdensome task in opposition to the purpose of God, God cast down their city and laid low their tower. From that time he diversified the tongues of men, *giving each a different language* [Gen. 11: 7]. The Sibyl indicated these events when she proclaimed that *wrath would come to the world* [*Or. Sib.* viii. 1].

---

30. [1] For Orpheus from Orphēn, Orphōndas, etc., cf. O. Kern, *Orphicorum fragmenta* (Berlin, 1922), test. 1, pp. 1–2; from ὄρη (mountains) and πέτραι (stones) following him, Agatharchides, *De mari erythraeo* i. 7.

Ἔφη δὲ οὕτως·

Ἀλλ' ὁπόταν μεγάλοιο θεοῦ τελέωνται ἀπειλαί,
ἅς ποτ' ἐπηπείλησε βροτοῖς, ὅτε πύργον ἔτευξαν
χώρῃ ἐν Ἀσσυρίῃ. ὁμόφωνοι δ' ἦσαν ἅπαντες,
καὶ βούλοντ' ἀναβῆναι εἰς οὐρανὸν ἀστερόεντα.
αὐτίκα δ' ἀθάνατος μεγάλην ἐπέθηκεν ἀνάγκην
πνεύμασιν· αὐτὰρ ἔπειτ' ἄνεμοι μέγαν ὑψόθι πύργον
ῥίψαν καὶ θνητοῖσιν ἐπ' ἀλλήλοις ἔριν ὦρσαν.
αὐτὰρ ἐπεὶ πύργος τ' ἔπεσεν, γλῶσσαί τ' ἀνθρώπων
εἰς πολλὰς θνητῶν ἐμερίσθησαν διαλέκτους.

καὶ τὰ ἑξῆς. ταῦτα μὲν οὖν ἐγενήθη ἐν γῇ Χαλδαίων. Ἐν δὲ τῇ γῇ Χαναὰν ἐγένετο πόλις ᾗ ὄνομα Χαρράν. κατ' ἐκείνους δὲ τοὺς χρόνους πρῶτος βασιλεὺς Αἰγύπτου ἐγένετο Φαραώ, ὃς καὶ Νεχαὼθ κατὰ Αἰγυπτίους ὠνομάσθη· καὶ οὕτως οἱ καθεξῆς βασιλεῖς ἐγένοντο. ἐν δὲ τῇ γῇ Σενναάρ, ἐν τοῖς καλουμένοις Χαλδαίοις, πρῶτος βασιλεὺς ἐγένετο Ἀριώχ· μετὰ δὲ τοῦτον ἕτερος Ἐλλάσαρ, καὶ μετὰ τοῦτον Χοδολλαγόμορ βασιλεὺς Αἰλάμ, καὶ μετὰ τοῦτον Θαργὰλ βασιλεὺς ἐθνῶν τῶν καλουμένων Ἀσσυρίων. ἄλλαι δὲ πόλεις ἐγένοντο πέντε ἐν τῇ μερίδι τοῦ Χὰμ υἱοῦ Νῶε· πρώτη ἡ καλουμένη Σόδομα, ἔπειτα Γόμορρα,[2] Ἀδαμὰ καὶ Σεβωεὶν καὶ Βαλάκ,[3] ἡ καὶ Σηγὼρ ἐπικληθεῖσα. καὶ τὰ ὀνόματα τῶν βασιλέων αὐτῶν ἐστιν ταῦτα· Βαλλὰς βασιλεὺς Σοδόμων, Βαρσὰς βασιλεὺς Γομόρρας, Σενναὰρ βασιλεὺς Ἀδάμας, Ὑμοὸρ βασιλεὺς Σεβωείν, Βαλὰχ βασιλεὺς Σηγώρ, τῆς καὶ Βαλὰκ[4] κεκλημένης. οὗτοι ἐδούλευσαν τῷ Χοδολλαγόμορ βασιλεῖ τῶν Ἀσσυρίων ἕως ἐτῶν δύο καὶ δέκα. ἐν δὲ τῷ τρισκαιδεκάτῳ ἔτει ἀπὸ τοῦ Χοδολλαγόμορ ἀπέστησαν. καὶ οὕτως ἐγένετο τότε τοὺς τέσσαρας βασιλεῖς τῶν Ἀσσυρίων συνάψαι πόλεμον πρὸς τοὺς πέντε βασιλεῖς. αὕτη ἀρχὴ ἐγένετο πρώτη τοῦ γίνεσθαι πολέμους ἐπὶ τῆς γῆς. καὶ κατέκοψαν τοὺς γίγαντας Καραναείν, καὶ ἔθνη ἰσχυρὰ ἅμα αὐτοῖς, καὶ τοὺς Ὀμμαίους ἐν αὐτῇ τῇ πόλει, καὶ τοὺς Χορραίους τοὺς ἐν τοῖς ὄρεσιν ἐπονομαζομένοις Σηεὶρ ἕως τῆς καλουμένης Τερεβίνθου τῆς Φαράν, ἥ ἐστιν ἐν τῇ ἐρήμῳ.

31. [2] Γόμορρα] Gesner: add. Σενναὰρ V   [3] καὶ Βαλάκ] Otto: om. V
[4] καὶ Βαλὰκ] Otto: κεφαλὰκ V

She spoke thus:

But when the warnings of the great God are accomplished,
Threats which he then made to mortals, when they built a tower
In the Assyrian land. They all spoke the same language,
And they wanted to ascend into the starry heaven.
Straightway the Immortal laid strong necessity
Upon the winds; straightway then the winds the great tower from above
Cast down, and roused strife among mortals [*Or. Sib.* iii. 97–103].
Straightway when the tower fell, the tongues of men [iii. 105][1]
Were divided into many languages of mortals [viii. 5],

and so on. These things took place in the land of the Chaldaeans.

In the *land of Canaan* there was a city named *Charran* [Gen. 11: 31]. In those times lived the first king of Egypt, Pharaoh, who was called Nechaoth by the Egyptians;[2] and thus the rest of the kings followed in succession. In the land of Sennaar among the so-called Chaldaeans the first *king* was *Arioch*; after him came another, *Ellasar*, and after him *Chodollagomor, king of Ailam*, and after him *Thargal, king of the nations* called Assyrian [cf. Gen. 14: 1]. There were five other cities in the part belonging to Cham the son of Noah; first that called *Sodoma*, then *Gomorrha, Adama, Seboein*, and *Balak*, which is also called *Segor*. And the names of their kings are these: *Ballas king of Sodoma, Barsas king of Gomorrha, Sennaar king of Adama, Hymoor king of Seboein, Balach king of Segor, which is also called Balak* [Gen. 14: 2]. These were *slaves of Chodollagomor* king of the Assyrians *for twelve years. In the thirteenth year they revolted* against Chodollagomor [Gen. 14: 4], and thus it happened that the four kings of the Assyrians then waged war against the five kings. This was the first beginning of wars on the earth. *And they cut to pieces the giants of Karanaein, and mighty nations with them, and the Ommaioi in the city* itself *and the Chorraioi in the mountains* called *Seeir up to* what is called *the terebinth of Pharan, which is in the desert* [Gen. 14: 5–6].

---

31. [1] *Or. Sib.* iii. 105 is almost identical with viii. 4.
[2] Cf. 2 Paralip. (2 Chron.) 25: 20; 4 Regn. (2 Kings) 23: 33. For Nechaos, also called Pharaoh, cf. Josephus, *Bell*. v. 379.

Κατὰ δὲ τὸν αὐτὸν καιρὸν ἐγένετο βασιλεὺς δίκαιος ὀνόματι Μελχισεδὲκ ἐν πόλει Σαλήμ, τῇ νῦν καλουμένῃ Ἱεροσόλυμα· οὗτος ἱερεὺς ἐγένετο πρῶτος πάντων ἱερέων τοῦ θεοῦ τοῦ ὑψίστου. ἀπὸ τούτου ἡ πόλις ὠνομάσθη Ἱερουσαλήμ, ἡ προειρημένη Ἱεροσόλυμα· ἀπὸ τούτου εὑρέθησαν καὶ ἱερεῖς γινόμενοι ἐπὶ πᾶσαν τὴν γῆν. μετὰ δὲ τοῦτον ἐβασίλευσεν Ἀβιμέλεχ ἐν Γεράροις· μετὰ δὲ τοῦτον ἕτερος Ἀβιμέλεχ· ἔπειτα ἐβασίλευσεν Ἔφρων καὶ ὁ Χετταῖος ἐπικληθείς. τὰ μὲν οὖν περὶ τούτων πρότερον γεγενημένων βασιλέων οὕτως τὰ ὀνόματα περιέχει· τῶν δὲ κατὰ Ἀσσυρίους πολλῶν ἐτῶν μεταξὺ οἱ λοιποὶ βασιλεῖς παρεσιγήθησαν τοῦ ἀναγραφῆναι· πάντων ἐσχάτων καθ' ἡμᾶς χρόνων ἀπομνημονεύονται γεγονότες βασιλεῖς τῶν Ἀσσυρίων Θεγλαφάσαρ, μετὰ δὲ τοῦτον Σελαμανάσαρ, εἶτα Σενναχαρείμ. τοῦ δὲ τρίαρχος ἐγένετο Ἀδραμέλεχ Αἰθίοψ, ὃς καὶ Αἰγύπτου ἐβασίλευσεν· καίπερ ταῦτα, ὡς πρὸς τὰ ἡμέτερα γράμματα, πάνυ νεώτερά ἐστιν.

32. Ἐντεῦθεν οὖν κατανοεῖν τὰς ἱστορίας ἐστὶν τοῖς φιλομαθέσιν καὶ φιλαρχαίοις, ὅτι οὐ[1] πρόσφατά ἐστιν τὰ ὑφ' ἡμῶν λεγόμενα διὰ τῶν ἁγίων προφητῶν. ὀλίγων γὰρ ὄντων ἐν πρώτοις τῶν τότε ἀνθρώπων ἐν τῇ Ἀραβικῇ γῇ καὶ Χαλδαϊκῇ, μετὰ τὸ διαμερισθῆναι τὰς γλώσσας αὐτῶν, πρὸς μέρος ἤρξαντο πολλοὶ γίνεσθαι καὶ πληθύνεσθαι ἐπὶ πάσης τῆς γῆς. καὶ οἱ μὲν ἔκλιναν οἰκεῖν πρὸς ἀνατολάς, οἱ δὲ ἐπὶ τὰ μέρη τὰ τῆς μεγάλης ἠπείρου καὶ τὰ πρὸς βόρειον, ὥστε διατείνειν μέχρι τῶν Βριττανῶν ἐν τοῖς ἀρκτικοῖς κλίμασιν, ἕτεροι δὲ γῆν Χαναναίαν, καὶ Ἰουδαίαν καὶ Φοινίκην ἐπικληθεῖσαν, καὶ τὰ μέρη τῆς Αἰθιοπίας καὶ Αἰγύπτου καὶ Λιβύης καὶ τὴν καλουμένην διακεκαυμένην καὶ τὰ μέχρι δυσμῶν κλίματα παρατείνοντα, οἱ δὲ λοιποὶ τὰ ἀπὸ τῆς παραλίου καὶ τῆς Παμφυλίας καὶ τὴν Ἀσίαν καὶ τὴν Ἑλλάδα καὶ τὴν Μακεδονίαν καὶ τὸ λοιπὸν τὴν Ἰταλίαν καὶ τὰς καλουμένας Γαλλείας καὶ Σπανίας καὶ Γερμανίας, ὥστε οὕτως τὰ νῦν ἐμπεπλῆσθαι τὴν σύμπασαν τῶν κατοικούντων αὐτήν. τριμεροῦς οὖν γεγενημένης τῆς κατοικήσεως τῶν ἀνθρώπων ἐπὶ τῆς γῆς κατ' ἀρχάς, ἔν τε ἀνατολῇ καὶ μεσημβρίᾳ καὶ δύσει, μετέπειτα καὶ τὰ λοιπὰ μέρη κατῳκήθη τῆς γῆς, χυδαίων τῶν ἀνθρώπων γενομένων.

32. [1] ὅτι οὐ] Nautin; cf. III. 16. 2: ὅπου V: εἴπου Humphry

At that time there was a righteous king named Melchisedek in the city of Salem, now called Jerusalem; he was the first priest [*hiereus*] of all the priests *of God Most High* [Gen. 14: 18]. From him the city was called Hierousalem (the previously mentioned Jerusalem); from his time priests are found in existence over the whole earth. After him Abimelech reigned in Gerara [Gen. 20: 2]; after him, another Abimelech [Gen. 26: 1]; then there reigned Ephron, who was also called the Chettaios [Gen. 23: 10]. As regards those early kings, these are their names. The rest of the kings in Assyria in the many intervening years were passed over in silence in the record; in the latest times of all, near our own, the kings of the Assyrians who are mentioned are Theglaphasar [4 Regn. 15: 29], and after him Selamanasar [17: 3], then Sennachareim [18: 13]. His triarch was Adramelech the Ethiopian, who also became king of Egypt.[3] But these matters are very recent in comparison with our scriptures.

How the World was Settled

32. Those who love learning and antiquities can judge whether what has been said by us through the holy prophets is merely recent or not by considering this: though there were originally only a few men at that time in Arabia and Chaldaea, after the division of their languages they gradually began to become many and to multiply over the whole earth. Some turned to dwell to the east, some to the parts of the great continent[1] and the regions to the north so that they reached the Britons in the arctic zones.[2] Others inhabited the land of Canaan, which is also called Judaea and Phoenicia, and the regions of Ethiopia and Egypt and Libya and the so-called torrid zone and the areas extending to the west. The rest, beginning with the lands from the sea coast and Pamphylia, inhabited Asia and Greece and Macedonia and finally Italy and the so-called Gauls and Spains and Germanies.[3] Thus the whole world is now filled with inhabitants. Since, then, the settlement of the world by mankind had a triple beginning, in the east and south and west, later the other parts of the earth were also inhabited when men came to be very numerous.

31. [3] According to 4 Regn. 19: 37 one of the king's three sons (hence a 'triarch' or ruler of a third part) was named Adramelech. The Lucianic text of 4 Regn. 17: 4 mentions an Adramelech as king of Egypt (A. Rahlfs, *Septuaginta-Studien* iii (Göttingen, 1911, 114–15). Theophilus or a predecessor identified the Adramelechs.

32. [1] Europe (Herodotus iv. 42, 45).

[2] At Antioch (lat. 36° N.) the arctic zone for Greek astronomers would begin at lat. 54° N. (B. Einarson).

[3] The plurals refer to Roman provinces.

Ταῦτα δὲ μὴ ἐπιστάμενοι οἱ συγγραφεῖς βούλονται τὸν κόσμον σφαιροειδῆ λέγειν καὶ ὡσπερεὶ κύβῳ συγκρίνειν αὐτόν. πῶς δὲ δύνανται ταῦτα ἀληθῆ φάσκειν, μὴ ἐπιστάμενοι τὴν ποίησιν τοῦ κόσμου μήτε τὴν κατοίκησιν αὐτοῦ; πρὸς μέρος αὐξανομένων τῶν ἀνθρώπων καὶ πληθυνομένων ἐπὶ τῆς γῆς, ὡς προειρήκαμεν, οὕτως κατῳκήθησαν καὶ αἱ νῆσοι τῆς θαλάσσης καὶ τὰ λοιπὰ κλίματα.

33. Τίς οὖν πρὸς ταῦτα ἴσχυσεν τῶν καλουμένων σοφῶν καὶ ποιητῶν ἢ[1] ἱστοριογράφων τὸ ἀληθὲς εἰπεῖν πολὺ μεταγενεστέρων αὐτῶν γεγενημένων καὶ πληθὺν θεῶν εἰσαγαγόντων, οἵτινες μετὰ τοσαῦτα ἔτη αὐτοὶ ἐγεννήθησαν τῶν πόλεων, ἔσχατοι καὶ τῶν βασιλέων καὶ ἐθνῶν καὶ πολέμων; ἐχρῆν γὰρ αὐτοὺς μεμνῆσθαι πάντων καὶ τῶν πρὸ κατακλυσμοῦ γεγονότων, περί τε κτίσεως κόσμου καὶ ποιήσεως ἀνθρώπου, τά τε ἑξῆς συμβάντα ἀκριβῶς ἐξειπεῖν τοὺς παρ' Αἰγυπτίοις προφήτας ἢ Χαλδαίους τούς τε ἄλλους συγγραφεῖς, εἴπερ θείῳ καὶ καθαρῷ πνεύματι ἐλάλησαν καὶ τὰ δι' αὐτῶν ῥηθέντα ἀληθῆ ἀνήγγειλαν· καὶ οὐ μόνον τὰ προγενόμενα ἢ ἐνεστῶτα ἀλλὰ καὶ τὰ ἐπερχόμενα τῷ κόσμῳ ἐχρῆν αὐτοὺς προκαταγγεῖλαι. διὸ δείκνυται πάντας τοὺς λοιποὺς πεπλανῆσθαι, μόνους δὲ Χριστιανοὺς τὴν ἀλήθειαν κεχωρηκέναι, οἵτινες ὑπὸ πνεύματος ἁγίου διδασκόμεθα, τοῦ λαλήσαντος ἐν τοῖς ἁγίοις προφήταις, καὶ τὰ πάντα προκαταγγέλλοντος.

34. Καὶ τὸ λοιπὸν ἔστω σοι φιλοφρόνως ἐρευνᾶν τὰ τοῦ θεοῦ, λέγω δὲ τὰ διὰ τῶν προφητῶν ῥηθέντα, ὅπως συγκρίνας τά τε ὑπὸ ἡμῶν λεγόμενα καὶ τὰ ὑπὸ τῶν λοιπῶν δυνήσει εὑρεῖν τὸ ἀληθές. Τὰ μὲν οὖν ὀνόματα τῶν καλουμένων θεῶν ὅτι παρ' αὐτοῖς ὀνόματα ἀνθρώπων εὑρίσκεται, καθὼς ἐν τοῖς ἐπάνω ἐδηλώσαμεν, ἐξ αὐτῶν τῶν ἱστοριῶν ὧν συνέγραψαν ἀπεδείξαμεν. αἱ δὲ εἰκόνες αὐτῶν τὸ καθ' ἡμέραν ἕως τοῦ δεῦρο ἐκτυποῦνται, εἴδωλα, ἔργα χειρῶν ἀνθρώπων. καὶ τούτοις μὲν λατρεύει τὸ πλῆθος τῶν ματαίων ἀνθρώπων· τὸν δὲ ποιητὴν καὶ δημιουργὸν τῶν ὅλων καὶ τροφέα πάσης πνοῆς ἀθετοῦσιν, πειθόμενοι δόγμασιν ματαίοις διὰ πλάνης πατροπαραδότου γνώμης ἀσυνέτου.

33. [1] ἢ] Fell: om. V

Writers who do not know these things want to call the world spherical or to compare it with a cube.[4] How can they speak truthfully in these matters when they do not know how the world was created or how it was inhabited? As men gradually *increased and multiplied* [Gen. 9: 1] on the earth, as we have said, the islands of the sea and the other regions were thus inhabited [cf. Gen. 10: 5].

All Greek Writers were Inferior to the Prophets

33. Which of the so-called wise men or poets or historiographers was able to say what was true in regard to these matters? They lived long after them and introduced a multitude of gods; indeed, they lived many years later than the foundation of the cities and came after the kings, nations, and wars. They should have made mention of all the events before the deluge, and the Egyptian prophets and the Chaldaeans and the other writers should have made accurate declarations concerning the creation of the world and the making of man and the later events, if they really spoke by a divine and pure spirit and if the utterances made through them were true. They should have announced not only past or present events but also those which were going to come upon the world. For this reason it is plain that all the rest were in error and that only the Christians have held the truth—we who are instructed by the Holy Spirit who spoke in the holy prophets and foretold everything.

The Teaching of the Prophets

34. Furthermore, you must devotedly search the things of God [cf. 1 Cor. 2: 10], I mean those spoken through the prophets, so that by comparing what is said by us with what is said by the others you will be able to discover the truth. We have shown from the very histories they composed that in their own writings the names of the so-called gods are names of men, as we have made clear above [I. 9; II. 2–7]. And their images, which are fashioned every day up to the present time, are *idols, the works of men's hands* [Ps. 113: 12; 1. 1]. The multitude of foolish men worships these, but they reject the Maker and Fashioner of the universe, the Nourisher of all breath, in obedience to vain doctrines because of the hereditary error of their unintelligent opinion.

---

32. [4] For these shapes cf. H. Diels, *Doxographi Graeci* 329 a 2, b 6–9 (cf. Pliny, *Nat. hist.* ii. 112); 334 a 19–20, b 10–11; also Tertullian, *Ad nat.* ii. 4.

'Ο μέντοι γε θεὸς καὶ πατὴρ καὶ κτίστης τῶν ὅλων οὐκ ἐγκατέλιπεν τὴν ἀνθρωπότητα, ἀλλὰ ἔδωκεν νόμον καὶ ἔπεμψεν προφήτας ἁγίους πρὸς τὸ καταγγεῖλαι καὶ διδάξαι[1] τὸ γένος τῶν ἀνθρώπων, εἰς τὸ ἕνα ἕκαστον ἡμῶν ἀνανῆψαι καὶ ἐπιγνῶναι ὅτι εἷς ἐστιν θεός· οἳ καὶ ἐδίδαξαν ἀπέχεσθαι ἀπὸ τῆς ἀθεμίτου εἰδωλολατρείας καὶ μοιχείας καὶ φόνου, πορνείας, κλοπῆς, φιλαργυρίας, ὅρκου ψεύδους, ὀργῆς καὶ πάσης ἀσελγείας καὶ ἀκαθαρσίας καὶ πάντα ὅσα ἂν μὴ βούληται ἄνθρωπος ἑαυτῷ γίνεσθαι ἵνα μηδὲ ἄλλῳ ποιῇ, καὶ οὕτως ὁ δικαιοπραγῶν ἐκφύγῃ τὰς αἰωνίους κολάσεις καὶ καταξιωθῇ τῆς αἰωνίου ζωῆς παρὰ τοῦ θεοῦ.

35. Ὁ μὲν οὖν θεῖος νόμος οὐ μόνον κωλύει τὸ εἰδώλοις προσκυνεῖν, ἀλλὰ καὶ τοῖς στοιχείοις, ἡλίῳ σελήνῃ ἢ τοῖς λοιποῖς ἄστροις, ἀλλ' οὔτε τῷ οὐρανῷ οὔτε γῇ οὔτε θαλάσσῃ ἢ πηγαῖς ἢ ποταμοῖς θρησκεύειν· ἀλλ' ἢ μόνῳ τῷ ὄντως θεῷ καὶ ποιητῇ τῶν ὅλων χρὴ λατρεύειν ἐν ὁσιότητι καρδίας καὶ εἰλικρινεῖ γνώμῃ. διό φησιν ὁ ἅγιος νόμος· "Οὐ μοιχεύσεις, οὐ φονεύσεις, οὐ κλέψεις, οὐ ψευδομαρτυρήσεις, οὐκ ἐπιθυμήσεις τὴν γυναῖκα τοῦ πλησίον σου." ὁμοίως καὶ οἱ προφῆται. Σολομὼν μὲν οὖν καὶ τὸ δι' ἐννεύματος[1] μὴ ἁμαρτάνειν διδάσκει ἡμᾶς, λέγων· "Οἱ ὀφθαλμοί σου ὀρθὰ βλεπέτωσαν, τὰ δὲ βλέφαρά σου νευέτω δίκαια."

Καὶ Ὡσηὲ[2] δὲ καὶ αὐτὸς προφήτης περὶ μοναρχίας θεοῦ λέγει· "Οὗτος ὁ θεὸς ὑμῶν ὁ στερεῶν τὸν οὐρανὸν καὶ κτίζων τὴν γῆν, οὗ αἱ χεῖρες κατέδειξαν πᾶσαν τὴν στρατιὰν τοῦ οὐρανοῦ, καὶ οὐ παρέδειξεν ὑμῖν αὐτὰ τοῦ ὀπίσω αὐτῶν πορεύεσθαι." Ἡσαΐας δὲ καὶ αὐτός φησιν· "Οὕτως λέγει κύριος ὁ θεός, ὁ στερεώσας τὸν οὐρανὸν καὶ θεμελιώσας τὴν γῆν καὶ τὰ ἐν αὐτῇ, καὶ διδοὺς πνοὴν τῷ λαῷ τῷ ἐπ' αὐτῆς καὶ πνεῦμα τοῖς πατοῦσιν αὐτήν. οὗτος κύριος ὁ θεὸς ὑμῶν." καὶ πάλιν δι' αὐτοῦ· "Ἐγώ, φησίν, ἐποίησα γῆν καὶ ἄνθρωπον ἐπ' αὐτῇ, ἐγὼ τῇ χειρί μου ἐστερέωσα τὸν οὐρανόν." καὶ ἐν ἑτέρῳ κεφαλαίῳ· "Οὗτος ὁ θεὸς ὑμῶν ὁ κατασκευάσας τὰ ἄκρα τῆς γῆς· οὐ πεινάσει οὐδὲ κοπιάσει, οὐδέ ἐστιν ἐξεύρησις τῆς φρονήσεως αὐτοῦ." ὁμοίως καὶ Ἱερεμίας ⟨ὅς⟩[3] καί φησιν·"Ὁ ποιήσας

34. [1] διδάξαι] Heumann ap. Otto: δεῖξαι V
35. [1] δι' ἐννεύματος] V; cf. Prov. 6: 13: διὰ νεύματος V[2] [2] Ὡσηὲ] Grant; cf. Hos. 13: 4: Μωσῆς V   [3] ὅς] Maran: om. V

The God and Father and Maker of the universe did not abandon mankind but gave a law and sent holy prophets to proclaim and to teach the human race so that each one of us might become sober and recognize that God is one. They also taught us to abstain from *unlawful idolatry* [1 Pet. 4: 3] and adultery and murder, fornication, theft, love of money, perjury, anger, and all licentiousness and uncleanness; they taught that 'whatever a man does not want done to himself he should not do to another' [Acts 15: 20, 29];[1] and that thus a person who acts righteously may escape the eternal punishments and be judged worthy of receiving eternal life from God [I. 14].

The Prophets on Idolatry

35. The divine law forbids not only the worship of idols but also the worship of the heavenly bodies such as *the sun, the moon,* or *the* other *stars* [Deut. 4: 19], or of heaven or earth or sea or springs or rivers. Only the real God who made the universe is to be worshipped, with holiness of heart and a sincere mind. For this reason the holy law said, 'You shall not commit adultery, you shall not kill, you shall not steal, you shall not bear false witness, you shall not covet your neighbour's wife' [Exod. 20: 13–17; cf. III. 9]. So also the prophets. Solomon teaches us not to sin even by a glance, saying, 'Let your eyes look straight and let your eyelids incline justly' [Prov. 4: 25; cf. III. 13].

And Hosea, who himself was a prophet, says of the sole rule of God: 'This is your God, who made firm the heaven and founded the earth, whose hands showed forth the whole host of heaven, and he did not show them to you so that you should follow them' [Hos. 13: 4]. Isaiah himself says: 'Thus says the Lord God, who made firm the heaven and established the earth and what is in it, and gave breath to the people upon it and spirit to those who walk upon it: this is the Lord your God' [Isa. 42: 5–6]. And again through him: 'I, he says, made the earth and man upon it; I made firm the heaven by my hand' [Isa. 45: 12]. And in another chapter: 'This is your God, who constructed the ends of the earth; he will not hunger or grow weary, and there is no searching out of his intelligence' [Isa. 40: 28]. Similarly also Jeremiah; and he says:

34. [1] This is the text of Codex Bezae and some other witnesses; cf. **Irenaeus,** *Adv. haer.* iii. 12. 14. The 'apostolic decree' in this form refers to idolatry, 'blood', and fornication and then quotes the 'negative golden rule'.

τὴν γῆν ἐπὶ τῇ ἰσχύϊ αὐτοῦ, ἀνορθώσας τὴν οἰκουμένην ἐν τῇ σοφίᾳ αὐτοῦ, καὶ ἐν τῇ φρονήσει αὐτοῦ ἐξέτεινεν τὸν οὐρανὸν καὶ πλῆθος ὕδατος ἐν οὐρανῷ καὶ ἀνήγαγεν νεφέλας ἐξ ἐσχάτου τῆς γῆς, ἀστραπὰς εἰς ὑετὸν ἐποίησεν καὶ ἐξήγαγεν ἀνέμους ἐκ θησαυρῶν αὐτοῦ."

Ὁρᾶν ἔστιν πῶς φίλα καὶ σύμφωνα ἐλάλησαν πάντες οἱ προφῆται, ἑνὶ καὶ τῷ αὐτῷ πνεύματι ἐκφωνήσαντες περί τε μοναρχίας θεοῦ καὶ τῆς τοῦ κόσμου γενέσεως καὶ τῆς ἀνθρώπου ποιήσεως. οὐ μὴν ἀλλὰ καὶ ὥδιναν, πενθοῦντες τὸ ἄθεον γένος τῶν ἀνθρώπων, καὶ τοὺς δοκοῦντας εἶναι σοφοὺς διὰ τὴν ἐν αὐτοῖς πλάνην καὶ πώρωσιν τῆς καρδίας κατῄσχυναν. ὁ μὲν Ἰερεμίας ἔφη· " Ἐμωράνθη πᾶς ἄνθρωπος ἀπὸ γνώσεως αὐτοῦ, κατῃσχύνθη πᾶς χρυσοχόος ἀπὸ τῶν γλυπτῶν αὐτοῦ, εἰς μάτην ἀργυροκόπος ἀργυροκοπεῖ, οὐκ ἔστιν πνεῦμα ἐν αὐτοῖς, ἐν ἡμέρᾳ ἐπισκοπῆς αὐτῶν ἀπολοῦνται." τὸ αὐτὸ καὶ ὁ Δαυὶδ λέγει· " Ἐφθάρησαν καὶ ἐβδελύχθησαν ἐν ἐπιτηδεύμασιν αὐτῶν, οὐκ ἔστιν ποιῶν χρηστότητα, οὐκ ἔστιν ἕως ἑνός· πάντες ἐξέκλιναν, ἅμα ἠχρειώθησαν." ὁμοίως καὶ Ἀββακούμ· " Τί ὠφελεῖ γλυπτὸν ἄνθρωπον, ὅτι ἔγλυψεν αὐτὸ φαντασίαν ψευδῆ; οὐαὶ τῷ λέγοντι τῷ λίθῳ ἐξεγέρθητι, καὶ τῷ ξύλῳ ὑψώθητι." ὁμοίως εἶπον καὶ οἱ λοιποὶ τῆς ἀληθείας προφῆται.

Καὶ τί μοι τὸ πλῆθος καταλέγειν τῶν προφητῶν, πολλῶν ὄντων καὶ μυρία φίλα καὶ σύμφωνα εἰρηκότων; οἱ γὰρ βουλόμενοι δύνανται ἐντυχόντες τοῖς δι' αὐτῶν εἰρημένοις ἀκριβῶς γνῶναι τὸ ἀληθὲς καὶ μὴ παράγεσθαι[4] ὑπὸ διανοίας καὶ ματαιοπονίας. οὗτοι οὖν οὓς προειρήκαμεν προφῆται ἐγένοντο ἐν Ἑβραίοις, ἀγράμματοι καὶ ποιμένες καὶ ἰδιῶται.

36. Σίβυλλα δέ, ἐν Ἕλλησιν καὶ ἐν τοῖς λοιποῖς ἔθνεσιν γενομένη προφῆτις, ἐν ἀρχῇ τῆς προφητείας αὐτῆς ὀνειδίζει τὸ τῶν ἀνθρώπων γένος, λέγουσα·

Ἄνθρωποι θνητοὶ καὶ σάρκινοι, οὐδὲν ἐόντες,
πῶς ταχέως ὑψοῦσθε, βίου τέλος οὐκ ἐσορῶντες,
οὐ τρέμετ' οὐδὲ[1] φοβεῖσθε θεόν, τὸν ἐπίσκοπον ὑμῶν,
ὕψιστον γνώστην, πανεπόπτην,[2] μάρτυρα πάντων,

---

35. [4] παράγεσθαι] Fell : παραγενέσθαι V
36. [1] οὐδὲ] Gesner : οὐ V   [2] πανεπόπτην] Castalio : παντεπόπτην V

'He who made the earth by his strength, who set up the world by his Wisdom, by his intelligence stretched out the heaven and the multitude of the water in heaven, and brought clouds from the end of the earth and made lightnings into rain and brought forth winds from his treasuries' [Jer. 10: 12–13; cf. 1. 6].

It is obvious how agreeably and harmoniously all the prophets spoke, making their proclamation by *one and the same Spirit* [1 Cor. 12: 11] concerning the sole rule of God and the origin of the world and the making of man. Moreover, they suffered pangs [cf. Gal. 4: 19], grieving over the godless race of mankind, and they put to shame those who thought they were wise [cf. Rom. 1: 22; 1 Cor. 3: 18] because of their error and hardness of heart. Jeremiah says: 'Every man was made foolish from his knowledge, every goldsmith was put to shame by his carvings; in vain the silversmith works silver. There is no spirit in them; in the day of their visitation they will perish' [Jer. 10: 14–15; 6: 29]. David also says the same: 'They were corrupted and made abominable in their ways of living; there is not one who does good, not even one; all have fallen away and have become useless' [Ps. 13: 1, 3]. Similarly also Habakkuk: 'What does a sculpture avail a man, that he carved it a false image? Woe to him who says to the stone, Be raised up, and to the wood, Be lifted up' [Hab. 2: 18–19]. The rest of the prophets of truth spoke similarly.

And why should I list the multitude of the prophets, since they are many and made countless statements in agreement and harmony? For those who desire to do so can read what was said through them and acquire accurate knowledge of what is true, and not be led astray by speculation and pointless labour. These persons whom we have mentioned were prophets among the Hebrews; they were illiterate men and shepherds and uneducated.

The Sibyl's Warning

36. And the Sibyl, who was a prophetess for the Greeks and the other nations, rebukes the human race at the beginning of her prophecy, saying [fr. 1 Geffcken]:

> Mortal and fleshly men, you who are nothing,
> How swiftly are you exalted, not noting the end of life!
> Do you not tremble or fear God, your overseer,
> The Most High who knows, sees all, witnesses all,

παντοτρόφον κτίστην, ὅστις γλυκὺ πνεῦμ' ἐν ἅπασιν
κάτθετο,³ χἠγητῆρα βροτῶν πάντων ἐποίησεν;
εἷς θεός, ὅς⁴ μόνος ἄρχει, ὑπερμεγέθης, ἀγένητος,
παντοκράτωρ, ἀόρατος, ὁρῶν μόνος⁵ αὐτὸς ἅπαντα,
αὐτὸς δ' οὐ βλέπεται θνητῆς ὑπὸ σαρκὸς ἁπάσης.
τίς γὰρ σὰρξ δύναται τὸν ἐπουράνιον καὶ ἀληθῆ
ὀφθαλμοῖσιν ἰδεῖν θεὸν ἄμβροτον, ὃς πόλον οἰκεῖ;
ἀλλ' οὐδ' ἀκτίνων κατεναντίον ἠελίοιο
ἄνθρωποι στῆναι δυνατοί,⁶ θνητοὶ γεγαῶτες,
ἄνδρες ἐν ὀστήεσσι,⁷ φλέβες καὶ σάρκες ἐόντες.
αὐτὸν τὸν μόνον ὄντα σέβεσθ' ἡγήτορα κόσμου,
ὃς μόνος εἰς αἰῶνα καὶ ἐξ αἰῶνος ἐτύχθη.
αὐτογενής, ἀγένητος, ἅπαντα κρατῶν διαπαντός,
πᾶσι βροτοῖσι νέμων⁸ τὸ κριτήριον ἐν φαΐ κοινῷ.
τῆς κακοβουλοσύνης δὲ τὸν ἄξιον ἕξετε μισθόν,
ὅττι⁹ θεὸν προλιπόντες ἀληθινὸν ἀεναόν τε
δοξάζειν, αὐτῷ τε θύειν ἱερὰς ἑκατόμβας,
δαίμοσι τὰς θυσίας ἐποιήσατε τοῖσιν ἐν ᾅδῃ·
τύφῳ καὶ μανίῃ δὲ βαδίζετε, καὶ τρίβον ὀρθὴν
εὐθεῖαν προλιπόντες ἀπήλθετε, καὶ δι' ἀκανθῶν
καὶ σκολόπων ἐπλανᾶσθε. βροτοὶ παύσασθε μάταιοι
ῥεμβόμενοι σκοτίῃ καὶ ἀφεγγέϊ νυκτὶ μελαίνῃ,
καὶ λίπετε σκοτίην νυκτός, φωτὸς δὲ λάβεσθε.
οὗτος ἰδοὺ πάντεσσι σαφὴς ἀπλάνητος ὑπάρχει.
ἔλθετε, μὴ σκοτίην δὲ διώκετε καὶ γνόφον αἰεί·
ἠελίου γλυκυδερκὲς ἰδοὺ φάος ἔξοχα λάμπει.
γνῶτε δὲ κατθέμενοι¹⁰ σοφίην ἐν στήθεσιν ὑμῶν·
εἷς θεὸς ἔστι, βροχάς, ἀνέμους, σεισμοὺς ἐπιπέμπων,
ἀστεροπάς, λιμούς, λοιμοὺς καὶ κήδεα λυγρὰ
καὶ νιφετούς, κρύσταλλα. τί δὴ καθ' ἓν ἐξαγορεύω;
οὐρανοῦ ἡγεῖται, γαίης κρατεῖ, αὐτὸς ὑπάρχει.

36. ³ κάτθετο] Castalio; cf. Lact. *Div. inst.* iv. 6. 5 (Brandt): κατέθετο V ⁴ ὅς] Ducaeus; cf. Lact. *Div. inst.* i. 6. 15 (Brandt): om. V ⁵ ὁρῶν μόνος] V: ὁρώμενος Friedlieb; cf. Ps.-Just. *Coh.* 16 (Otto) ⁶ δυνατοί] Fell; cf. Clem. *Protr.* lxxi. 4; *Strom.* v. 108. 6 (Stählin): δύναντ' V: δύνανται V² ⁷ ὀστήεσσι] V: ὀστείοισι Nauck ⁸ βροτοῖσι νέμων] Maran: βροτοῖσιν ἐνὼν V ⁹ ὅττι] Castalio: ὅτι V ¹⁰ κατθέμενοι] Wolf: κατεθμενοι V

All-nourishing creator, who sweet spirit in all
Did place and made it the guide of all mortals?
God is one, who alone rules, immense, uncreated,
Almighty, invisible, alone himself seeing all,
Himself yet not viewed by any mortal flesh.
For what flesh can see with eyes the heavenly
And true immortal God, who dwells in heaven?
Not even against the sun's rays
Can men stand, born to be mortal,
Men who dwell in bones and are veins and flesh.
Worship him alone who is ruler of the universe,
Who alone exists from eternity to eternity,
Self-generated, ungenerated, ruling all forever,
To all mortals dispensing judgement in common light.
Of your evil counsel you will receive the just reward,
For forsaking the worship of God, the true and eternal,
Nor sacrificing to him holy hecatombs,
You offer sacrifices to demons who are in Hades.
In infatuation and madness you walk, and the right way
And straight you have abandoned; through thistles
And thorns you have wandered. Cease, vain mortals,
Your roaming in dark and obscure black night,
And leave the darkness of night; receive the light.
Behold, he exists changeless and sure for all.
Come, pursue not gloom and darkness forever;
Behold, the sweet-glancing light of the sun shines bright.
Know this, setting wisdom in your hearts:
There is one God, who sends rains, winds, earthquakes,
Lightnings, famines, plagues, and baneful griefs,
And snow and ice. Why should I tell forth each one?
He guides the heaven, rules the earth, himself exists.[1]

36. [1] This 'fragment' of the *Sibylline Oracles* (cf. J. Geffcken, *Die Oracula Sibyllina*, Leipzig, 1902, 227–9) originally stood at the beginning of Book iii, from which Theophilus probably took his quotation (cf. Lactantius, *Div. inst.* iv. 6. 5). Books iii–v of the *Oracles* were composed in Hellenistic Jewish circles and were also in circulation among early Christians. Verses from this 'fragment' were quoted by Clement of Alexandria, the unknown apologist who wrote the *Cohortatio ad gentes*, and Lactantius.

καὶ πρὸς τοὺς γενητοὺς λεγομένους ἔφη·

Εἰ δὲ γενητὸν ὅλως καὶ φθείρεται, οὐ δύνατ' ἀνδρὸς
ἐκ μηρῶν μήτρας τε θεὸς τετυπωμένος εἶναι.
ἀλλὰ θεὸς μόνος[11] εἷς πανυπέρτατος, ὃς πεποίηκεν
οὐρανὸν ἠέλιόν τε καὶ ἀστέρας ἠδὲ σελήνην,
καρποφόρον γαῖάν τε καὶ ὕδατος οἴδματα[12] πόντου,
οὔρεα θ' ὑψήεντα καὶ ἀέναα χεύματα πηγῶν·
τῶν τ' ἐνύδρων πάλι γεννᾷ ἀνήριθμον πολὺ πλῆθος.
ἕρπετα δὲ γαίης κινούμενα ψυχοτροφεῖται,
ποικίλα τε πτηνῶν[13] λιγυρόθροα, τραυλίζοντα,
ξουθά, λιγυπτερόφωνα,[14] ταράσσοντ' ἀέρα ταρσοῖς,
ἐν δὲ νάπαις ὀρέων ἀγρίαν γένναν θέτο θηρῶν·
ἡμῖν τε κτήνη ὑπέταξεν πάντα βροτοῖσιν,
πάντων δ' ἡγητῆρα κατέστησεν θεότευκτον,
ἀνδρὶ δ' ὑπαίταξεν παμποίκιλα κοὐ καταληπτά.
τίς γὰρ σὰρξ δύναται θνητῶν γνῶναι τάδ' ἅπαντα;
ἀλλ' αὐτὸς μόνος οἶδεν ὁ ποιήσας τάδ' ἀπ' ἀρχῆς
ἄφθαρτος κτίστης αἰώνιος, αἰθέρα ναίων,
τοῖς ἀγαθοῖς ἀγαθὸν προφέρων πολὺ πλείονα μισθόν,
τοῖς δὲ κακοῖς ἀδίκοις τε χόλον καὶ θυμὸν ἐγείρων,
καὶ πόλεμον καὶ λοιμὸν ἰδ' ἄλγεα δακρυόεντα.
ἄνθρωποι, τί μάτην ὑψούμενοι ἐκριζοῦσθε;
Αἰσχύνθητε γαλᾶς[15] καὶ κνώδαλα θειοποιοῦντες.
οὐ μανίη καὶ λύσσα φρενῶν αἴσθησιν ἀφαιρεῖ,[16]
εἰ λοπάδας κλέπτουσι θεοί, συλοῦσι δὲ χύτρας;
ἀντὶ δὲ χρυσήεντα πόλον κατὰ πίονα ναίειν
σητόβρωτα δέδορκε, πυκναῖς δ' ἀράχναις δεδίασται·
προσκυνέοντες ὄφεις κύνας αἰλούρους, ἀνόητοι,
καὶ πετεηνὰ σέβεσθε καὶ ἑρπετὰ θηρία γαίης
καὶ λίθινα ξόανα καὶ ἀγάλματα χειροποίητα,
καὶ παρ' ὁδοῖσι[17] λίθων συγχώσματα· ταῦτα σέβεσθε
ἄλλα τε πολλὰ μάταια, ἃ δὴ κ' αἰσχρὸν ἀγορεύειν,

36. [11] μόνος] B; cf. Lact. *Div. inst.* i. 6. 15 (Brandt): om. V   [12] οἴδματα] B; cf. Lact. *Div. inst.* i. 6. 15 (Brandt): οἶδμα V   [13] πτηνῶν] Thienemann: κτηνῶν V   [14] λιγυπτερόφωνα] Opsopoeus: λιγυροπτερόφωνα V   [15] γαλᾶς] Opsopoeus: γάλας Gesner: τάλας V   [16] αἴσθησιν ἀφαιρεῖ] Alexandre: καὶ ἐστησι αφαρη V   [17] παρ' ὁδοῖσι] Wilamowitz: ἐν παρόδοις V

And in regard to those (gods) who are called created she said [fr. 3 Geffcken]:

> If what comes to be certainly perishes,
> No god can take shape from loins and a womb.
> There is but one who is God, most exalted, who made
> Heaven, sun, stars, and moon,
> The fruitful earth and the billows of sea water,
> The lofty mountains and ever-flowing streams of springs.
> He also generates the countless throng of marine animals;
> He sustains the life of reptiles moving on the earth
> And of the various sweet-sounding birds that twitter,
> Rustling and whirring, stirring the air with their feathers;
> In the glens of mountains he set the fierce race of wild beasts,
> But to us mortals he subjected all flocks,
> And established man, made by God, as ruler of all;
> To man he subjected the varied and countless animals.
> What mortal flesh can know all this?
> He alone knows who made them from the beginning,
> The immortal, eternal creator, who dwells in the aether.
> To the good he offers good as the greatest reward,
> On the evil and unjust arousing anger and wrath
> And war and plague and tearful pains.
> Men, why are you vainly exalted and then uprooted?
> Be ashamed that you make gods of weasels and brute beasts.
> Do not madness and fury deprive you of sense,
> If the gods steal dishes and plunder pots?
> Instead of dwelling in the golden rich heaven
> Their god has a worm-eaten look and is woven over with thick spider-webs.
> You stupidly worship snakes and dogs and cats
> And you reverence birds and wild reptiles of earth
> And statues, made by hands, of stone and wood,
> And even roadside piles of stones; these you worship
> As well as other pointless things, shameful to mention.

εἰσὶ[18] θεοὶ μερόπων δόλῳ ἡγητῆρες[19] ἀβούλων
τῶν δὴ κὰκ στόματος χεῖται[20] θανατηφόρος ἰός.
ὃς δ᾽[21] ἔστι ζωή τε καὶ ἄφθιτον ἀέναον φῶς,
καὶ μέλιτος ⌣⌣ — [22] γλυκερώτερον ἀνδράσι χάρμα
ἐκπροχέει ⌣⌣ — [23] τῷ δὴ[24] μόνῳ αὐχένα κάμπτειν,
καὶ τρίβον αἰώνεσσιν ἐν εὐσεβέεσσ᾽ ἀνακλίνοις.[25]
ταῦτα λιπόντες ἅπαντα, δίκης μεστὸν τὸ[26] κύπελλον
ζωρότερον, στιβαρόν, βεβαρημένον, εὖ μάλ᾽ ἄκρητον,
εἱλκύσατ᾽ ἀφροσύνῃ μεμανηότι πνεύματι πάντες·
κοὺ θέλετ᾽ ἐκνῆψαι καὶ σώφρονα πρὸς νόον ἐλθεῖν,
καὶ γνῶναι βασιλῆα θεόν, τὸν παντ᾽ ἐφορῶντα.
τοὔνεκεν αἰσθομένοιο πυρὸς σέλας ἔρχετ᾽ ἐφ᾽ ὑμᾶς·
λαμπάσι καυθήσεσθε δι᾽ αἰῶνος τὸ πανῆμαρ,
ψευδέσιν αἰσχυνθέντες ἐπ᾽ εἰδώλοισιν ἀχρήστοις.
οἱ δὲ θεὸν τιμῶντες ἀληθινὸν ἀέναόν τε
ζωὴν κληρονομοῦσι,[27] τὸν αἰῶνος χρόνον αὐτοί
οἰκοῦντες παραδείσου ὁμῶς[28] ἐριθηλέα κῆπον,
δαινύμενοι γλυκὺν ἄρτον ἀπ᾽ οὐρανοῦ ἀστερόεντος.

ὅτι μὲν οὖν ταῦτα ἀληθῆ καὶ ὠφέλιμα καὶ δίκαια καὶ προφιλῆ πᾶσιν ἀνθρώποις τυγχάνει, δῆλόν ἐστιν, καὶ ὅτι οἱ κακῶς δράσαντες ἀναγκαίως ἔχουσιν κατ᾽ ἀξίαν τῶν πράξεων κολασθῆναι.

37. Ἤδη δὲ καὶ τῶν ποιητῶν τινες ὡσπερεὶ λόγια ἑαυτοῖς ἐξεῖπον ταῦτα καὶ εἰς μαρτύριον τοῖς τὰ ἄδικα πράσσουσι λέγοντες ὅτι μέλλουσιν κολάζεσθαι. Αἰσχύλος ἔφη·

Δράσαντι γάρ τοι καὶ παθεῖν ὀφείλεται.

Πίνδαρος δὲ καὶ αὐτὸς ἔφη·

Ἐπεὶ
ῥέζοντά τι καὶ παθεῖν ἔοικεν.

36. [18] εἰσί] Opsopoeus: add. γὰρ V   [19] δόλῳ ἡγητῆρες] Wilamowitz: δολοήτορες V   [20] χεῖται] Castalio: κεῖται V   [21] ὃς δ᾽] Rzach: οὐδέ V   [22] ⌣⌣ –] Geffcken: γλυκεροῦ Opsopoeus: om. V   [23] ⌣⌣ –] Geffcken: om. V   [24] δὴ] Gesner: δεῖ V   [25] ἀνακλίνοις] Geffcken: ἀνακλινοῖ V   [26] τὸ Opsopoeus: τε V   [27] κληρονομοῦσι] Wolf; cf. Lact. Div. inst. ii. 12. 19 (Brandt): κληρονομήσουσιν V   [28] ὁμῶς] Castalio; cf. Lact. Div. inst. ii. 12. 19 (Brandt): om. V

These gods are crafty leaders of thoughtless men,
And from their mouth pours death-dealing poison.
The one who is life and unceasing, ever-flowing light,
Who pours forth joy for men, sweeter than honey,
[. . . .] to him alone must one bend one's neck
And incline one's way in pious lives.
Leaving all this, the cup full of just punishment,
Most pure, strong, pressed down, quite unmixed,
You all have quaffed with mindlessness and mad spirit;
You do not wish to become sober and come to sober mind,
Nor to know God as king, the all-seeing.
Therefore a flame of burning fire is coming upon you;
You will be burned in flames daily forever,
Put to shame for your false useless idols.
But those who worship God, the true and eternal,
Receive life, for eternal time
Dwelling in the luxuriant garden of paradise,
Eating sweet bread from the starry heaven.[2]

Now that these statements are *true* and useful and *just* and *lovely* [Phil. 4: 8] is obvious to all men, and also that those who act in evil fashion must necessarily be punished in accordance with their actions.

The Poets on Justice and Punishment

37. Now it has happened that some of the poets too expressed these things as (so to speak) oracles for themselves and as testimony against those whose actions are unjust, saying that they will be punished. Aeschylus said [fr. 456 Nauck]:

He who causes suffering must also suffer.[1]

And Pindar himself said [*Nem.* iv. 51–2]:

For
He who does something should also suffer.[2]

---

36. [2] Like the preceding passage from the *Sibylline Oracles*, this is a 'fragment' which originally stood in Book iii (cf. Geffcken, op. cit., 230–2); but cf. Zeegers-Vander Vorst, i. 184–91. Quotations from it are to be found not only in Clement of Alexandria and Lactantius but also among the Gnostic Peratae mentioned by Hippolytus (*Ref.* v. 16. 1).

37. [1] Stob. i. 3. 24 (I, 56, 23 Wachsmuth); cf. Orion vi. 6, schol. ad Pind. *Nem.* iv. 51–2, Arrian, *Anab.* vi. 13. 5.

[2] Stob. iv. 5. 8 (IV, 199, 4–5).

ὡσαύτως καὶ Εὐριπίδης·

Ἀνάσχου πάσχων· δρῶν γὰρ ἔχαιρες.
νόμου τὸν ἐχθρὸν δρᾶν, ὅπου λάβῃς, κακῶς.

καὶ πάλιν ὁ αὐτός·

Ἐχθροὺς[1] κακῶς δρᾶν ἀνδρὸς ἡγοῦμαι μέρος.

ὁμοίως καὶ Ἀρχίλοχος·

Ἓν δ' ἐπίσταμαι μέγα,
τὸν κακῶς[2] δρῶντα δεινοῖς ἀνταμείβεσθαι κακοῖς.

Καὶ ὅτι ὁ θεὸς τὰ πάντα ἐφορᾷ καὶ οὐδὲν αὐτὸν λανθάνει, μακρόθυμος δὲ ὢν ἀνέχεται ἕως οὗ μέλλει κρίνειν, καὶ περὶ τούτου Διονύσιος εἴρηκεν·

Ὁ τῆς Δίκης ὀφθαλμὸς ὡς δι' ἡσύχου
λεύσσων προσώπου πάνθ' ὁμῶς ἀεὶ βλέπει.

Καὶ ὅτι μέλλει ἡ τοῦ θεοῦ κρίσις γίνεσθαι καὶ τὰ κακὰ[3] τοὺς πονηροὺς αἰφνιδίως καταλαμβάνειν, καὶ τοῦτο Αἰσχύλος ἐσήμανεν λέγων·

τό τοι[4] κακὸν ποδῶκες ἔρχεται βροτοῖς,
κατ' ἀμπλάκημα τῷ περῶντι τὴν θέμιν.
ὁρᾷς Δίκην ἄναυδον, οὐχ ὁρωμένην
εὕδοντι καὶ στείχοντι καὶ καθημένῳ·
ἑξῆς ὀπάζει δόχμιον, ἄλλοθ' ὕστερον.
οὐκ ἐγκαλύπτει νὺξ κακῶς εἰργασμένον·
ὅ τι δ' ἂν ποιῇς δεινὸν νόμιζ' ὁρᾶν τινά.

τί δ' οὐχὶ καὶ ὁ Σιμωνίδης;

Οὐκ ἔστιν κακὸν
ἀνεπιδόκητον ἀνθρώποις· ὀλίγῳ δὲ χρόνῳ
πάντα μεταρρίπτει θεός.

πάλιν Εὐριπίδης·

Οὐδέποτ' εὐτυχίαν κακοῦ ἀνδρὸς ὑπέρφρονά τ' ὄλβον
βέβαιον εἰκάσαι χρεών,
οὐδ' ἀδίκων γενεάν· ὁ γὰρ οὐδενὸς ἐκφὺς χρόνος
δείκνυσιν ἀνθρώπων κακότητας.[5]

37. [1] ἐχθροὺς] Otto: ἐχθροῦ V   [2] κακῶς] V: add. με Diels   [3] κακὰ] Wolf: κατὰ V   [4] τοι] Fell: om. V   [5] κακότητας] V: add. ἐμοί Stob. Flor. iii. 2. 13

Similarly also Euripides [fr. 1090–1 Nauck]:
> Suffer patiently, for you were glad to act.
> It is lawful to mistreat an enemy when you have caught him.

And again the same [fr. 1092]:
> I think it is a man's part to treat enemies badly.

Similarly also Archilochus [fr. 65 Bergk]:
> One great thing I know,
> To repay with dire evils him who does me harm.

And that God oversees everything and nothing escapes him, but being patient he forbears until he is about to judge, of this Dionysius said [fr. 5 Kock]:
> The eye of justice, how looking from a gentle
> Face, ever looks at everything alike.[3]

And that the judgement of God is going to take place, and that evils are suddenly going to overtake the wicked, is also indicated by Aeschylus, who says:
> Evil comes with swift step to mortals,
> To him who sinfully transgresses right [fr. 22 Nauck].
> You see justice silent and unseen;
> She follows obliquely after when one sleeps, walks, sits;
> At other times comes late [trag. adesp. fr. 493 Nauck].
> Night does not veil the evildoer;
> Whatever evil you do, consider that someone sees
> [com. adesp. fr. 148 Kock].[4]

And what of Simonides [fr. 62 Bergk]?
> There is no evil
> Unexpected by men; in a short time
> God overturns everything.

Again, Euripides [*Bellerophon* fr. 303 Nauck]:
> Never the fortune of an evil man and his proud riches
> Should you consider stable,
> Nor the generation of the wicked; for time, produced from nothing
> Shows forth the evil deeds of men.[5]

---

37. [3] Stob. i. 3. 19 (I, 55, 17–18).   [4] Stob. i. 3. 26–9 (I, 57, 5–13).
[5] Stob. iii. 2. 13 (III, 181, 2–6).

ἔτι ὁ Εὐριπίδης·

> Οὐ γὰρ ἀσύνετον τὸ θεῖον, ἀλλ' ἔχει συνιέναι
> τοὺς κακῶς παγέντας ὅρκους καὶ κατηναγκασμένους.

καὶ ὁ Σοφοκλῆς·

> Εἰ δείν' ὄρεξας, δεινὰ καὶ παθεῖν σε δεῖ.

Ἤτοι οὖν περὶ ἀδίκου ὅρκου ἢ καὶ περὶ ἄλλου τινὸς πταίσματος ὅτι μέλλει ὁ θεὸς ἐξετάζειν, καὶ αὐτοὶ σχεδὸν προειρήκασιν, ἢ καὶ περὶ ἐκπυρώσεως κόσμου θέλοντες καὶ μὴ θέλοντες ἀκόλουθα ἐξεῖπαν τοῖς προφήταις, καίπερ πολὺ μεταγενέστεροι γενόμενοι καὶ κλέψαντες ταῦτα ἐκ τοῦ νόμου καὶ τῶν προφητῶν.

38. Καὶ τί γὰρ ἤτοι ἔσχατοι ἢ καὶ πρῶτοι ἐγένοντο; πλὴν ὅτι γοῦν καὶ αὐτοὶ ἀκόλουθα τοῖς προφήταις εἶπον. περὶ μὲν οὖν ἐκπυρώσεως Μαλαχίας ὁ προφήτης προείρηκεν· " Ἰδοὺ ἡμέρα ἔρχεται κυρίου ὡς κλίβανος καιόμενος, καὶ ἀνάψει πάντας τοὺς ἀσεβεῖς." καὶ Ἠσαΐας· " Ἥξει γὰρ ὀργὴ θεοῦ ⟨ὡς πῦρ καὶ⟩[1] ὡς χάλαζα συγκαταφερομένη βίᾳ καὶ ὡς ὕδωρ σύρον ἐν φάραγγι."

Τοίνυν Σίβυλλα καὶ οἱ λοιποὶ προφῆται, ἀλλὰ μὴν καὶ οἱ ποιηταὶ καὶ φιλόσοφοι καὶ αὐτοὶ[2] δεδηλώκασιν περὶ δικαιοσύνης καὶ κρίσεως καὶ κολάσεως· ἔτι μὴν καὶ περὶ προνοίας, ὅτι[3] φροντίζει ὁ θεὸς οὐ μόνον περὶ τῶν ζώντων ἡμῶν ἀλλὰ καὶ τῶν τεθνεώτων, καίπερ ἄκοντες[4] ἔφασαν· ἠλέγχοντο γὰρ ὑπὸ τῆς ἀληθείας. καὶ τῶν μὲν προφητῶν Σολομὼν περὶ τῶν τεθνηκότων εἶπεν· " Ἔσται ἴασις ταῖς σαρξὶν καὶ ἐπιμέλεια τῶν ὀστέων." τὸ δ' αὐτὸ καὶ Δαυίδ· " Ἀγαλλιάσεται ὀστᾶ τεταπεινωμένα." τούτοις ἀκόλουθα εἴρηκεν καὶ Τιμοκλῆς, λέγων·

> Τεθνεῶσιν ἔλεος ἐπιεικὴς θεός.

καὶ περὶ πλήθους οὖν θεῶν οἱ συγγραφεῖς εἰπόντες καθῆλθον εἰς μοναρχίαν, καὶ περὶ ἀπρονοησίας λέγοντες εἶπον περὶ προνοίας καὶ περὶ ἀκρισίας φάσκοντες ὡμολόγησαν ἔσεσθαι κρίσιν, καὶ οἱ μετὰ

---

38. [1] ⟨ὡς πῦρ καὶ⟩] Grant; cf. Isa. 30: 27: om. V [2] αὐτοί] V: om. edd.
[3] ὅτι] Humphry: om. V [4] ἄκοντες] Humphry: ἅπαντες V

Further, Euripides [*Iphigen. Aul.* 394a–5]:
> The deity is not unintelligent, but has knowledge
> Of oaths badly established and sworn.[6]

And Sophocles [fr. 877 Nauck]:
> If you have given evil, you must suffer evil.[7]

Whether, then, they spoke of an unjust oath or any other fault they virtually predicted that God would inquire into it; and willing or unwilling they made declarations about the conflagration of the world in harmony with the prophets, though they were much more recent and stole these things from the law and the prophets.[8]

Poets and Prophets on Conflagration and Death

38. And what difference does it make whether they were last or first? In any event, they spoke in harmony with the prophets. Concerning the conflagration Malachi the prophet made this prediction: 'Behold, the day of the Lord comes like a burning oven, and it will kindle all the ungodly' [Mal. 3: 19]. And Isaiah: 'For the wrath of God will come like fire and like hail borne down with force and like water rushing through a ravine' [Isa. 30: 27, 30, 28].

Therefore the Sibyl and the other prophets, as well as the poets and philosophers themselves, also spoke about justice and judgement [cf. John 16: 8] and punishment, and furthermore about providence; God cares not only for us who are living but also for the dead. All of them said these things, for they were convinced by the truth [cf. John 16: 13]. Among the prophets, Solomon said concerning the dead: 'There will be healing for the flesh and treatment for the bones' [Prov. 3: 8]. Similarly David: 'The humiliated bones will rejoice' [Ps. 50: 10]. In harmony with them, Timocles too spoke these words:

> For the dead,
> Pity is a gentle god [fr. 31 Kock].[1]

So even though the writers spoke of a multitude of gods, they ended with monotheism; though they denied providence they also spoke of providence; though they said there was no judgement they

37. [6] Stob. iii. 28. 2 (III, 617, 1–2).   [7] Stob. i. 3. 48a (I, 61, 4).
[8] The appropriate quotations from the poets on this subject have been lost from the text. Perhaps one of them was Sophocles, fr. (fals.) 1027 Nauck, cited by Clement, *Str.* v. 121. 4–122. 1, and Pseudo-Justin, *De monarchia* 3.
38. [1] Stob. iv. 57. 8 (V, 1139, 1 Wachsmuth–Hense).

θάνατον ἀρνούμενοι εἶναι αἴσθησιν ὡμολόγησαν. Ὅμηρος μὲν οὖν εἰπών·

Ψυχὴ δ'⁵ ἠΰτ' ὄνειρος ἀποπταμένη πεπότηται,

ἐν ἑτέρῳ λέγει·

Ψυχὴ δ' ἐκ ῥεθέων πταμένη Ἄϊδόσδε βεβήκει,

καὶ πάλιν·

Θάπτε με ὅττι τάχιστα πύλας Ἀΐδαο περήσω.

Τὰ δὲ περὶ τῶν λοιπῶν, οὓς ἀνέγνωκας, ἡγοῦμαί σε ἀκριβῶς ἐπίστασθαι ᾧ τρόπῳ εἰρήκασιν. ταῦτα δὲ πάντα συνήσει πᾶς ὁ ζητῶν τὴν σοφίαν τοῦ θεοῦ καὶ εὐαρεστῶν αὐτῷ διὰ πίστεως καὶ δικαιοσύνης καὶ ἀγαθοεργίας. καὶ γάρ τις εἶπεν προφήτης ὢν προεγράψαμεν, ὀνόματι Ὠσηέ· "Τίς σοφός καὶ συνήσει ταῦτα, συνετός καὶ γνώσεται; ὅτι εὐθεῖαι αἱ ὁδοὶ τοῦ κυρίου, καὶ δίκαιοι εἰσελεύσονται ἐν αὐταῖς, οἱ δὲ ἀσεβεῖς ἀσθενήσουσιν ἐν αὐταῖς." χρὴ οὖν τὸν φιλομαθῆ καὶ φιλομαθεῖν. πειράθητι οὖν πυκνότερον συμβαλεῖν, ὅπως καὶ ζώσης ἀκούσας φωνῆς ἀκριβῶς μάθῃς τἀληθές.

8. ⁵ δ'] Otto; cf. Hom. *Od.* xi. 221 : om. V

admitted that there will be a judgement; those who denied the existence of sensation after death also admitted it.

Homer, after saying [*Od.* xi. 222],[2]

The soul, like a dream, takes flight away,

elsewhere says [*Il.* xvi. 856 = xxii. 362],

The soul, taking flight from the limbs, goes down to Hades,

and again [*Il.* xxiii. 71],[3]

Bury me so that swiftly I may pass the gates of Hades.

As far as the other writers whose works you have read are concerned, I think you have accurate knowledge of the way they spoke. All these matters will be understood by everyone who seeks for the Wisdom of God and is pleasing to him through faith and righteousness and good deeds. For a certain prophet named Hosea, one of those whom we have already mentioned, said: 'Who is wise and will understand these things, understanding and will know them? For straight are the paths of the Lord, and the righteous will come in by them, but the ungodly will grow weak on them' [Hos. 14: 10]. He who loves learning must really love it. Endeavour to meet with us more often, so that by hearing a living voice you may accurately learn what is true.

---

[2] Cf. Porphyry, Περὶ Στυγός, in Stob. i. 49. 50 (I, 420, 14).

[3] Cf. Porphyry, op. cit., in Stob. i. 49. 53 (I, 426, 4).

Τὸ γ'[1]

1. Θεόφιλος Αὐτολύκῳ χαίρειν.

Ἐπειδὴ οἱ συγγραφεῖς βούλονται πληθὺν βίβλων συγγράφειν πρὸς κενὴν δόξαν, οἱ μὲν περὶ θεῶν καὶ πολέμων ἢ χρόνων, τινὲς δὲ καὶ μύθων ἀνωφελῶν καὶ τῆς λοιπῆς ματαιοπονίας, ἧς ἤσκεις καὶ σὺ ἕως τοῦ δεῦρο, κἀκείνου μὲν τοῦ καμάτου οὐκ ὀκνεῖς ἀνεχόμενος, ἡμῖν δὲ συμβαλὼν ἔτι λῆρον ἡγῇ τυγχάνειν τὸν λόγον τῆς ἀληθείας, οἰόμενος προσφάτους καὶ νεωτερικὰς εἶναι τὰς παρ' ἡμῖν γραφάς, διὸ δὴ κἀγὼ οὐκ ὀκνήσω ἀνακεφαλαιώσασθαί σοι παρέχοντος θεοῦ τὴν ἀρχαιότητα τῶν παρ' ἡμῖν γραμμάτων, ὑπόμνημά σοι ποιούμενος δι' ὀλίγων, ὅπως μὴ ὀκνήσῃς ἐντυγχάνειν αὐτῷ, ἐπιγνῶς δὲ τῶν λοιπῶν συνταξάντων τὴν φλυαρίαν.

2. Ἐχρῆν γὰρ τοὺς συγγράφοντας αὐτοὺς αὐτόπτας γεγενῆσθαι περὶ ὧν διαβεβαιοῦνται, ἢ ἀκριβῶς μεμαθηκέναι ὑπὸ τῶν τεθεαμένων αὐτά. τρόπῳ γάρ τινι οἱ τὰ ἄδηλα συγγράφοντες ἀέρα δέρουσιν.

Τί γὰρ ὠφέλησεν Ὅμηρον συγγράψαι τὸν Ἰλιακὸν πόλεμον καὶ πολλοὺς ἐξαπατῆσαι, ἢ Ἡσίοδον ὁ κατάλογος τῆς θεογονίας τῶν παρ' αὐτῷ θεῶν ὀνομαζομένων, Ὀρφέα οἱ τριακόσιοι ἑξήκοντα πέντε θεοί, οὓς αὐτὸς ἐπὶ τέλει τοῦ βίου ἀθετεῖ, ἐν ταῖς Διαθήκαις αὐτοῦ λέγων ἕνα εἶναι θεόν; τί δὲ ὠφέλησεν Ἄρατον ἡ σφαιρογραφία τοῦ κοσμικοῦ κύκλου, ἢ τοὺς τὰ ὅμοια αὐτῷ εἰπόντας, πλὴν τῆς κατ' ἄνθρωπον δόξης, ἧς οὐδὲ αὐτῆς κατ' ἀξίαν ἔτυχον; τί δὲ καὶ ἀληθὲς εἰρήκασιν; ἢ τί ὠφέλησεν Εὐριπίδην καὶ Σοφοκλέα ἢ τοὺς λοιποὺς τραγῳδιογράφους αἱ τραγῳδίαι, ἢ Μένανδρον καὶ Ἀριστοφάνην καὶ τοὺς λοιποὺς κωμικοὺς αἱ κωμῳδίαι, ἢ Ἡρόδοτον καὶ Θουκυδίδην αἱ ἱστορίαι αὐτῶν, ἢ Πυθαγόραν τὰ ἄδυτα καὶ Ἡρακλέους στῆλαι, ἢ Διογένην ἡ κυνικὴ φιλοσοφία, ἢ Ἐπίκουρον τὸ δογματίζειν μὴ εἶναι πρόνοιαν, ἢ Ἐμπεδοκλέα τὸ διδάσκειν ἀθεότητα, ἢ Σωκράτην τὸ ὀμνύειν τὸν κύνα καὶ τὸν χῆνα καὶ τὴν

[1] τὸ γ'] VB: Θεοφίλου πατριάρχου ἕκτου Ἀντιοχείας πρὸς Αὐτόλυκον ἕλληνα περὶ τῆς τῶν Χριστιανῶν πίστεως P: cf. liber de temporibus ad Autolycum, Lactantius, *Div. inst.* i. 23. 2

Book III

1. Theophilus to Autolycus, greetings.

Since historians desire to write a multitude of books for vainglory's sake, some about gods and wars or chronology and others about useless myths and other pointless labour such as you yourself have been engaged in up to the present time (you do not shrink from enduring that labour, though after meeting us you still regard the word of truth as silly, fancying that our scriptures are new and modern), therefore I too will not shrink from summing up for you, with God's help, the antiquity of our writings. I will make a brief memorandum for you so that you will not shrink from reading it but will recognize the nonsense of other writers.

Greek Literature is Useless

2. Writers ought to have been eye-witnesses of the events about which they make affirmations or else they should have learned about them accurately from those who witnessed them [cf. Luke 1 : 2–3].[1] Those who write down uncertain statements are, so to speak, striking the air [cf. 1 Cor. 9 : 26].

What did it avail Homer that he wrote the *Trojan War* and led many astray? or Hesiod, the catalogue of the 'theogony' of those whom he called gods? or Orpheus, the 365 gods whom he himself rejected at the end of his life, saying in his *Testaments* that there is one god [cf. O. Kern, *Orphicorum fragmenta*, 255–6]? Of what avail to Aratus was his description of the sphere of the cosmic circle,[2] or to those who made statements like his—except for human fame, which they did not rightly acquire? What truth did they speak? Or what did their tragedies avail for Euripides and Sophocles and the other tragic poets, or their comedies for Menander and Aristophanes and the other comic poets, or their histories for Herodotus and Thucydides? Or the shrines and the pillars of Heracles for Pythagoras? or the Cynic philosophy for Diogenes? or the dogmatic denial of providence for Epicurus? or the teaching of atheism for Empedocles? or the oath by dog and goose and plane-tree for Socrates, not to mention his oath by the lightning-struck

---

2. [1] Cf. Josephus, *C. Ap.* i. 53.

[2] Not a book title, according to E. Maass, *Arati Phaenomena* (Berlin, 1893), xix. Theophilus may mention Aratus because the Orphic *Testaments* imitate the *Phaenomena*; cf. Maass, *Aratea* (Berlin, 1892), 253–4.

πλάτανον καὶ τὸν κεραυνωθέντα Ἀσκλήπιον καὶ τὰ δαιμόνια ἃ ἐπεκαλεῖτο; πρὸς τί δὲ καὶ ἑκὼν ἀπέθνησκεν, τίνα καὶ ὁποῖον μισθὸν μετὰ θάνατον ἀπολαβεῖν ἐλπίζων; τί δὲ ὠφέλησεν Πλάτωνα ἡ κατ' αὐτὸν παιδεία, ἢ τοὺς λοιποὺς φιλοσόφους τὰ δόγματα αὐτῶν ἵνα μὴ τὸν ἀριθμὸν αὐτῶν καταλέγω πολλῶν ὄντων; ταῦτα δέ φαμεν εἰς τὸ ἐπιδεῖξαι τὴν ἀνωφελῆ καὶ ἄθεον διάνοιαν αὐτῶν.

3. Δόξης γὰρ κενῆς καὶ ματαίου πάντες οὗτοι ἐρασθέντες οὔτε αὐτοὶ τὸ ἀληθὲς ἔγνωσαν οὔτε μὴν ἄλλους ἐπὶ τὴν ἀλήθειαν προετρέψαντο. καὶ γὰρ ἃ ἔφασαν αὐτὰ ἐλέγχει αὐτούς, ἢ ἀσύμφωνα εἰρήκασιν, καὶ τὰ ἴδια δόγματα οἱ πλείους αὐτῶν κατέλυσαν· οὐ γὰρ ἀλλήλους μόνον ἀνέτρεψαν, ἀλλ' ἤδη τινὲς καὶ τὰ ἑαυτῶν δόγματα ἄκυρα ἐποίησαν, ὥστε ἡ δόξα αὐτῶν εἰς ἀτιμίαν καὶ μωρίαν ἐχώρησεν· ὑπὸ γὰρ τῶν συνετῶν καταγινώσκονται.

Ἤτοι γὰρ περὶ θεῶν ἔφασαν, αὐτοὶ δ'[1] ὕστερον ἀθεότητα ἐδίδαξαν, ἢ εἰ καὶ περὶ κόσμου γενέσεως, ἔσχατον αὐτοματισμὸν εἶπον εἶναι τῶν πάντων, ἀλλὰ καὶ περὶ προνοίας λέγοντες πάλιν ἀπρονόητον εἶναι κόσμον ἐδογμάτισαν. τί δ'; οὐχὶ καὶ περὶ σεμνότητος πειρώμενοι γράφειν ἀσελγείας καὶ πορνείας καὶ μοιχείας ἐδίδαξαν ἐπιτελεῖσθαι, ἔτι μὴν καὶ τὰς στυγητὰς ἀρρητοποιίας εἰσηγήσαντο; καὶ πρώτους γε τοὺς θεοὺς αὐτῶν κηρύσσουσιν ἐν ἀρρήτοις μίξεσιν συγγίνεσθαι ἔν τε ἀθέσμοις βρώσεσιν. τίς γὰρ οὐκ ᾄδει Κρόνον τεκνοφάγον, Δία δὲ τὸν παῖδα αὐτοῦ τὴν Μῆτιν καταπίνειν καὶ δεῖπνα μιαρὰ τοῖς θεοῖς ἑτοιμάζειν· ἔνθα καὶ χωλὸν Ἥφαιστόν τινα χαλκέα φασὶν διακονεῖν αὐτοῖς· τήν τε Ἥραν ἰδίαν ἀδελφὴν αὐτοῦ μὴ μόνον τὸν Δία γαμεῖν, ἀλλὰ καὶ διὰ στόματος ἀνάγνου ἀρρητοποιεῖν; τάς τε λοιπὰς περὶ αὐτοῦ πράξεις, ὅποσας ᾄδουσιν οἱ ποιηταί, εἰκὸς ἐπίστασαι. τί μοι λοιπὸν καταλέγειν τὰ περὶ Ποσειδῶνος καὶ Ἀπόλλωνος ἢ Διονύσου καὶ Ἡρακλέους, Ἀθηνᾶς τῆς φιλομόλπου[2] καὶ Ἀφροδίτης τῆς ἀναισχύντου, ἀκριβέστερον πεποιηκότων ἡμῶν ἐν ἑτέρῳ τὸν περὶ αὐτῶν λόγον;

4. Οὐδὲ γὰρ ἐχρῆν ἡμᾶς ταῦτα ἀνασκευάζειν, εἰ μὴ ὅτι σε θεωρῶ νυνὶ διστάζοντα περὶ τὸν λόγον τῆς ἀληθείας. φρόνιμος γὰρ ὢν

3. [1] δ'] Maran: om. V   [2] φιλομόλπου] Roscher; cf. Nonn. *Dionys*. xxiv. 36: φιλοκόλπου V

Asclepius and his invocation of the demons? For what purpose was he willing to die? What kind of reward did he hope to receive after death? And what did Plato's form of education avail him? What did their doctrines avail the other philosophers—not to list the whole number, since there are so many?[3] We say these things to demonstrate their useless and godless notions.

The Inconsistency and Immorality of Greek Authors

3. All these, as lovers of empty and useless fame, neither knew the truth themselves nor impelled others toward the truth. The very things they said convict them: their statements are inconsistent and most of them demolished their own doctrines. They not only refuted one another but in some instances even nullified their own doctrines so that their fame ended in dishonour and foolishness; for they are condemned by intelligent persons.

If they spoke about the gods, they later taught atheism; if about the creation of the world, they said that everything came about spontaneously; and if they spoke about providence, at another time they decreed that the world is without providence [cf. II. 4, 8]. And more—undertaking to write about purity, did they not advocate lascivious acts and fornication and adultery and even introduce abominable obscenities? They proclaim that their gods were the first to unite in unspeakable unions and unlawful meals. What poet does not sing of Kronos the child-eater [I. 9] and Zeus, who consumed his daughter Metis[1] and prepared disgusting banquets for the gods at which, they say, a certain lame smith, Hephaestus, served them.[2] Hera, his own sister, not only married Zeus but acted obscenely with impure mouth [III. 8]. You probably know the rest of his deeds about which the poets sing. Why should I list the stories about Poseidon, Apollo, Dionysus, Heracles, the danceloving Athena and the shameless Aphrodite, when we have given a more detailed account of them elsewhere [I. 9–10]?

How Can Learned Men Believe Charges against Christians?

4. There would be no need for us to refute these notions were it not that I see you still in doubt about the word of truth. For *being wise*,

---

[3] For a similar list of writings studied by grammarians cf. Sext. Emp. *Adv. math.* i. 57–8.

3. [1] Hesiod, *Theog.* 886–900; cf. *SVF* ii. 908–9.
　　[2] Homer, *Il.* i. 568–611.

ἡδέως μωρῶν ἀνέχῃ· ἐπεί τοι οὐκ ἂν ἐκινήθης ὑπὸ ἀνοήτων ἀνθρώπων κενοῖς λόγοις ἀπάγεσθαι καὶ φήμῃ πείθεσθαι προκατεσχηκυίῃ, στομάτων ἀθέων ψευδῶς συκοφαντούντων ἡμᾶς, τοὺς θεοσεβεῖς καὶ χριστιανοὺς καλουμένους, φασκόντων ὡς κοινὰς ἁπάντων οὔσας τὰς γυναῖκας ἡμῶν καὶ ἀδιαφόρῳ[1] μίξει ζῶντας, ἔτι μὴν καὶ ταῖς ἰδίαις ἀδελφαῖς συμμίγνυσθαι, καί, τὸ ἀθεώτατον καὶ ὠμότατον πάντων,[2] σαρκῶν ἀνθρωπίνων ἐφάπτεσθαι ἡμᾶς. ἀλλὰ καὶ ὡς προσφάτου ὁδεύοντος τοῦ καθ' ἡμᾶς λόγου, καὶ μηδὲν ἔχειν ἡμᾶς λέγειν εἰς ἀπόδειξιν ἀληθείας τῆς καθ' ἡμᾶς καὶ διδασκαλίας, μωρίαν δὲ εἶναι τὸν λόγον ἡμῶν φασιν. ἐγὼ μὲν οὖν θαυμάζω μάλιστα ἐπὶ σοί, ὃς ἐν μὲν τοῖς λοιποῖς γενόμενος σπουδαῖος καὶ ἐκζητητὴς ἁπάντων πραγμάτων, ἀμελέστερον ἡμῶν ἀκούεις. εἰ γάρ σοι δυνατόν, καὶ νύκτωρ οὐκ ὤκνεις διατρίβειν ἐν βιβλιοθήκαις.

5. Ἐπειδὴ οὖν πολλὰ ἀνέγνως, τί σοι ἔδοξεν τὰ Ζήνωνος ἢ τὰ Διογένους καὶ Κλεάνθους ὁπόσα περιέχουσιν αἱ βίβλοι αὐτῶν, διδάσκουσαι ἀνθρωποβορίας, πατέρας μὲν ὑπὸ ἰδίων τέκνων ἕψεσθαι[1] καὶ βιβρώσκεσθαι, καὶ εἴ τις οὐ βούλοιτο ἢ μέλος τι τῆς μυσερᾶς τροφῆς ἀπορρίψειεν, αὐτὸν κατεσθίεσθαι[2] τὸν μὴ φαγόντα; πρὸς τούτοις ἀθεωτέρα τις φωνὴ εὑρίσκεται, ἡ τοῦ Διογένους, διδάσκοντος τὰ τέκνα τοὺς ἑαυτῶν γονεῖς εἰς θυσίαν ἄγειν καὶ τούτους κατεσθίειν. τί δ'; οὐχὶ καὶ Ἡρόδοτος ὁ ἱστοριογράφος μυθεύει τὸν Καμβύσην τὰ τοῦ Ἁρπάγου τέκνα σφάξαντα καὶ ἑψήσαντα παρατεθεικέναι τῷ πατρὶ βοράν; ἔτι δὲ καὶ παρὰ Ἰνδοῖς μυθεύει κατεσθίεσθαι[3] τοὺς πατέρας ὑπὸ τῶν ἰδίων τέκνων.

Ὢ τῆς ἀθέου διδασκαλίας τῶν τὰ τοιαῦτα ἀναγραψάντων μᾶλλον δὲ διδαξάντων, ὢ τῆς ἀσεβείας καὶ ἀθεότητος αὐτῶν, ὢ τῆς διανοίας τῶν οὕτως ἀκριβῶς φιλοσοφησάντων καὶ φιλοσοφίαν ἐπαγγελλομένων! οἱ γὰρ ταῦτα δογματίσαντες τὸν κόσμον ἀσεβείας ἐνέπλησαν.

6. Καὶ γὰρ περὶ ἀθέσμου πράξεως σχεδὸν πᾶσιν συμπεφώνηκεν τοῖς περὶ τὸν χορὸν τῆς φιλοσοφίας πεπλανημένοις. καὶ πρῶτός γε

4. [1] ἀδιαφόρῳ] Ducaeus; cf. III. 15. 1: διαφόρῳ V   [2] πάντων] Maran; cf. III. 15. 2: πασῶν V
5. [1] ἕψεσθαι] Ducaeus: ὄψεσθαι V   [2] κατεσθίεσθαι] Wolf: κατεσθέσθαι V
[3] κατεσθίεσθαι] Wolf: κατεσθέσθαι V

you suffer fools gladly [2 Cor. 11 : 19] ; otherwise you would not have been influenced by unintelligent men so that you were led astray by pointless words and believed a prejudiced rumour when godless mouths falsely accused us, the godly who are called Christians. They said that our wives are the common property of all and live in promiscuity, that we have intercourse with our own sisters, and—most godless and savage of all—that we partake of human flesh. They also say that our message has been made public only recently, and that we have nothing to say in proof of our truth and our teaching; they call our message *foolishness* [1 Cor. 1 : 18]. I marvel especially in your case. In other matters you are diligent and investigate all subjects, but you listen to us with indifference. For if you could, you would not hesitate to spend even the night in libraries.

Cannibalism in Greek Literature

5. Since you have read so much, what do you think of the ideas of Zeno or Diogenes and Cleanthes as contained in their books which advocate cannibalism and the cooking and eating of fathers by their own children, and teach that if anyone refuses to eat or rejects some part of the abominable food, he who does not eat is to be eaten [*SVF* i. 254 = 584 = iii. 750]? In addition to these, a more godless voice is heard, that of Diogenes, who teaches that children should lead their own parents to the slaughter and eat them [cf. Diog. Laert. vi. 73]. And more—does not the historian Herodotus relate how Cambyses slew the children[1] of Harpagus and after cooking them placed them before their father as food [i. 119]? Further, he tells the story that among the Indians fathers are eaten by their own children [iii. 99].

O the godless teaching of those who described or rather advocated such actions! O the impiety and godlessness of those men! O the understanding of those who thus accurately pursued and professed philosophy! Those who laid down such doctrines have filled the world with impiety.

Philosophers Contradict Laws on Sexual Behaviour

6. Also in the case of unlawful action there is agreement among practically all those who have gone astray with the chorus of

---

5. [1] According to Herodotus, Astyages slew one child of Harpagus.

Πλάτων, ὁ δοκῶν ἐν αὐτοῖς σεμνότερον πεφιλοσοφηκέναι, διαρρήδην ἐν τῇ πρώτῃ βίβλῳ τῶν πολιτειῶν ἐπιγραφομένῃ, τρόπῳ τινὶ νομοθετεῖ χρῆν εἶναι κοινὰς ἁπάντων τὰς γυναῖκας, χρώμενος παραδείγματι τῷ Διὸς καὶ Κρητῶν νομοθέτῃ, ὅπως διὰ προφάσεως παιδοποιΐα πολλὴ γίνηται ἐκ τῶν τοιούτων, καὶ ὡς δῆθεν τοὺς λυπουμένους διὰ τοιούτων ὁμιλιῶν χρῆν παραμυθεῖσθαι. Ἐπίκουρος δὲ καὶ αὐτὸς σὺν τῷ ἀθεότητα διδάσκειν συμβουλεύει καὶ μητράσι καὶ ἀδελφαῖς συμμίγνυσθαι, καὶ πέρα[1] τῶν νόμων τῶν τόδε[2] κωλυόντων. ὁ γὰρ Σόλων[3] καὶ περὶ τούτου σαφῶς ἐνομοθέτησεν, ὅπως ἐκ τοῦ γήμαντος οἱ παῖδες νομίμως γίνωνται, πρὸς τὸ μὴ ἐκ μοιχείας τοὺς γεννωμένους εἶναι, ἵνα μὴ τὸν οὐκ ὄντα πατέρα τιμήσῃ τις ὡς πατέρα, ἢ τὸν ὄντως πατέρα ἀτιμάσῃ τις ἀγνοῶν ὡς μὴ πατέρα. ὁπόσα τε οἱ λοιποὶ νόμοι κωλύουσιν Ῥωμαίων τε καὶ Ἑλλήνων τὰ τοιαῦτα πράσσεσθαι.

Πρὸς τί οὖν Ἐπίκουρος καὶ οἱ Στωϊκοὶ δογματίζουσιν ἀδελφοκοιτίας καὶ ἀρρενοβασίας ἐπιτελεῖσθαι, ἐξ ὧν διδασκαλιῶν μεστὰς βιβλιοθήκας πεποιήκασιν, εἰς τὸ ἐκ παίδων μανθάνειν τὴν ἄθεσμον κοινωνίαν; καὶ τί μοι λοιπὸν καταρίβεσθαι περὶ αὐτῶν, ὅπου γε καὶ περὶ τῶν θεῶν παρ' αὐτοῖς λεγομένων τὰ ὅμοια κατηγγέλκασιν;

7. Θεοὺς γὰρ φήσαντες εἶναι πάλιν εἰς οὐδὲν αὐτοὺς ἡγήσαντο. οἱ μὲν γὰρ ἐξ ἀτόμων αὐτοὺς ἔφασαν συνεστάναι, ἢ[1] δ' αὖ χωρεῖν εἰς ἀτόμους, καὶ μηδὲν πλεῖον ἀνθρώπων δύνασθαι τοὺς θεούς φασιν. Πλάτων δέ, θεοὺς εἰπὼν εἶναι, ὑλικοὺς αὐτοὺς βούλεται συνιστᾶν. Πυθαγόρας δέ, τοσαῦτα μοχθήσας περὶ θεῶν καὶ τὴν ἄνω κάτω πορείαν ποιησάμενος, ἔσχατον ὁρίζει φύσιν καὶ αὐτοματισμὸν εἶναί φησιν τῶν πάντων· θεοὺς ἀνθρώπων μηδὲν φροντίζειν. ὁπόσα δὲ Κλειτόμαχος ὁ Ἀκαδημαϊκὸς περὶ ἀθεότητος εἰσηγήσατο. τί δ' οὐχὶ καὶ Κριτίας καὶ Πρωταγόρας ὁ Ἀβδηρίτης λέγων· "Εἴτε γάρ[2] εἰσιν θεοί, οὐ δύναμαι περὶ αὐτῶν λέγειν, οὔτε ὁποῖοί εἰσιν δηλῶσαι· πολλὰ γάρ ἐστιν τὰ κωλύοντά με"; τὰ γὰρ περὶ Εὐημέρου τοῦ ἀθεωτάτου περισσὸν ἡμῖν καὶ λέγειν. πολλὰ γὰρ περὶ θεῶν

6. [1] πέρα] Gesner: περὶ V [2] τόδε] Otto: τότε V [3] Σόλων] Wolf: Σολομῶν V

7. [1] ἢ] V; cf. Diels, Dox. 589, 8: οἱ V[2] [2] εἴτε γάρ] V: εἴπερ Wilamowitz

philosophy. First Plato, who is thought to have philosophized most chastely among them, gives explicit legislation, so to speak, in the first book of the *Republic* [*Rep.* v. 457 d]. He holds that the wives of all ought to be common property and uses as a model the son of Zeus who was legislator for the Cretans—so that on this 'pretext' [460 b] there might be much procreation of offspring from such women and so that, no doubt, men who grieve might be consoled by such occasions for intercourse. And Epicurus, along with his teaching of atheism, recommends intercourse with mothers and sisters [cf. H. Usener, *Epicurea*, p. 323] in spite of the laws which forbid this. For Solon [cf. fr. 19 Diehl] gave clear legislation on this very subject, so that children might be lawfully produced from the husband and so that the offspring might not be produced from adultery. He intended that no one would honour someone not his father as his father or slight his real father, not knowing him to be his father. Things of this sort are forbidden by the other laws of Romans and Greeks alike.

Why then do Epicurus and the Stoics [*SVF* iii. 750] decree incest and homosexual acts and fill libraries with their teachings, so that unlawful intercourse can be learned from childhood? Why should I waste any more time on them, when they have made similar statements about those whom they call gods?

The Contradictions of Philosophers and Poets

7. After saying that gods exist, once more they reduced them to nothing. For some said that they were composed of atoms, or on the other hand that they return to atoms [Diels, *Dox.* 589, 8]; and they say that the power of the gods is no greater than that of men. Plato, who said that gods exist, wanted them to consist of matter. And Pythagoras, who went through such great labours over the gods and made his way up and down,[1] finally defines their nature and says that everything was produced spontaneously [ibid., 589, 9–10: Epicurus]; the gods do not take thought for men [ibid., 572, 6: Epicurus]. Furthermore, Clitomachus the Academic philosopher introduced many arguments for atheism. And what of Critias, and Protagoras the Abderite who said: 'Whether or not there are gods, I cannot say anything about them or explain their nature; for there are many things that hinder me' [cf. Sext. Emp. *Adv. math.* ix. 56]? It would be pointless for us to speak of the theories of the most godless Euhemerus. For after venturing to make many statements about the gods he finally denied their existence entirely [ibid., ix. 53: Diagoras], and held that everything is governed by spontaneity.

7. [1] 'Up and down' is actually related to the Pythagorean definition of bodies; cf. Sext. Emp. *Adv. math.* ix. 367; Diels, *Dox.* 339 b 9–10.

τολμήσας φθέγξασθαι ἔσχατον καὶ τὸ ἐξόλου μὴ εἶναι θεούς, ἀλλὰ τὰ πάντα αὐτοματισμῷ διοικεῖσθαι βούλεται. Πλάτων[3] δέ, ὁ τοσαῦτα εἰπὼν περὶ μοναρχίας θεοῦ καὶ ψυχῆς ἀνθρώπου, φάσκων ἀθάνατον εἶναι τὴν ψυχήν, οὐκ αὐτὸς ὕστερον εὑρίσκεται ἐναντία ἑαυτῷ λέγων, τὰς μὲν ψυχὰς μετέρχεσθαι εἰς ἑτέρους ἀνθρώπους, ἐνίων δὲ καὶ εἰς ἄλογα ζῶα χωρεῖν; πῶς οὐ δεινὸν καὶ ἀθέμιτον δόγμα αὐτοῦ τοῖς γε νοῦν ἔχουσι φανήσεται, ἵνα ὅ ποτε ἄνθρωπος πάλιν ἔσται λύκος ἢ κύων ἢ ὄνος ἢ ἄλλο τι ἄλογον κτῆνος; τούτῳ ἀκόλουθα καὶ Πυθαγόρας εὑρίσκεται φλυαρῶν, πρὸς τῷ καὶ πρόνοιαν ἐκκόπτειν.

Τίνι οὖν αὐτῶν πιστεύσωμεν, Φιλήμονι τῷ κωμικῷ λέγοντι·

Οἱ γὰρ[4] θεὸν σέβοντες ἐλπίδας καλὰς
ἔχουσιν[5] εἰς σωτηρίαν,

ἢ οἷς προειρήκαμεν Εὐημέρῳ καὶ Ἐπικούρῳ καὶ Πυθαγόρᾳ καὶ τοῖς λοιποῖς ἀρνουμένοις εἶναι θεοσέβειαν καὶ πρόνοιαν ἀναιροῦσιν. περὶ μὲν οὖν θεοῦ καὶ προνοίας Ἀρίστων ἔφη·

Θάρσει, βοηθεῖν πᾶσι μὲν[6] τοῖς ἀξίοις
εἴωθεν ὁ θεός, τοῖς δὲ τοιούτοις σφόδρα.
εἰ μὴ πάρεσται προεδρία τις κειμένη
τοῖς ζῶσιν ὡς δεῖ, τί πλέον ἐστὶν εὐσεβεῖν;
εἴη γὰρ οὕτως, ἀλλὰ καὶ λίαν ὁρῶ
τοὺς εὐσεβῶς μὲν ἑλομένους διεξάγειν
πράττοντας ἀτόπως, τοὺς δὲ μηδὲν ἕτερον ἢ
τὸ λυσιτελὲς τὸ κατ' αὐτοὺς μόνον,
ἐντιμοτέραν ἔχοντες ἡμῶν διάθεσιν.
ἐπὶ τοῦ παρόντος· ἀλλὰ δεῖ πόρρω βλέπειν
καὶ τὴν ἁπάντων ἀναμένειν καταστροφήν.
οὐχ ὃν τρόπον γὰρ παρ' ἐνίοις ἴσχυσέ τις
δόξα κακοήθης τῷ βίῳ τ' ἀνωφελής,
φορά τις ἔστ' αὐτόματος ἢ βραβεύεται
ὡς ἔτυχε· ταῦτα γὰρ πάντα κρίνουσιν ἔχειν
ἐφόδια πρὸς τὸν ἴδιον οἱ φαῦλοι τρόπον.
ἔστιν δὲ καὶ τοῖς ζῴοις ὁσίως προεδρία,
καὶ τοῖς πονηροῖς ὡς προσῆκ' ἐπιθυμία·
χωρὶς προνοίας γίνεται γὰρ οὐδὲ ἕν.

---

[3] Πλάτων] Fell: πάντων V   [4] γὰρ] V: ἕνα Epiphanius, *Ancoratus* civ. 3
[5] ἐλπίδας καλὰς ἔχουσιν] V: ἐλπίδας ἔχουσι καλὰς Epiphanius   [6] μὲν] Meineke: om. V

And did not Plato, who said so many things about the sole rule of God and about the human soul, saying that the soul is immortal, later contradict himself and say that souls pass into other men and, in some cases, into irrational animals? How is it possible that his teaching will not seem evil and unlawful for those who possess reason, when he holds that one formerly a human being will become a wolf or dog or ass or some other irrational animal? Pythagoras also spoke nonsense which agrees with Plato, in addition to rejecting providence [Diels, *Dox.* 589, 7: Epicurus].

Which of them, then, shall we believe [cf. II. 8]? Philemon the comic poet, who says [fr. 181 Kock]:

> Those who worship God have good hopes
> Of safety,

or the previously mentioned Euhemerus and Epicurus and Pythagoras and the rest who deny the existence of religion and destroy providence?

Of God and providence, then, Ariston said:[2]

Be of good cheer, for God is accustomed to aid all who are worthy, and indeed especially such men. If there is no reward awaiting those who live as they ought, what use is religion?

It may be so; but I clearly see those who wish to live piously experiencing misfortune, while those who look for nothing but their own advantage have a more honourable state than we do.

For the present; but one must look further and wait for the final ending of all. Not true, though prevalent among some, is the wicked opinion, useless for living, that there is a certain spontaneous motion, or that chance is in control. Wicked men suppose they have all these things as supports of their ways. But there is a reward for those who live piously, and for the evil a fitting punishment; for nothing at all takes place apart from providence.

[2] Cf. A. Meineke, *Fragmenta comicorum graecorum* i (Berlin, 1839), ix–x.

ὁπόσα τε καὶ ἄλλοι καὶ σχεδόν γε οἱ πλείους εἶπον περὶ θεοῦ καὶ προνοίας, ὁρᾶν ἔστιν πῶς ἀνακόλουθα ἀλλήλοις ἔφασαν· οἱ μὲν γὰρ τὸ ἐξόλου θεὸν καὶ πρόνοιαν εἶναι ἀνεῖλον, οἱ δ' αὖ συνέστησαν θεὸν καὶ πάντα προνοίᾳ διοικεῖσθαι ὡμολόγησαν. τὸν οὖν συνετὸν ἀκροατὴν καὶ ἀναγινώσκοντα προσέχειν ἀκριβῶς τοῖς λεγομένοις δεῖ,[7] καθὼς καὶ ὁ Σιμύλος ἔφη·

> Κοινῶς ποιητὰς ἔθος ἐστὶν καλεῖν,
> καὶ τοὺς περιττοὺς τῇ φύσει καὶ τοὺς κακούς·[8]
> ἔδει δὲ κρίνειν.

καθάπερ ἐν τόπῳ τινι[9] καὶ ὁ Φιλήμων·

> Χαλεπὸν ἀκροατὴς ἀσύνετος καθήμενος·
> ὑπὸ γὰρ ἀνοίας οὐχ ἑαυτὸν μέμφεται.

χρὴ οὖν προσέχειν καὶ νοεῖν τὰ λεγόμενα κριτικῶς ἐξετάζοντα τὰ ὑπὸ τῶν φιλοσόφων καὶ τῶν λοιπῶν ποιητῶν εἰρημένα.

8. Ἀρνούμενοι γὰρ θεοὺς εἶναι πάλιν ὁμολογοῦσιν αὐτοί, καὶ τούτους πράξεις ἀθέσμους ἐπιτελεῖν ἔφασαν. καὶ πρώτου γε Διὸς οἱ ποιηταὶ εὐφωνότερον ᾄδουσι τὰς χαλεπὰς πράξεις. Χρύσιππος δέ, ὁ πολλὰ φλυαρήσας, πῶς οὐχὶ εὑρίσκεται σημαίνων τὴν Ἥραν στόματι μιαρῷ συγγίνεσθαι τῷ Διΐ; τί γάρ μοι καταλέγειν τὰς ἀσελγείας τῆς μητρὸς θεῶν λεγομένης ἢ Διὸς τοῦ Λατεαρίου διψῶντος αἵματος ἀνθρωπείου, ἢ Ἄττου τοῦ ἀποκοπτομένου, ἢ ὅτι ὁ Ζεὺς ὁ καλούμενος Τραγῳδός, κατακαύσας[1] τὴν ἑαυτοῦ χεῖρα, ὥς φασιν, νῦν παρὰ Ῥωμαίοις θεὸς τιμᾶται; σιγῶ τὰ Ἀντινόου τεμένη καὶ τὰ τῶν λοιπῶν καλουμένων θεῶν. καὶ γὰρ ἱστορούμενα τοῖς συνετοῖς καταγέλωτα φέρει.

Ἤτοι οὖν περὶ ἀθεότητος αὐτοὶ ὑπὸ τῶν ἰδίων δογμάτων ἐλέγχονται οἱ τὰ τοιαῦτα φιλοσοφήσαντες, ἢ καὶ περὶ πολυμιξίας καὶ ἀθέσμου κοινωνίας· ἔτι μὴν καὶ ἀνθρωποβορία παρ' αὐτοῖς εὑρίσκεται δι' ὧν συνέγραψαν γραφῶν, καὶ πρώτους γε οὓς τετιμήκασιν θεοὺς ταῦτα πεπραχότας ἀναγράφουσιν.

9. Ἡμεῖς δὲ καὶ θεὸν ὁμολογοῦμεν, ἀλλ' ἕνα, τὸν κτίστην καὶ ποιητὴν καὶ δημιουργὸν τοῦδε τοῦ παντὸς κόσμου, καὶ προνοίᾳ τὰ

---

[7] δεῖ] P: om. V   [8] κακούς] Wolf: καλούς V   [9] ἐν τόπῳ τινι] Grant: ἐξ οὗ τινι V: om. P
8. [1] κατακαύσας] Otto; cf. Epiphan. *Ancor.* cvi. 2 : κατακλύσας V

And whatever the others, though practically a majority, said about God and providence, it is easy to see how they contradicted one another; for some absolutely rejected the existence of God and providence, while others gave proof of God and admitted that everything is governed by providence. The intelligent listener and reader must pay close attention to what they say, as Simylos observes:[3]

> It is the custom to call poets equally
> Those of exceptional nature and those who are bad;
> One must differentiate.

In the same vein, Philemon [fr. 143 Kock] says somewhere:

> A bad thing is an unintelligent listener in his seat,
> For because of his stupidity he does not blame himself.

One must therefore pay attention and understand what is said, critically examining the remarks of philosophers and of poets as well.

8. For after denying the existence of gods they admit it once more, and have said that they perform unlawful actions. Notably in the case of Zeus the poets sing of his wicked deeds most euphoniously. And did not Chrysippus, who uttered so much nonsense, indicate that Hera with impure mouth had intercourse with Zeus [*SVF* ii. 1073]?[1] Why should I list the lascivious acts of the so-called Mother of the gods, or of Zeus Latiaris, thirsty for human blood, or of castrated Attis? Why should I relate that the Zeus called Tragedian, after burning his own hand, as they say, is now worshipped among the Romans as a god? I do not mention the temples of Antinous and those of the other so-called gods, for descriptions of them result in ridicule from intelligent people.

The persons who philosophized in this way are convicted by their own teaching either of atheism or of promiscuity and unlawful intercourse. Furthermore, cannibalism exists among them, according to their writings, and they describe the gods they have honoured as being the first to perform such actions.

The Ten Divine Commandments

9. We acknowledge a god, but only one, the Founder and Maker and Demiurge of this whole universe. We know that everything is

---

[3] Cf. T. Kock, *Comicorum graecorum fragmenta* ii (Leipzig, 1884), 444.
8. [1] Chrysippus allegorized not only this story but also the story of Metis (iii. 4).

πάντα διοικεῖσθαι ἐπιστάμεθα, ἀλλ' ὑπ' αὐτοῦ μόνου, καὶ νόμον ἅγιον μεμαθήκαμεν, ἀλλὰ νομοθέτην ἔχομεν τὸν ὄντως θεόν, ὃς καὶ διδάσκει ἡμᾶς δικαιοπραγεῖν καὶ εὐσεβεῖν καὶ καλοποιεῖν.[1]

Καὶ περὶ μὲν εὐσεβείας λέγει· "Οὐκ ἔσονταί σοι θεοὶ ἕτεροι πλὴν ἐμοῦ. οὐ ποιήσεις σεαυτῷ εἴδωλον οὐδὲ παντὸς ὁμοίωμα ὅσα ἐν τῷ οὐρανῷ ἄνω ἢ ὅσα ἐν τῇ γῇ κάτω ἢ ὅσα ἐν τοῖς ὕδασιν ὑποκάτω τῆς γῆς. οὐ προσκυνήσεις αὐτοῖς, οὐδὲ μὴ λατρεύσεις αὐτοῖς· ἐγὼ γάρ εἰμι κύριος ὁ θεός σου."

Περὶ δὲ τοῦ καλοποιεῖν ἔφη· "Τίμα τὸν πατέρα σου καὶ τὴν μητέρα σου, ἵνα εὖ σοι γένηται καὶ ἵνα μακροχρόνιος ἔσῃ ἐπὶ τῆς γῆς, ἧς ἐγὼ δίδωμί σοι κύριος ὁ θεός."

Ἔτι περὶ δικαιοσύνης· "Οὐ μοιχεύσεις, οὐ φονεύσεις, οὐ κλέψεις, οὐ ψευδομαρτυρήσεις κατὰ τοῦ πλησίον σου μαρτυρίαν ψευδῆ, οὐκ ἐπιθυμήσεις τὴν γυναῖκα τοῦ πλησίον σου, οὐκ ἐπιθυμήσεις τὴν οἰκίαν αὐτοῦ οὐδὲ τὸν ἀγρὸν αὐτοῦ οὐδὲ τὸν παῖδα αὐτοῦ οὐδὲ τὴν παιδίσκην αὐτοῦ οὐδὲ τοῦ βοὸς αὐτοῦ οὐδὲ τοῦ ὑποζυγίου αὐτοῦ οὐδὲ παντὸς κτήνους αὐτοῦ, οὔτε ὅσα ἐστὶν τῷ πλησίον σου. οὐ διαστρέψεις κρίμα πένητος ἐν κρίσει αὐτοῦ, ἀπὸ παντὸς ῥήματος ἀδίκου διαποστήσει, ἀθῷον καὶ δίκαιον οὐκ ἀποκτενεῖς, οὐ δικαιώσεις τὸν ἀσεβῆ καὶ δῶρα οὐ λήψῃ· τὰ γὰρ δῶρα ἀποτυφλοῖ ὀφθαλμοὺς βλεπόντων καὶ λυμαίνεται ῥήματα δίκαια."

Τούτου μὲν οὖν τοῦ θείου νόμου διάκονος γεγένηται Μωσῆς, ὁ καὶ θεράπων τοῦ θεοῦ, παντὶ μὲν τῷ κόσμῳ, παντελῶς δὲ τοῖς Ἑβραίοις, τοῖς καὶ Ἰουδαίοις καλουμένοις, οὓς κατεδουλώσατο ἀρχῆθεν βασιλεὺς Αἰγύπτου, τυγχάνοντας σπέρμα δίκαιον ἀνδρῶν θεοσεβῶν καὶ ὁσίων, Ἀβραὰμ καὶ Ἰσαὰκ καὶ Ἰακώβ· ὧν[2] ὁ θεὸς μνησθεὶς καὶ ποιήσας[3] θαυμάσια καὶ τέρατα διὰ Μωσέως παράδοξα ἐρρύσατο αὐτούς, καὶ ἐξήγαγεν ἐκ τῆς Αἰγύπτου, ἀγαγὼν αὐτοὺς διὰ τῆς ἐρήμου καλουμένης· οὓς καὶ ἀπεκατέστησεν εἰς τὴν Χαναναίαν γῆν, μετέπειτα δὲ Ἰουδαίαν ἐπικληθεῖσαν, καὶ νόμον[4] παρέθετο καὶ ἐδίδαξεν αὐτοὺς ταῦτα. τοῦ μὲν οὖν νόμου μεγάλου καὶ θαυμασίου πρὸς πᾶσαν δικαιοσύνην ὑπάρχοντος δέκα κεφάλαια ἃ προειρήκαμεν, τοιαῦτά ἐστιν.

9. [1] καὶ καλοποιεῖν] BP: om. καὶ V   [2] ὧν] Humphry: om. V   [3] μνησθεὶς καὶ ποιήσας] BP: ποιήσας καὶ μνησθεὶς V   [4] καὶ νόμον] Gesner: κατὰ νόμον V

governed by providential care, but by him alone. We have learned a holy law, but we have as legislator the real God, who teaches us to practise justice and piety and beneficence.

Concerning piety he says, 'You shall have no other gods but me. You shall not make for yourself an idol or the likeness of anything in the heaven above or in the earth below or in the waters under the earth. You shall not worship them or serve them, for I am the Lord your God' [Exod. 20: 3–5].

Concerning beneficence he said, 'Honour your father and your mother, so that it may be well for you and that you may live long upon the land which I, the Lord God, give you' [Exod. 20: 12].

And concerning justice: 'You shall not commit adultery; you shall not kill; you shall not steal; you shall not bear false witness against your neighbour; you shall not covet your neighbour's wife, you shall not covet his house or his field or his servant or his servant girl or his ox or his ass or any of his animals or anything that belongs to your neighbour [Exod. 20: 13–17; cf. II. 35]. You shall not pervert the judgement of the poor man in judging him: from every unjust word you shall stand aloof. You shall not kill the innocent and righteous man. You shall not vindicate the ungodly man and you shall not take bribes, for bribes blind the eyes of those who see and they do harm to just words' [Exod. 23: 6–8].

Of this divine law the minister was Moses, the servant of God, not only to all the world but especially to the Hebrews (also called Jews), whom the king of Egypt had originally enslaved though they were the righteous seed of pious and holy men, Abraham, Isaac, and Jacob. God remembered them and delivered them from Egypt, working miracles and strange wonders through Moses, and took them through what is called the desert. He restored them to the land of Canaan, afterwards called Judaea, and gave the law and taught them these things. The ten chapters[1] of this great and marvellous law, which suffices for all righteousness [cf. Matt. 3: 15],[2] are those we have just mentioned.

9. [1] Theophilus' ten commandments thus do not include the third (taking God's name in vain) or the fourth (Sabbath observance), though allusions to both occur in II. 10 and 12. He may regard the first two commandments as a unity and therefore adds three 'judgements' from Exod. 23.
[2] Theophilus' predecessor Ignatius also alludes to this verse (*Smyrn.* i. 1).

10. Ἐπειδὴ οὖν προσήλυτοι ἐγενήθησαν ἐν γῇ Αἰγύπτῳ ὄντες τὸ γένος Ἑβραῖοι ἀπὸ γῆς τῆς Χαλδαϊκῆς (κατ' ἐκεῖνο καιροῦ λιμοῦ γενομένης ἀνάγκην ἔσχον μετελθεῖν εἰς Αἴγυπτον σιτίων ἐκεῖ πιπρασκομένων, ἔνθα καὶ χρόνῳ παρῴκησαν· ταῦτα δὲ αὐτοῖς συνέβη κατὰ προαναφώνησιν θεοῦ), παροικήσαντες οὖν ἐν Αἰγύπτῳ ἔτεσι τετρακοσίοις καὶ τριάκοντα, ἐν τῷ τὸν Μωσῆν μέλλειν ἐξάγειν αὐτοὺς εἰς τὴν ἔρημον ὁ θεὸς ἐδίδαξεν αὐτοὺς διὰ τοῦ νόμου λέγων· "Προσήλυτον οὐ θλίψετε· ὑμεῖς γὰρ οἴδατε τὴν ψυχὴν τοῦ προσηλύτου· αὐτοὶ γὰρ προσήλυτοι ἦτε ἐν τῇ γῇ Αἰγύπτῳ."

11. Τὸν μὲν οὖν νόμον, τὸν ὑπὸ τοῦ θεοῦ δεδομένον αὐτοῖς, ἐν τῷ παραβῆναι τὸν λαόν, ἀγαθὸς ὢν καὶ οἰκτίρμων ὁ θεός, μὴ βουλόμενος διαφθεῖραι αὐτούς, πρὸς τῷ δεδωκέναι τὸν νόμον ὕστερον καὶ προφήτας ἐξέπεμψεν αὐτοῖς ἐκ τῶν ἀδελφῶν αὐτῶν, πρὸς τὸ διδάσκειν καὶ ἀναμιμνήσκειν τὰ τοῦ νόμου αὐτοὺς καὶ ἐπιστρέφειν εἰς μετάνοιαν τοῦ μηκέτι ἁμαρτάνειν· εἰ δὲ ἐπιμένοιεν ταῖς φαύλαις πράξεσιν, προανεφώνησαν ὑποχειρίους αὐτοὺς παραδοθῆναι πάσαις ταῖς βασιλείαις τῆς γῆς καὶ ὅτι ταῦτα αὐτοῖς ἤδη ἀπέβη, φανερὸν μέν ἐστιν.

Περὶ μὲν οὖν τῆς μετανοίας Ἡσαΐας ὁ προφήτης κοινῶς μὲν πρὸς πάντας, διαρρήδην δὲ πρὸς τὸν λαὸν λέγει· "Ζητήσατε τὸν κύριον, καὶ ἐν τῷ εὑρίσκειν αὐτὸν ἐπικαλέσασθε· ἡνίκα δ' ἂν ἐγγίζῃ ὑμῖν, ἀπολιπέτω ὁ ἀσεβὴς τὰς ὁδοὺς αὐτοῦ, καὶ ἀνὴρ ἄνομος τὰς βουλὰς αὐτοῦ, καὶ ἐπιστραφήτω ἐπὶ κύριον τὸν θεὸν αὐτοῦ, καὶ ἐλεηθήσεται, ὅτι ἐπὶ πολὺ ἀφήσει τὰς ἁμαρτίας ὑμῶν." καὶ ἕτερος προφήτης Ἐζεχιὴλ φησιν· "Ἐὰν ἀποστραφῇ ὁ ἄνομος ἀπὸ πασῶν τῶν ἀνομιῶν ὧν ἐποίησεν καὶ φυλάξῃ τὰς ἐντολάς μου καὶ ποιήσῃ τὰ δικαιώματά μου, ζωῇ ζήσεται καὶ οὐ μὴ ἀποθάνῃ· πᾶσαι αἱ ἀδικίαι αὐτοῦ ἃς ἐποίησεν οὐ μὴ μνησθῶσιν, ἀλλὰ τῇ δικαιοσύνῃ ᾗ ἐποίησεν ζήσεται, ὅτι οὐ βούλομαι τὸν θάνατον τοῦ ἀνόμου, λέγει κύριος, ὡς ἐπιστρέψαι ἀπὸ τῆς ὁδοῦ τῆς πονηρᾶς καὶ ζῆν αὐτόν." πάλιν ὁ Ἡσαΐας· "Ἐπιστράφητε οἱ τὴν βαθεῖαν βουλὴν βουλευόμενοι καὶ ἄνομον, ἵνα σωθήσεσθε." καὶ ἕτερος, Ἱερεμίας· "Ἐπιστράφητε ἐπὶ κύριον τὸν θεὸν ὑμῶν, ὡς ὁ τρυγῶν ἐπὶ τὸν κάρτελλον αὐτοῦ, καὶ ἐλεηθήσεσθε."

Proselytes and the Law

10. Since, then, they had become sojourners[1] in the land of Egypt, though by birth they were Hebrews from the land of Chaldaea—at that time when there was a famine they had to migrate to Egypt because grain was sold there, and they stayed there for a time; these things happened to them in accordance with God's prediction [Gen. 15: 13]—when they had stayed in Egypt for 430 years [Exod. 12: 40], as Moses was about to lead them forth into the desert, God taught them through the law and said: 'You shall not oppress the sojourner, for you know the life of the sojourner; you yourselves were sojourners in the land of Egypt' [Exod. 23: 9].

Through the Prophets God Taught Repentance

11. Now when the people transgressed the law which God had given them, because God is good and merciful and did not want to destroy them he not only gave the law but later sent prophets *from among their brothers* [Deut. 18: 15] to *teach and remind* them [John 14: 26] of the content of the law and to convert them to repentance so that they would no longer sin. But the prophets predicted that if they continued in their evil deeds they would be delivered *under the hand of all the kingdoms* [Baruch 2: 4][1] of the earth; and it is obvious that these things have already happened to them.

Concerning repentance, then, Isaiah the prophet speaks generally to all men but especially to the people: 'Seek the Lord and when you find him call upon him; but after he has approached you, let the impious man leave his ways and the lawless man his counsels, and let him be converted to the Lord his God, and he will obtain mercy because he will abundantly forgive your sins' [Isa. 55: 6–7]. And another prophet, Ezekiel, says: 'If the lawless man is converted from all the lawless deeds he has done and keeps my commandments and performs my ordinances, he will truly live and will not die; all his iniquities which he has done will not be remembered, but by the righteousness which he has done he will live; for I do not desire the death of the lawless man, says the Lord, so much as that he may be converted from the evil way and live' [Ezek. 18: 21–3]. Again Isaiah: 'Be converted, you who take deep and lawless counsel [Isa. 31: 6], so that you may be saved' [45: 22]. And another, Jeremiah: 'Be converted to the Lord your God, as the harvester of grapes to his basket [Jer. 6: 9], and you will obtain mercy.'

10. [1] The Greek word means both 'sojourners' and 'proselytes'.
11. [1] This was a penalty for cannibalism (Baruch 2: 3).

Πολλὰ μὲν οὖν μᾶλλον δὲ ἀναρίθμητά ἐστιν τὰ ἐν ἁγίαις γραφαῖς εἰρημένα περὶ μετανοίας, ἀεὶ τοῦ θεοῦ βουλομένου ἐπιστρέφειν τὸ γένος τῶν ἀνθρώπων ἀπὸ πασῶν τῶν ἁμαρτιῶν.

12. Ἔτι μὴν καὶ περὶ δικαιοσύνης, ἧς ὁ νόμος εἴρηκεν, ἀκόλουθα εὑρίσκεται καὶ τὰ τῶν προφητῶν καὶ τῶν εὐαγγελίων ἔχειν, διὰ τὸ τοὺς πάντας πνευματοφόρους ἑνὶ πνεύματι θεοῦ λελαληκέναι. ὁ γοῦν Ἡσαΐας οὕτως ἔφη· " Ἀφέλετε τὰς πονηρίας ἀπὸ τῶν ψυχῶν ὑμῶν, μάθετε καλὸν ποιεῖν, ἐκζητήσατε κρίσιν, ῥύσασθε ἀδικούμενον, κρίνατε ὀρφανῷ καὶ δικαιώσατε χήραν." ἔτι ὁ αὐτός· "Διάλυε, φησίν, πάντα σύνδεσμον ἀδικίας, λύε στραγγαλίας βιαίων συναλλαγμάτων, ἀπόστελλε τεθραυσμένους ἐν ἀφέσει, καὶ πᾶσαν συγγραφὴν ἄδικον διάσπα, διάθρυπτε πεινῶντι τὸν ἄρτον σου καὶ πτωχοὺς ἀστέγους εἰσάγαγε εἰς τὸν οἶκόν σου· ἐὰν ἴδῃς γυμνόν, περίβαλλε, καὶ ἀπὸ τῶν οἰκείων τοῦ σπέρματός σου οὐχ ὑπερόψῃ. τότε ῥαγήσεται πρώϊμον τὸ φῶς σου, καὶ τὰ ἱμάτια σου ταχὺ ἀνατελεῖ καὶ προπορεύσεται ἔμπροσθέν σου ἡ δικαιοσύνη σου." ὁμοίως καὶ Ἱερεμίας· "Στῆτε, φησίν, ἐπὶ ταῖς ὁδοῖς καὶ ἴδετε, καὶ ἐπερωτήσατε ποία ἐστὶν ἡ ὁδὸς κυρίου τοῦ θεοῦ ἡμῶν ἡ ἀγαθή, καὶ βαδίζετε ἐν αὐτῇ, καὶ εὑρήσετε ἀνάπαυσιν ταῖς ψυχαῖς ὑμῶν. κρίμα δίκαιον κρίνετε, ὅτι ἐν τούτοις ἐστὶν τὸ θέλημα κυρίου τοῦ θεοῦ ὑμῶν." ὡσαύτως καὶ Ὡσηὲ[1] λέγει· "Φυλάσσεσθε κρίμα καὶ ἐγγίζετε πρὸς κύριον τὸν θεὸν ὑμῶν, τὸν στερεώσαντα τὸν οὐρανὸν καὶ κτίσαντα τὴν γῆν." καὶ ἕτερος Ἰωὴλ ἀκόλουθα τούτοις ἔφη· "Συναγάγετε λαόν, ἁγιάσατε ἐκκλησίαν, εἰσδέξασθε πρεσβυτέρους, συναγάγετε νήπια θηλάζοντα μαστούς· ἐξελθέτω νυμφίος ἐκ τοῦ κοιτῶνος αὐτοῦ καὶ νύμφη ἐκ τοῦ παστοῦ αὐτῆς. καὶ εὔξασθε πρὸς κύριον τὸν θεὸν ὑμῶν ἐκτενῶς, ὅπως ἐλεήσῃ ὑμᾶς, καὶ ἐξαλείψει τὰ ἁμαρτήματα ὑμῶν." ὁμοίως καὶ ἕτερος Ζαχαρίας· "Τάδε λέγει κύριος παντοκράτωρ· Κρίμα ἀληθείας κρίνετε, καὶ ἔλεος καὶ οἰκτιρμὸν ποιεῖτε ἕκαστος πρὸς τὸν πλησίον αὐτοῦ, καὶ χήραν καὶ ὀρφανὸν καὶ προσήλυτον μὴ καταδυναστεύσητε, καὶ κακίαν ἕκαστος μὴ μνησικακείτω τῷ ἀδελφῷ αὐτοῦ ἐν ταῖς καρδίαις ὑμῶν, λέγει κύριος παντοκράτωρ."

13. Καὶ περὶ σεμνότητος οὐ μόνον διδάσκει ἡμᾶς ὁ ἅγιος λόγος τὸ μὴ ἁμαρτάνειν ἔργῳ, ἀλλὰ καὶ μέχρις ἐννοίας, τὸ μηδὲ τῇ καρδίᾳ

12. [1] Ὡσηὲ] Wolf (cf. II. 35. 11) : Μωσῆς V

There are many other passages, or rather innumerable other passages, in the holy scriptures concerning repentance, for God always wants the human race to turn away from all its sins.

Consistent Christian Teaching on Justice

12. Furthermore, concerning the justice of which the law spoke, the teaching of the prophets and the gospels is consistent with it because all the inspired men made utterances by means of the one Spirit of God. For Isaiah thus spoke: 'Take away wickedness from your souls, learn to do good, seek judgement, free the oppressed, judge for the orphan, and vindicate the widow' [Isa. 1: 16–17]. And again the same: 'Dissolve', he says, 'every bond of iniquity, loosen the knots of violent dealings, send away the wounded with forgiveness, and tear asunder every unjust contract, break your bread for the hungry, and bring the homeless poor into your house; if you see someone naked, clothe him, and do not despise your own relatives. Then your light will break forth in the morning and your healings will swiftly rise, and your righteousness will go forth before you' [Isa. 58: 6–8]. Similarly also Jeremiah: 'Stand', he says, 'in the roads and see, and ask what is the good way of the Lord our God, and walk in it, and you will find rest for your souls [Jer. 6: 16]. Judge a just judgement [Zech. 9: 9], for in this is the will of the Lord your God [cf. Jer. 9: 23].' So also Hosea says: 'Keep judgement and approach the Lord your God, who made firm the heaven and established the earth' [Hos. 12: 7; 13: 4]. And another, Joel, said in agreement with these: 'Assemble the people, sanctify the congregation, assemble the elders, gather infants at the breast; let the bridegroom come out of his chamber and the bride out of her room [Joel 2: 16]; and pray constantly to the Lord your God [Joel 1: 14] so that he may have mercy on you, and he will blot out your sins [cf. Isa. 43: 25].' Similarly also another, Zechariah: 'Thus says the Lord Almighty, Judge a judgement of truth, and show mercy and pity each to his neighbour, and do not oppress the widow and the orphan and the sojourner, and let each one not bear malice to his brother in your hearts [Zech. 7: 9–10], says the Lord Almighty.'[1]

Consistent Christian Teaching on Chastity

13. Concerning chastity the holy Word teaches us not to sin either in deed or even in thought, not to imagine any evil in our heart or

---

12. [1] The gospel passages dealing with justice (righteousness) have been lost from this chapter, but presumably they came from Matthew. For Matthew 3: 15 cf. III. 9.

ἐννοηθῆναι περί τινος κακοῦ, ἢ θεασάμενον τοῖς ὀφθαλμοῖς ἀλλοτρίαν γυναῖκα ἐπιθυμῆσαι. Σολομὼν μὲν οὖν, ὁ βασιλεὺς καὶ προφήτης γενόμενος, ἔφη· "Οἱ ὀφθαλμοί σου ὀρθὰ βλεπέτωσαν, τὰ δὲ βλέφαρά σου νευέτω δίκαια· ὀρθὰς ποίει τροχιὰς σοῖς ποσίν." ἡ δὲ εὐαγγέλιος φωνὴ ἐπιτατικώτερον διδάσκει περὶ ἁγνείας λέγουσα· "Πᾶς ὁ ἰδὼν γυναῖκα ἀλλοτρίαν πρὸς τὸ ἐπιθυμῆσαι αὐτὴν ἤδη ἐμοίχευσεν αὐτὴν ἐν τῇ καρδίᾳ αὐτοῦ. καὶ ὁ γαμῶν", φησίν, "ἀπολελυμένην ἀπὸ ἀνδρὸς μοιχεύει, καὶ ὃς ἀπολύει γυναῖκα παρεκτὸς λόγου πορνείας ποιεῖ αὐτὴν μοιχευθῆναι." ἔτι[1] ὁ Σολομών φησιν· " Ἀποδήσει τις πῦρ ἐν ἱματίῳ, τὰ δὲ ἱμάτια αὐτοῦ οὐ κατακαύσει; ἢ περιπατήσει τις ἐπ' ἀνθράκων πυρός, τοὺς δὲ πόδας οὐ κατακαύσει; οὕτως ὁ εἰσπορευόμενος πρὸς γυναῖκα ὕπανδρον οὐκ ἀθῳωθήσεται."

14. Καὶ τοῦ μὴ μόνον ἡμᾶς εὐνοεῖν τοῖς ὁμοφύλοις,[1] ὡς οἴονταί τινες, Ἠσαΐας ὁ προφήτης ἔφη· "Εἴπατε τοῖς μισοῦσιν ὑμᾶς καὶ τοῖς βδελυσσομένοις· ἀδελφοὶ ἡμῶν ἔστε, ἵνα τὸ ὄνομα κυρίου δοξασθῇ καὶ ὀφθῇ ἐν τῇ εὐφροσύνῃ αὐτῶν." τὸ δὲ εὐαγγέλιον· " Ἀγαπᾶτε, φησίν, τοὺς ἐχθροὺς ὑμῶν καὶ προσεύχεσθε ὑπὲρ τῶν ἐπηρεαζόντων ὑμᾶς. ἐὰν γὰρ ἀγαπᾶτε τοὺς ἀγαπῶντας ὑμᾶς, ποῖον μισθὸν ἔχετε; τοῦτο καὶ οἱ λῃσταὶ καὶ οἱ τελῶναι ποιοῦσιν."

Τοὺς δὲ ποιοῦντας τὸ ἀγαθὸν διδάσκει μὴ καυχᾶσθαι, ἵνα μὴ ἀνθρωπάρεσκοι ὦσιν. "Μὴ γνώτω γάρ", φησίν, "ἡ χείρ σου ἡ ἀριστερὰ τί ποιεῖ ἡ χείρ σου ἡ δεξιά." ἔτι μὴν καὶ περὶ τοῦ ὑποτάσσεσθαι ἀρχαῖς καὶ ἐξουσίαις καὶ εὔχεσθαι ὑπὲρ αὐτῶν κελεύει ἡμᾶς ὁ θεῖος λόγος, ὅπως ἤρεμον καὶ ἡσύχιον βίον διάγωμεν. καὶ διδάσκει ἀποδιδόναι πᾶσιν τὰ πάντα, τῷ τὴν τιμὴν τὴν τιμήν, τῷ τὸν φόβον τὸν φόβον, τῷ τὸν φόρον τὸν φόρον, μηδένι μηδὲν ὀφελεῖν ἢ μόνον τὸ ἀγαπᾶν πάντας.

15. Σκόπει τοίνυν εἰ οἱ τὰ τοιαῦτα μανθάνοντες δύνανται ἀδιαφόρως ζῆν καὶ συμφύρεσθαι ταῖς ἀθεμίτοις μίξεσιν, ἢ τὸ ἀθεώτατον πάντων, σαρκῶν ἀνθρωπείων ἐφάπτεσθαι, ὅπου γε καὶ τὰς θέας τῶν μονομάχων ἡμῖν ἀπείρηται ὁρᾶν, ἵνα μὴ κοινωνοὶ καὶ συνίστορες φόνων γενώμεθα. ἀλλ' οὐδὲ τὰς λοιπὰς θεωρίας ὁρᾶν χρή, ἵνα μὴ μολύνωνται

13. [1] ἔτι] Otto: ὅτι V   14. [1] ὁμοφύλοις Clauser: ἀλοφύλοις V

to covet another person's wife when we see her with our eyes. Solomon, who was a king and a prophet, said, 'Let your eyes look straight and let your eyelids incline justly [cf. II. 35]; make straight paths for your feet' [Prov. 4: 25 f.]. The gospel voice provides a stricter teaching about purity when it says, 'Everyone who looks upon another person's wife to desire her has already committed adultery with her in his heart' [Matt. 5: 28]. 'And he who marries', it says, 'a woman divorced by her husband commits adultery, and whoever divorces his wife except for fornication makes her a partner in adultery' [Matt. 5: 32]. Further, Solomon said, 'Will anyone bind up fire in his cloak without burning it? Or will anyone walk on coals without burning his feet? So he who approaches a married woman will not be guiltless' [Prov. 6: 27–9].

Other Examples of Consistent Christian Teaching

14. And concerning the good will which we exercise not only toward our own people, as some suppose, Isaiah the prophet said: 'Say to those who hate you and to those who abominate you, "You are our brothers", so that the name of the Lord may be glorified and may be seen in their gladness' [Isa. 66: 5]. And the gospel: 'Love', it says, 'your enemies and pray for those who insult you. For if you love those who love you, what reward do you have? Brigands and tax-collectors do this' [Matt. 5: 44, 46].

It teaches those who do good not to boast, lest they be sycophantic. For it says: 'Let not your left hand know what your right hand is doing' [Matt. 6: 3]. Furthermore, the divine Word gives us orders about *subordination to principalities and powers* [Rom. 13: 1–3] and *prayer for them, so that we may lead a quiet and tranquil life* [1 Tim. 2: 1–2]; and it teaches us to *render all things to all men, honour to whom honour is due, fear to whom fear, tribute to whom tribute; to owe no man anything except to love all* [Rom. 13: 7–8].

The Conduct of Christians

15. Consider, therefore, whether those who learn such teachings can live promiscuously and be united in unlawful intercourse or, most godless of all, partake of human flesh, when we are forbidden even to witness gladiatorial shows lest we should become participants and accomplices in murders. And we are not allowed to

ἡμῶν οἱ ὀφθαλμοὶ καὶ τὰ ὦτα, γινόμενα συμμέτοχα τῶν ἐκεῖ φωνῶν ᾀδομένων. εἰ γὰρ εἴποι τις περὶ ἀνθρωποβορίας, ἐκεῖ τὰ Θυέστου καὶ Τηρέως τέκνα ἐσθιόμενα· εἰ δὲ περὶ μοιχείας, οὐ μόνον περὶ ἀνθρώπων ἀλλὰ καὶ περὶ θεῶν, ὧν καταγγέλλουσιν εὐφώνως μετὰ τιμῶν καὶ ἄθλων, παρ' αὐτοῖς τραγῳδεῖται. μακρὰν δὲ ἀπείη χριστιανοῖς ἐνθυμηθῆναί τι τοιοῦτο πρᾶξαι, παρ' οἷς σωφροσύνη πάρεστιν, ἐγκράτεια ἀσκεῖται, μονογαμία τηρεῖται, ἁγνεία φυλάσσεται, ἀδικία ἐκπορθεῖται, ἁμαρτία ἐκριζοῦται, δικαιοσύνη μελετᾶται, νόμος πολιτεύεται, θεοσέβεια πράσσεται, θεὸς ὁμολογεῖται, ἀλήθεια βραβεύει, χάρις συντηρεῖ, εἰρήνη περισκέπει, λόγος ἅγιος ὁδηγεῖ, σοφία διδάσκει, ζωὴ βραβεύει, θεὸς βασιλεύει.

Πολλὰ μὲν οὖν ἔχοντες λέγειν περὶ τῆς καθ' ἡμᾶς πολιτείας καὶ τῶν δικαιωμάτων τοῦ θεοῦ καὶ δημιουργοῦ πάσης κτίσεως, τὰ νῦν αὐτάρκως ἡγούμεθα ἐπιμεμνῆσθαι, εἰς τὸ καί σε ἐπιστῆσαι μάλιστα ἐξ ὧν ἀναγινώσκεις ἕως τοῦ δεῦρο, ἵνα ὡς φιλομαθὴς ἐγενήθης ἕως τοῦ δεῦρο[1] οὕτως καὶ φιλομαθὴς ἔσῃ.

16. Θέλω δέ σοι καὶ τὰ τῶν χρόνων θεοῦ παρέχοντος νῦν ἀκριβέστερον ἐπιδεῖξαι, ἵνα ἐπιγνῷς ὅτι οὐ πρόσφατος οὐδὲ μυθώδης ἐστίν ὁ καθ' ἡμᾶς λόγος, ἀλλ' ἀρχαιότερος καὶ ἀληθέστερος ἁπάντων ποιητῶν καὶ συγγραφέων, τῶν ἐπ' ἀδήλῳ συγγραψάντων. οἱ μὲν γὰρ τὸν κόσμον ἀγένητον εἰπόντες εἰς τὸ[1] ἀπέραντον ἐχώρησαν, ἕτεροι δὲ γενητὸν φήσαντες εἶπον ὡς ἤδη μυριάδας ἐτῶν πεντεκαίδεκα ἐληλυθέναι καὶ τρισχίλια ἑβδομήκοντα πέντε ἔτη. ταῦτα μὲν οὖν Ἀπολλώνιος ὁ Αἰγύπτιος ἱστορεῖ. Πλάτων δέ, ὁ δοκῶν Ἑλλήνων σοφώτερος γεγενῆσθαι, εἰς πόσην φλυαρίαν ἐχώρησεν! ἐν γὰρ ταῖς Πολιτείαις αὐτοῦ ἐπιγραφομέναις ῥητῶς κεῖται· "Πῶς γὰρ ἄν,[2] εἴ γε ἔμενε τάδε οὕτως πάντα χρόνον ὡς νῦν διακοσμεῖται, καινὸν ἀνευρίσκετό ποτε ὁτιοῦν τοῦτο; ὅτι μὲν μυριάκις μυρία ἔτη διελάνθανεν ἄρα τοὺς τότε· χίλια δ' ἀφ' οὗ[3] γέγονεν ἢ δὶς τοσαῦτα

15. [1] ἕως τοῦ δεῦρο post ἐγενήθης] Otto: post ἔσῃ V
16. [1] τὸ] P: τὸν V   [2] πῶς γὰρ ἄν] Otto: λέγοντος V: λέγων P   [3] χίλια δ' ἀφ' οὗ] Fell: ἔχειν ἀδελφοὺς V

witness the other spectacles, lest our eyes and ears should be defiled by taking part in the songs which are sung there. If anyone should mention cannibalism, there the children of Thyestes and Tereus are eaten; if adultery, it is the subject of their tragedies not only as regards men but also as regards the gods whom they euphoniously proclaim for honours and prizes. Far be it from Christians to think of doing any such thing, for among them temperance is present, continence is exercised, monogamy is preserved, purity is guarded; injustice is driven out, sin is uprooted, righteousness is practised, law is the guiding principle, piety is performed, God is acknowledged; truth controls, grace preserves, peace protects; holy Logos leads, Sophia teaches, Life controls, God reigns.[1]

Although we have many things to say about our way of life and the ordinances of the God and Fashioner of the whole creation, we consider that we have now made sufficient mention of them that you too may know them from what you have read thus far, so that as you have hitherto been a lover of learning, you may become (a real) one [cf. II. 38].

Chronology
The Question of the Deluge

16. Now I wish with God's help to demonstrate the chronology for you more exactly, so that you may recognize that our doctrine is neither modern nor mythical but more ancient and true than all the poets and historians who wrote on what they knew nothing about. For some declared that the world was not created and went off into endless time; others called it created and said that 153,075 years had already passed. This statement is made by Apollonius the Egyptian.[1] And Plato, who is thought to have been the wisest of the Greeks—to what nonsense did he not attain! For in his book entitled *Republic* it says explicitly [*Leg.* iii. 677 c–d]: 'If these things had remained for all time just as they are now arranged, how would anything new ever be found? On the one hand, they must have escaped the knowledge of those who lived then for a myriad myriad years; on the other, one or two thousand years ago, some things have been discovered from the time of Daedalus, some from that of Orpheus, and some from that of Palamedes.' When he says that these things took place, he indicates that his

---

15. [1] On this passage cf. Grant, *After the New Testament* (Philadelphia, 1967), 60–1.

16. [1] The figure, which bears no relation to the Egyptian 'Sothic period' of 1,461 years, is given as ιε̄. ͵γοε΄ in III. 26. Conceivably this is an error for the figure ροε. ͵γσ΄ (1,753,200) provided by Lydus, *De mensibus* iii. 16, equal to 1,200 Sothic periods.

ἔτη· τὰ μὲν ἀπὸ Δαιδάλου καταφανῆ γέγονεν, τὰ δὲ ἀπὸ Ὀρφέως, τὰ δὲ ἀπὸ Παλαμήδους." καὶ ταῦτα εἰπὼν γεγενῆσθαι, τὰ μὲν μυριάκις μυρία ἔτη ἀπὸ κατακλυσμοῦ ἕως Δαιδάλου δηλοῖ. καὶ πολλὰ φήσας περὶ πολέων καὶ κατοικισμῶν[4] καὶ ἐθνῶν, ὁμολογεῖ εἰκασμῷ ταῦτα εἰρηκέναι. λέγει γάρ· "Εἰ γοῦν, ὦ ξένε, τις ἡμῖν ὑπόσχηται θεὸς ὥς, ἂν ἐπιχειρήσωμεν ⟨τὸ β'⟩[5] τῇ τῆς νομοθεσίας σκέψει, τῶν νῦν εἰρημένων ⟨λόγων οὐ χείρους οὐδ' ἐλάττους ἀκουσόμεθα, μακρὰν ἂν ἔλθοιμι ἔγωγε⟩."[6] δηλονότι εἰκασμῷ ἔφη· εἰ δὲ εἰκασμῷ, οὐκ ἄρα ἀληθῆ ἐστιν τὰ ὑπ' αὐτοῦ εἰρημένα.

17. Δεῖ οὖν μᾶλλον μαθητὴν γενέσθαι τῆς νομοθεσίας τοῦ θεοῦ, καθὼς καὶ αὐτὸς ὡμολόγηκεν ἄλλως μὴ δύνασθαι τὸ ἀκριβὲς μαθεῖν, ἐὰν μὴ ὁ θεὸς διδάξῃ διὰ τοῦ νόμου. τί δέ; οὐχὶ καὶ οἱ ποιηταὶ Ὅμηρος καὶ Ἡσίοδος καὶ Ὀρφεὺς ἔφασαν ἑαυτοὺς ἀπὸ θείας προνοίας μεμαθηκέναι; ἔτι μὴν μάντεις καὶ προγνώστας γεγενῆσθαι κατὰ τοὺς συγγραφεῖς, καὶ τοὺς παρ' αὐτῶν μαθόντας ἀκριβῶς συγγεγραφέναι φασίν. πόσῳ οὖν μᾶλλον ἡμεῖς τὰ ἀληθῆ εἰσόμεθα οἱ μανθάνοντες ἀπὸ τῶν ἁγίων προφητῶν, τῶν χωρησάντων τὸ ἅγιον πνεῦμα τοῦ θεοῦ; διὸ σύμφωνα καὶ φίλα ἀλλήλοις οἱ πάντες προφῆται εἶπον, καὶ προεκήρυξαν τὰ μέλλοντα ἔσεσθαι παντὶ τῷ κόσμῳ. τοὺς γὰρ φιλομαθεῖς μᾶλλον δὲ φιλαληθεῖς δύναται αὐτὴ ἡ ἔκβασις τῶν προαναπεφωνημένων πραγμάτων καὶ ἤδη ἀπηρτισμένων ἐκδιδάσκειν ὄντως ἀληθῆ εἶναι τὰ δι' αὐτῶν κεκηρυγμένα περί τε χρόνων καὶ καιρῶν τῶν πρὸ κατακλυσμοῦ, ἀφ' οὗ ἔκτισται ὁ κόσμος ἕως τοῦ δεῦρο, ὡς συνέστηκε τὰ ἔτη, εἰς τὸ ἐπιδεῖξαι τὴν φλυαρίαν τοῦ ψεύδους τῶν συγγραφέων, ὅτι οὐκ ἀληθῆ ἐστιν τὰ δι' αὐτῶν ῥηθέντα.

18. Πλάτων γάρ, ὡς προειρήκαμεν, δηλώσας κατακλυσμὸν γεγενῆσθαι, ἔφη μὴ πάσης τῆς γῆς ἀλλὰ τῶν πεδίων μόνον γεγενῆσθαι, καὶ τοὺς διαφυγόντας ἐπὶ τοῖς ὑψηλοτάτοις ὄρεσιν αὐτοὺς διασεσῶσθαι. ἕτεροι δὲ λέγουσι γεγονέναι Δευκαλίωνα καὶ Πύρραν, καὶ τούτους ἐν λάρνακι διασεσῶσθαι καὶ τὸν Δευκαλίωνα μετὰ τὸ ἐλθεῖν ἐκ τῆς λάρνακος λίθους εἰς τὰ ὀπίσω πεπομφέναι καὶ ἀνθρώπους ἐκ τῶν

---

[4] καὶ κατοικισμῶν] Einarson: κατακοσμῶν καὶ οἰκήσεων V   [5] ⟨τὸ β'⟩]
Einarson; cf. Plat. *Leg.* 683 b (des Places); om. V   [6] ⟨λόγων–ἔγωγε⟩]
Einarson; cf. Plat. *Leg.* 683 c (des Places): om. V

'myriad myriad years' are from the deluge [cf. *Leg.* iii. 677 a] to the time of Daedalus. And when he makes many statements about the various cities in the world and the habitations and nations, he admits that these statements are made by conjecture. For he says [*Leg.* iii. 683 b–c]: 'If, then, stranger, some god should promise us that if we could undertake for a second time our examination of the laws, we should hear discourses not inferior or shorter than the discourses so far spoken, I should go a great way.' Obviously he spoke by conjecture; and if by conjecture, then his statements are not true.

17. One must, instead, become a student of the legislation of God, as Plato himself admitted when he said that accurate learning cannot be obtained unless God teaches it through the law [*Meno* 99 e]. Did not the poets Homer, Hesiod, and Orpheus say that they had been instructed by divine providence? Furthermore, it is said that there were diviners and seers at the time of the historians, and that people who learned from them wrote accurate histories. How much more, then, shall we know the truth, since we learn it from the holy prophets, who were filled with the holy Spirit of God? For this reason all the prophets spoke harmoniously and in agreement with one another when they predicted what was going to happen to the whole world. The very outcome of the previously predicted and fulfilled events can teach those who love learning—or rather, love truth—that their proclamations are really true, those which were made concerning the times and seasons before the deluge and the number of years from the creation of the world up to the present. This will demonstrate the nonsensical falsehood of the historians and show that their statements are not true.

18. Plato, as we have already said [III. 16], showed that there was a deluge, but he says that it took place not over the entire earth but only over the plains, and that those who fled to the highest mountains were saved [*Leg.* iii. 677 a–b]. Others say that there were persons named Deucalion and Pyrrha and that they were saved in an ark, and that after Deucalion came out of the ark he cast stones behind him, and that men came into existence out of the stones

λίθων γεγενῆσθαι· ὅθεν φασὶν λαοὺς προσαγορεύεσθαι τὸ πλῆθος ἀνθρώπων. ἄλλοι δ' αὖ Κλύμενον εἶπον ἐν δευτέρῳ κατακλυσμῷ γεγονέναι.

Ὅτι μὲν οὖν ἄθλιοι καὶ πάνυ δυσσεβεῖς καὶ ἀνόητοι εὑρίσκονται οἱ τὰ τοιαῦτα συγγράψαντες καὶ φιλοσοφήσαντες ματαίως, ἐκ τῶν προειρημένων δῆλόν ἐστιν. ὁ δὲ ἡμέτερος προφήτης καὶ θεράπων τοῦ θεοῦ Μωσῆς περὶ τῆς γενέσεως τοῦ κόσμου ἐξιστορῶν διηγήσατο τίνι τρόπῳ γεγένηται ὁ κατακλυσμὸς ἐπὶ τῆς γῆς, οὐ μὴν ἀλλὰ καὶ τὰ τοῦ κατακλυσμοῦ ᾧ τρόπῳ γέγονεν, οὐ Πύρραν οὔτε Δευκαλίωνα ἢ Κλύμενον μυθεύων, οὐδὲ μὴν τὰ πεδία μόνον κατακεκλύσθαι, καὶ τοὺς διαφυγόντας ἐπὶ τοῖς ὄρεσι μόνους διασεσῶσθαι.

19. Ἀλλ' οὐδὲ δεύτερον κατακλυσμὸν γεγονέναι δηλοῖ, ἀλλὰ μὲν οὖν ἔφη μηκέτι τῷ κόσμῳ κατακλυσμὸν ὕδατος ἔσεσθαι, οἷον[1] οὔτε γέγονεν οὔτε μὴν ἔσται. ὀκτὼ δέ φησιν τὰς πάσας ψυχὰς ἀνθρώπων ἐν τῇ κιβωτῷ διασεσῶσθαι, ἐν τῇ κατασκευασθείσῃ προστάγμασι θεοῦ, οὐχ ὑπὸ Δευκαλίωνος, ἀλλ' ὑπὸ τοῦ Νῶε ἑβραϊστί, ὃς διερμηνεύεται τῇ ἑλλάδι γλώσσῃ ἀνάπαυσις, καθὼς καὶ ἐν ἑτέρῳ λόγῳ ἐδηλώσαμεν ὡς Νῶε, καταγγέλλων τοῖς τοτε ἀνθρώποις μέλλειν κατακλυσμὸν ἔσεσθαι, προεφήτευσεν αὐτοῖς λέγων· Δεῦτε, καλεῖ ὑμᾶς ὁ θεὸς εἰς μετάνοιαν· διὸ οἰκείως Δευκαλίων ἐκλήθη. τούτῳ δὲ τῷ Νῶε υἱοὶ τρεῖς ἦσαν, καθὼς καὶ ἐν τῷ δευτέρῳ τόμῳ ἐδηλώσαμεν, ὧν τὰ ὀνόματά ἐστιν Σὴμ καὶ Χὰμ καὶ Ἰάφεθ, οἷς καὶ γυναῖκες τρεῖς ἦσαν τὸ καθ' ἕνα αὐτῶν, καὶ αὐτός, καὶ ἡ γυνὴ αὐτοῦ. Τοῦτον τὸν ἄνδρα ἔνιοι Εὐνοῦχον προσηγορεύκασιν. ὀκτὼ οὖν αἱ πᾶσαι ψυχαὶ ἀνθρώπων διεσώθησαν, οἱ ἐν τῇ κιβωτῷ εὑρεθέντες.

Τὸν δὲ κατακλυσμὸν ἐσήμανεν ὁ Μωσῆς ἐπὶ ἡμέρας τεσσαράκοντα καὶ νύκτας τεσσαράκοντα γεγενῆσθαι, ἀπὸ τοῦ οὐρανοῦ τῶν καταρακτῶν ῥυέντων καὶ πασῶν[2] τῶν πηγῶν τῆς ἀβύσσου βλυσάντων, ὥστε τὸ ὕδωρ ὑψωθῆναι ἐπάνω παντὸς ὄρους ὑψηλοῦ πεντεκαίδεκα πήχεις. καὶ οὕτως διεφθάρη τὸ γένος πάντων τῶν τότε ἀνθρώπων, μόνοι δὲ διεσώθησαν οἱ φυλαχθέντες ἐν τῇ κιβωτῷ, οὓς προειρήκαμεν ὀκτώ· ἧς κιβωτοῦ τὰ λείψανα μέχρις τοῦ δεῦρο δείκνυται εἶναι ἐν τοῖς Ἀραβικοῖς ὄρεσιν.

Τὰ μὲν οὖν τοῦ κατακλαυσμοῦ κεφαλαιωδῶς τοιαύτην ἔχει τὴν ἱστορίαν.

19. [1] οἷον] Gesner: δι' ὃν V   [2] πασῶν] Otto; cf. Gen. 7: 11: ἀπὸ V

(*lithoi*). For this reason, they say, the multitude of men is called 'peoples' (*laoi*). Still others mention Klymenos, who was in a second deluge.[1]

From what we have already said it is obvious that those who wrote and pointlessly speculated on such matters were wretched, exceedingly ungodly, and stupid. Moses, our prophet and the minister of God, in his account of the creation of the world narrated not only the way in which the deluge took place upon the earth but also the way in which the events accompanying the deluge occurred. He tells no myth about a Pyrrha or a Deucalion or a Klymenos, nor does eh say that only the plains were inundated or that those who fled to the mountains were saved.

19. He does not state that a second deluge took place. On the contrary, he said that there would not be another deluge of water upon the world [cf. Gen. 9: 11]; this has not taken place and never will take place. He says that eight was the total number of human lives saved in the ark [cf. 1 Pet. 3: 20], which was constructed at God's command not by Deucalion but by Noah, whose Hebrew name is translated in Greek as 'rest'. (We have explained in another treatise how Noah, proclaiming the coming of a deluge to the men of that time, prophesied to them, saying; 'Come (*deute*), God calls (*kalei*) you to repentance.' For this reason he is fittingly called Deucalion.) This Noah had three sons, as we have explained in the second volume [II. 30–1]; their names are Sem and Cham and Iapheth. They had three wives, one for each, and there were Noah himself and his wife. (Some persons call this man a eunuch.) Eight human lives, then, were saved in all—those who were in the ark.

Moses indicated that the deluge lasted for *forty days and forty nights*, when *cataracts* flowed from *heaven* and all *the springs of the abyss gushed forth* [Gen. 7: 11 f.] so that the water was raised *fifteen cubits above even the highest mountain* [Gen. 7: 20]. Thus the whole human race then existing was destroyed; the only ones saved were those who were preserved in the ark, the eight already mentioned. The remains of the ark are to be seen to this day in the Arabian mountains.

In summary, this is the story of the deluge.

18. [1] The father of Phaethon, first king after the deluge, was Klymenos (Hyginus, *Fab.* 154).

20. Ὁ δὲ Μωσῆς ὁδηγήσας τοὺς Ἰουδαίους, ὡς ἔφθημεν εἰρηκέναι, ἐκβεβλημένους ἀπὸ γῆς Αἰγύπτου ὑπὸ βασιλέως Φαραώ, οὗ τοὔνομα Τέθμωσις,[1] ὅς, φασίν, μετὰ τὴν ἐκβολὴν τοῦ λαοῦ ἐβασίλευσεν ἔτη εἴκοσι πέντε καὶ μῆνας δ΄, ὡς ὑφήρηται Μαναιθώς. καὶ μετὰ τοῦτον Χεβρῶν[2] ἔτη ιγ΄. μετὰ δὲ τοῦτον Ἀμένωφις ἔτη κ΄, μῆνας ἑπτά. μετὰ δὲ τοῦτον ἡ ἀδελφὴ αὐτοῦ Ἀμέσση ἔτη κα΄, μῆνας ἐννέα.[3] μετὰ δὲ ταύτην Μήφρης ἔτη ιβ΄, μῆνας θ΄. μετὰ δὲ τοῦτον Μηφραμμούθωσις ἔτη κε΄,[4] μῆνας ι΄. καὶ μετὰ τοῦτον Τυθμώσης ἔτη θ΄, μῆνας η΄. καὶ μετὰ τοῦτον Ἀμένωφις[5] ἔτη λ΄, μῆνας ι΄. μετὰ δὲ τοῦτον Ὧρος ἔτη λς΄, μῆνας πέντε. τούτου δὲ θυγάτηρ Ἀκεγχερὴς ἔτη ιβ΄, μῆνα α΄.[6] μετὰ δὲ ταύτην Ῥαθῶτις ἔτη θ΄. μετὰ δὲ τοῦτον Ἀκεγχήρης ἔτη ιβ΄, μῆνας ε΄. μετὰ δὲ τοῦτον[7] Ἀκεγχήρης[8] ἔτη ιβ΄, μῆνας γ΄. τοῦ δὲ Ἀρμαῒς ἔτη δ΄, μῆνα α΄. καὶ μετὰ τοῦτον Ῥαμέσσης ἐνιαυτόν, μῆνας δ΄. μετὰ δὲ τοῦτον Ἀρμέσσης Μιαμμοῦ ἔτη ξς΄ καὶ μῆνας β΄.[9] καὶ μετὰ τοῦτον Ἀμένωφις ἔτη ιθ΄, μῆνας ς΄. τοῦ δὲ Σέθως[10] καὶ Ῥαμέσσης ἔτη ξ΄,[11] οὕς φασιν ἐσχηκέναι πολλὴν δύναμιν ἱππικῆς καὶ παράταξιν ναυτικῆς κατὰ τοὺς ἰδίους χρόνους.

Οἱ μὲν Ἑβραῖοι, κατ᾽ ἐκεῖνο καιροῦ παροικήσαντες ἐν γῇ[12] Αἰγύπτῳ καὶ καταδουλωθέντες ὑπὸ βασιλέως ὃς προείρηται Τέθμωσις, ᾠκοδόμησαν αὐτῷ πόλεις ὀχυράς, τήν τε Πειθὼ καὶ Ῥαμεσσῆ καὶ Ὤν, ἥτις ἐστὶν Ἡλίου πόλις· ὥστε καὶ τῶν πόλεων τῶν τότε ὀνομαστῶν κατ᾽ Αἰγυπτίους δείκνυνται προγενέστεροι οἱ Ἑβραῖοι ὄντες, οἳ καὶ προπάτορες ἡμῶν, ἀφ᾽ ὧν καὶ τὰς ἱερὰς βίβλους ἔχομεν ἀρχαιοτέρας οὔσας ἁπάντων συγγραφέων, καθὼς προειρήκαμεν.

Αἴγυπτος δὲ ἡ χώρα ἐκλήθη ἀπὸ τοῦ βασιλέως Σέθως· ὁ[13] γὰρ Σέθως, φασίν, Αἴγυπτος καλεῖται. τῷ δὲ Σέθως ἦν ἀδελφὸς ᾧ

---

20. [1] Τέθμωσις] Clauser; cf. Jos. C. Ap. i. 94: Μωσῆς V   [2] τοῦτον Χεβρῶν] Gesner: τὸν Χεβρῶν V   [3] μῆνας ἐννέα] Grant; cf. Jos. C. Ap. i. 95: μῆνα α΄ (= ἕνα) V   [4] ἔτη κε΄] Grant; cf. Jos., ibid.: ἔτη κ΄ V   [5] Ἀμένωφις] Grant; cf. Jos. C. Ap. i. 96: Δαμφενοφις V (τοῦ δ᾽ Ἀμένοφις, Jos.)   [6] Ἀκεγχερὴς–α΄] Grant; cf. Jos., ibid.: ἔτη ι΄ μῆνας γ΄ V   [7] Ῥαθῶτις–τοῦτον] Grant; cf. Jos., ibid.: om. V   [8] Ἀκεγχήρης] Grant; cf. Jos. C. Ap. i. 97: Μερχερὴς V   [9] καὶ μετὰ τοῦτον–μῆνας β΄] Otto; cf. Jos. C. Ap. i. 97: μετὰ δὲ τοῦτον Μέσσης Μιαμμοῦ ἔτη ς΄ καὶ μετὰ τοῦτον Ῥαμέσσης ἐνιαυτόν, μῆνας δ΄ καὶ μῆνας β΄ V   [10] Σέθως] Grant; cf. Jos. C. Ap. i. 98: θοῖσσος V   [11] ξ΄] Grant; cf. Jos. C. Ap. i. 231: ι΄ V   [12] γῇ] V: τῇ Gesner   [13] ὁ] Humphry; cf. Jos. C. Ap. i. 102: τὸ V

The Testimony of Manetho

20. Now Moses was the leader of the Jews, as we have already said [III. 9–10], who were expelled from the land of Egypt by king Pharaoh, whose name was Tethmosis. This king is said to have reigned for 25 years and 4 months after the expulsion of the people, as Manetho counts it [Josephus, *C. Ap.* i. 94–7]. And after him Chebron for 13 years; after him Amenophis for 20 years, 7 months; after him his sister Amesse for 21 years, 9 months; after her Mephres for 12 years, 9 months; after him Mephrammouthosis for 25 years, 10 months. And after him Tuthmoses for 9 years, 8 months. And after him Amenophis for 30 years, 10 months; after him Oros for 36 years, 5 months; his daughter Akencheres for 12 years, 1 month; after her Rathotis for 9 years; after him Akencheres for 12 years, 5 months; after him Akencheres for 12 years, 3 months; his son Armais for 4 years, 1 month. And after him Ramesses for a year, 4 months; after him Armesses Miammou for 66 years and 2 months. And after him Amenophis for 19 years, 6 months. His sons Sethos and Ramesses for 60 years; they say these kings had great cavalry strength and naval forces in their time.

The Hebrews, who at that time sojourned in Egypt and had been enslaved by king Tethmosis, already mentioned, built fortified cities for him; these were Peitho and Ramesses and On, which is Heliopolis [cf. Exod. 1:11]. The Hebrews, therefore, are shown to be older than the cities which were then famous in Egypt. These Hebrews were our forefathers, and from them we possess the sacred books which are older than all other writers, as we have already said [III. 1].

The land of Egypt received its name from king Sethos; for Sethos, they say [Josephus, *C. Ap.* i. 102], is called 'Egypt'. The brother of

ὄνομα Ἁρμαῖς·[14] οὗτος Δαναὸς κέκληται ὁ εἰς Ἄργος ἀπὸ Αἰγύπτου παραγενόμενος, οὗ μέμνηται οἱ λοιποὶ συγγραφεῖς ὡς πάνυ ἀρχαίου τυγχάνοντος.

21. Μαναιθὼς δὲ ὁ κατ' Αἰγυπτίους πολλὰ φλυαρήσας, ἔτι μὴν καὶ βλάσφημα εἰπὼν εἴς τε[1] Μωσέα καὶ τοὺς σὺν αὐτῷ Ἑβραίους, ὡς δῆθεν διὰ λέπραν ἐκβληθέντας[2] ἐκ τῆς Αἰγύπτου, οὐχ εὗρεν τὸ ἀκριβὲς τῶν χρόνων εἰπεῖν.[3] ποιμένας μὲν γὰρ αὐτοὺς εἰπὼν καὶ πολεμίους Αἰγυπτίων, τὸ μὲν[4] ποιμένας ἄκων εἶπεν, ἐλεγχόμενος ὑπὸ τῆς ἀληθείας· ἦσαν γὰρ ὄντως ποιμένες οἱ προπάτορες ἡμῶν, οἱ παροικήσαντες ἐν Αἰγύπτῳ, ἀλλ' οὐ λεπροί. παραγενόμενοι γὰρ εἰς τὴν γῆν τὴν καλουμένην Ἰουδαίαν,[5] ἔνθα καὶ μεταξὺ κατῴκησαν, δηλοῦται ᾧ τρόπῳ οἱ ἱερεῖς αὐτῶν διὰ προστάγματος θεοῦ προσκαρτεροῦντες τῷ ναῷ, τότε ἐθεράπευον πᾶσαν νόσον ὥστε καὶ λεπρῶντας καὶ πάντα μῶμον ἰῶντο. ναὸν ᾠκοδόμησεν Σολομὼν ὁ βασιλεὺς τῆς Ἰουδαίας.

Περὶ δὲ τοῦ πεπλανῆσθαι τὸν Μαναιθὼ περὶ τῶν χρόνων ἐκ τῶν ὑπ' αὐτοῦ εἰρημένων δῆλόν ἐστιν· ἀλλὰ καὶ περὶ τοῦ βασιλέως τοῦ ἐκβαλόντος αὐτούς, Φαραὼ τοὔνομα. οὐκέτι γὰρ αὐτῶν ἐβασίλευσεν· καταδιώξας γὰρ Ἑβραίους μετὰ τοῦ στρατεύματος κατεποντίσθη εἰς τὴν ἐρυθρὰν θάλασσαν. ἔτι μὴν καὶ οὓς ἔφη ποιμένας πεπολεμηκέναι τοὺς Αἰγυπτίους ψεύδεται· πρὸ ἐτῶν γάρ λϟγ'[6] ἐξῆλθον ἐκ τῆς Αἰγύπτου καὶ ᾤκησαν ἔκτοτε τὴν χώραν, τὴν ἔτι καὶ νῦν καλουμένην Ἰουδαίαν, πρὸ τοῦ καὶ Δαναὸν εἰς Ἄργος ἀφικέσθαι. ὅτι δὲ τοῦτον ἀρχαιότερον ἡγοῦνται τῶν λοιπῶν κατὰ Ἕλληνας οἱ πλείους, σαφές ἐστιν.

Ὥστε ὁ Μαναιθὼς δύο τάξεις ἄκων τῆς ἀληθείας μεμήνυκεν ἡμῖν διὰ τῶν αὐτοῦ γραμμάτων, πρῶτον μὲν ποιμένας αὐτοὺς ὁμολογήσας, δεύτερον εἰπὼν καὶ τὸ ἐξεληλυθέναι αὐτοὺς ἐκ γῆς Αἰγύπτου· ὥστε καὶ ἐκ τούτων τῶν ἀναγραφῶν δείκνυσθαι προγενέστερον εἶναι τὸν Μωσῆν καὶ τοὺς σὺν αὐτῷ ἐνακοσίους ἢ καὶ χιλίους ἐνιαυτοὺς[7] πρὸ τοῦ Ἰλιακοῦ πολέμου.

[14] Ἁρμαῖς] Otto; cf. Jos. C. Ap. i. 102: Ἁρμαῒν V
21. [1] εἴς τε] Wolf: ὥστε V   [2] ἐκβληθέντας] Ducaeus: ἐκβληθέντος VB: ἐκβληθῆναι P   [3] οὐχ–εἰπεῖν post Αἰγύπτου] transp. Maran: post Αἰγυπτίων V
[4] τὸ μὲν] Humphry: add. γὰρ V   [5] Ἰουδαίαν] Grant; cf. l. 21; III. 22. 1: Ἱεροσόλυμα V   [6] λϟγ'] Grant; cf. Jos. C. Ap. i. 103; Tert. Apol. xix. 3: τριακοσίων δεκατριῶν (= λιγ') V   [7] ἐνιαυτοὺς] P: om. VB

Sethos was named Armais; he was called Danaus and came to Argos from Egypt. Other writers mention him as being exceedingly ancient [i. 103].

Manetho's Errors and Admissions

21. Manetho, who expressed much nonsense in Egyptian fashion and actually uttered outrageous slanders about Moses and the Hebrews with him by claiming that they were expelled from Egypt because of leprosy, was unable to make an exact chronological statement. He called them shepherds and enemies of the Egyptians, for he was forced by the truth; our forefathers who sojourned in Egypt actually were shepherds, but not lepers. When they reached the land called Judaea, where they afterwards settled, it is well known how their priests, devoting themselves to the temple by God's command, at that time cured every disease [cf. Matt. 4: 23] so that they healed lepers and every blemish.[1] Solomon, king of Judaea, built the temple.

The chronological error of Manetho is evident from his own statements. It is also clear in the case of the king who expelled them, Pharaoh by name. For he no longer reigned over them; in his pursuit of the Hebrews he and his army were drowned in the Red Sea. Furthermore, he falsely says that those whom he called shepherds were warring against the Egyptians; they had left Egypt and were inhabiting the land which is still called Judaea, 393 years before Danaus came to Argos. It is well known that most writers consider him more ancient than other persons among the Greeks.[2]

Therefore Manetho has involuntarily admitted two points of truth for us in his writings: first, he admitted that they were shepherds, and second, he said that they came out of the land of Egypt. Therefore from these chronicles it is proved that Moses and those with him are nine hundred or even a thousand years prior to the Trojan war.[2]

21. [1] Cf. Clement, *Hypot.* fr. 12 Stählin.
  [2] Josephus, *C. Ap.* i. 104.

22. Ἀλλὰ καὶ περὶ τοῦ ναοῦ τῆς οἰκοδομῆς τοῦ ἐν Ἰουδαίᾳ, ὃν ᾠκοδόμησεν ὁ βασιλεὺς Σολομὼν μετὰ ἔτη πεντακόσια ἑξήκοντα ἓξ τῆς Αἰγύπτου ἐξοδίας τῶν Ἰουδαίων, παρὰ Τυρίοις ἀναγέγραπται ὡς ὁ ναὸς ᾠκοδόμηται, καὶ ἐν τοῖς ἀρχείοις αὐτῶν πεφύλακται τὰ γράμματα, ἐν αἷς ἀναγραφαῖς εὑρίσκεται γεγονὼς ὁ ναὸς πρὸ τοῦ τοὺς Τυρίους τὴν Καρχηδόνα κτίσαι θᾶττον ἔτεσιν ἑκατὸν τεσσαράκοντα τρισίν,[1] μησὶν ὀκτώ· (ἀνεγράφη ὑπὸ Ἱερώμου τοὔνομα βασιλέως Τυρίων, υἱοῦ δὲ Ἀβειβάλου, διὰ τὸ ἐκ πατρικῆς συνηθείας τὸν Ἱέρωμον γεγενῆσθαι φίλον τοῦ Σολομῶνος, ἅμα καὶ διὰ τὴν ὑπερβάλλουσαν σοφίαν, ἣν ἔσχεν ὁ Σολομών. ἐν γὰρ προβλήμασιν ἀλλήλους συνεχῶς ἐγύμναζον· τεκμήριον δὲ τούτου, καὶ ἀντίγραφα ἐπιστολῶν αὐτῶν φασιν[2] μέχρι τοῦ δεῦρο παρὰ τοῖς Τυρίοις πεφυλαγμένα· γράμματά τε ἀλλήλοις διέπεμπον.)—καθὼς μέμνηται Μένανδρος ὁ Ἐφέσιος, ἱστορῶν περὶ τῆς Τυρίων βασιλείας, λέγων οὕτως· "Τελευτήσαντος γὰρ Ἀβειβάλου" βασιλέως Τυρίων "διεδέξατο τὴν βασιλείαν ὁ υἱὸς αὐτοῦ Ἱέρωμος, ὃς[3] βιώσας ἔτη πεντήκοντα τρία ⟨ἐβασίλευσεν ἔτη τριάκοντα τέσσαρα⟩.[4] τοῦτον δὲ διεδέξατο Βαλεάζωρος,[5] βιώσας ἔτη μγ΄, ὃς ἐβασίλευσεν ἔτη ιζ΄. ⟨μετὰ τοῦτον Ἀβδάστρατος, ὃς βιώσας ἔτη κθ΄ ἐβασίλευσεν ἔτη θ΄.⟩ [6]μετὰ δὲ τοῦτον Μεθουάσταρτος, βιώσας ἔτη νδ΄, ἐβασίλευσεν ἔτη ιβ΄. μετὰ δὲ τοῦτον ὁ ἀδελφὸς αὐτοῦ Ἀθάρυμος, βιώσας ἔτη νη΄, ἐβασίλευσεν ἔτη θ΄. τοῦτον ἀνεῖλεν ὁ ἀδελφὸς αὐτοῦ Ἕλλης[7] τοὔνομα, ὃς βιώσας ἔτη ν΄ ἐβασίλευσεν μῆνας ὀκτώ. τοῦτον ἀνεῖλεν Ἰουθώβαλος, ἱερεὺς τῆς Ἀστάρτης, ὃς βιώσας ἔτη μ΄ ἐβασίλευσεν ἔτη λβ΄.[8] τοῦτον διεδέξατο ὁ υἱὸς αὐτοῦ Βαλέζωρος,[9] ὃς βιώσας ἔτη με΄ ἐβασίλευσεν ἔτη ς΄.[10] υἱὸς δὲ τούτου Μέττηνος, βιώσας ἔτη λβ΄, ἐβασίλευσεν ἔτη κθ΄.[11] τοῦτον διεδέξατο Πυγμαλίων,[12] ὃς βιώσας ἔτη νς΄ ἐβασίλευσεν ἔτη μζ΄.[13] ἐν δὲ τῷ ἑβδόμῳ ἔτει τῆς βασιλείας αὐτοῦ ⟨ἡ

---

22. [1] τεσσαράκοντα τρισίν] Fell; cf. Jos. C. Ap. i. 126 (μγ΄): τριάκοντα τέσσαρσιν VB: τεσσαράκοντα τέσσαρσι P   [2] φασιν] Otto: φησιν V   [3] Ἱέρωμος ὃς] Fell; cf. Jos. C. Ap. i. 117: ἱερωμένος V   [4] ⟨ἐβασίλευσεν–τέσσαρα⟩] Fell; cf. Jos. C. Ap. i. 117: om. V   [5] Βαλεάζωρος] Grant; cf. Jos. C. Ap. i. 121: Βάζωρος V   [6] ⟨μετὰ τοῦτον–ἔτη θ΄⟩] Grant; cf. Jos. C. Ap. i. 122: om. V   [7] Ἕλλης] V: Φέλλης Wolf; cf. Jos. C. Ap. i. 123   [8] λβ΄] Fell; cf. Jos. C. Ap. i. 123: ιβ΄ V   [9] Βαλέζωρος] Grant; cf. Jos. C. Ap. i. 124: Βάζωρος V   [10] ς΄ Grant; cf. Jos. C. Ap. i. 124: ζ΄ V   [11] κθ΄] V: ἔννεα (= θ΄) Jos. C. Ap. i. 124   [12] Πυγμαλίων] Otto: ἐν πυγμαλίων Φυγμαλίουμ V; cf. Φυγμαλίου Jos. C. Ap. i. 125 (cod. L)   [13] μζ΄] Fell; cf. Jos. C. Ap. i. 125: ζ΄ V

The Temple in Jerusalem: Phoenician Chronology

22. But as regards the building of the temple in Judaea which king Solomon built 566 years after the exodus of the Jews from Egypt,[1] it is recorded among the Tyrians how the temple was built, and in their archives the records have been preserved. In these we find that the temple was built 143 years and 8 months before the Tyrians founded Carthage [cf. Josephus, *C. Ap.* i. 108]. These records were made by a certain Hieromos, king of Tyre, son of Abeibalos; because of his father's friendship with Solomon, Hieromos was also his friend, especially because of the extraordinary wisdom which Solomon possessed. They constantly exercised each other in solving problems (the proof of this is found in the copies of their letters, said to be preserved even now in Tyre) and sent letters to each other [cf. Josephus, *C. Ap.* i. 109, 111].

As Menander of Ephesus observes in his history of the Tyrian kingdom, speaking thus [Josephus, *C. Ap.* i. 117, 121–6]:

'At the death of Abeibalos (king of the Tyrians) his son Hieromos succeeded to the throne; he lived 53 years and reigned 34 years. His successor was Beleazoros, who lived 43 years and reigned 17 years. After him, Abdastratos, who lived 29 years and reigned 9 years. After him, Methouastartos, who lived 54 years and reigned 12 years. After him, his brother Atharymos, who lived 58 years and reigned 9 years. He was killed by his brother named Helles, who lived 50 years and reigned 8 months. He was killed by Iouthobalos, priest of Astarte, who lived 40 years and reigned 32 years. He was succeeded by his son Balezoros, who lived 45 years and reigned 6 years. His son was Mettenos, who lived 32 years and reigned 29 years. He was succeeded by Pygmalion, who lived 56 years and

---

22. [1] It is difficult to tell what number Theophilus may have written, for Josephus provides not only 612 (*C. Ap.* ii. 19; *Ant.* xx. 230) but also 592 (*Ant.* viii. 61).

ἀδελφὴ αὐτοῦ⟩[14] εἰς Λιβύην φυγοῦσα πόλιν ᾠκοδόμησεν τὴν μέχρι τοῦ δεῦρο Καρχηδονίαν καλουμένην. συνάγεται οὖν ὁ πᾶς χρόνος ἀπὸ τῆς Ἱερώμου βασιλείας μέχρι Καρχηδόνος κτίσεως ἔτη ρνε′, μῆνες ὀκτώ. τῷ δὲ δωδεκάτῳ ἔτει τῆς Ἱερώμου βασιλείας ἐν Ἱεροσολύμοις ὁ ναὸς ᾠκοδομήθη, ὥστε τὸν πάντα χρόνον γεγενῆσθαι ἀπὸ τῆς τοῦ ναοῦ οἰκοδομῆς μέχρι Καρχηδόνος κτίσεως ἔτη ρμγ′,[15] μῆνες η′."

23. Τῆς μὲν οὖν Φοινίκων καὶ Αἰγυπτίων μαρτυρίας, ὡς ἱστορήκασιν περὶ τῶν καθ' ἡμᾶς χρόνων οἱ συγγράψαντες Μαναιθὼς ὁ Αἰγύπτιος καὶ ὁ Μένανδρος ὁ Ἐφέσιος, ἔτι δὲ καὶ Ἰώσηππος ὁ ἀναγράψας τὸν Ἰουδαϊκὸν πόλεμον τὸν γενόμενον αὐτοῖς ὑπὸ Ῥωμαίων, ἀρκετῶς ἤτω ἡμῖν τὰ εἰρημένα. ἐκ γὰρ τούτων τῶν ἀρχαίων δείκνυται καὶ τὰ τῶν λοιπῶν συγγράμματα ἔσχατα εἶναι τῶν διὰ Μωσέως ἡμῖν δεδομένων γραμμάτων, ἔτι μὴν καὶ τῶν μεταξὺ προφητῶν· ὁ γὰρ ὕστερος τῶν προφητῶν γενόμενος Ζαχαρίας ὀνόματι ἤκμασεν κατὰ τὴν Δαρείου βασιλείαν.

Ἀλλὰ καὶ οἱ νομοθέται πάντες μεταξὺ εὑρίσκονται νομοθετοῦντες. εἰ γάρ τις εἴποι Σόλωνα τὸν Ἀθηναῖον, οὗτος γέγονεν κατὰ τοὺς χρόνους Κύρου καὶ Δαρείου τῶν βασιλέων, κατὰ τὸν χρόνον Ζαχαρίου τοῦ προειρημένου προφήτου, μεταξὺ γεγενημένου πάνυ πολλοῖς ἔτεσιν· ἤτοι καὶ περὶ Λυκούργου ἢ Δράκοντος ἢ Μίνω τῶν νομοθετῶν, τούτων ἀρχαιότητι[1] προάγουσιν αἱ ἱεραὶ βίβλοι, ὅπου γε καὶ τοῦ Διὸς τοῦ Κρητῶν βασιλεύσαντος, ἀλλὰ μὴν καὶ τοῦ Ἰλιακοῦ πολέμου δείκνυται προάγοντα τὰ γράμματα τοῦ θείου νόμου τοῦ διὰ Μωσέως ἡμῖν δεδομένου.

Ἵνα δὲ ἀκριβεστέραν ποιήσωμεν τὴν ἀπόδειξιν τῶν καιρῶν καὶ χρόνων, θεοῦ ἡμῖν παρέχοντος οὐ μόνον τὰ μετὰ κατακλυσμὸν ἱστοροῦντες ἀλλὰ καὶ τὰ πρὸ κατακλυσμοῦ εἰς τὸ καὶ τῶν ἁπάντων κατὰ τὸ δυνατὸν εἰπεῖν ἡμῖν τὸν ἀριθμόν, νυνὶ ποιησόμεθα, ἀναδραμόντες ἐπὶ τὴν ἀνέκαθεν ἀρχὴν τῆς τοῦ κόσμου κτίσεως, ἣν ἀνέγραψεν Μωσῆς ὁ θεράπων τοῦ θεοῦ διὰ πνεύματος ἁγίου. εἰπὼν γὰρ τὰ περὶ κτίσεως καὶ γενέσεως κόσμου, τοῦ πρωτοπλάστου ἀνθρώπου, καὶ τὰ τῶν ἑξῆς γεγενημένων, ἐσήμανεν καὶ τὰ πρὸ κατακλυσμοῦ

[14] ⟨ἡ ἀδελφὴ αὐτοῦ⟩] Maran; cf. Jos. C. Ap. i. 125: om. V   [15] ρμγ′ Wolf; cf. Jos. C. Ap. i. 126: ρλγ′ V
23. [1] τούτων ἀρχαιότητι] Otto: γράφων λέγει τοῖς VB, γράφων τὶς λέγει ἐν τοῖς P

reigned 47 years. In the seventh year of his reign his sister fled to Libya and founded a city still known as Carthage. The total period of time from the reign of Hieromos to the founding of Carthage is 155 years and 8 months. In the twelfth year of the reign of Hieromos the temple in Jerusalem was built, so that the whole time from the building of the temple to the foundation of Carthage is 143 years and 8 months.'

History and Legislation; the True Chronology

23. As for the testimony of the Phoenicians [cf. Josephus, *C. Ap.* i. 127] and the Egyptians, as related concerning our chronology by the historians Manetho the Egyptian and Menander the Ephesian —and further by Josephus, who described the Jewish war which was brought upon them by the Romans—what we have said should suffice. For from these ancient authors it is proved that the writings of the others are later than the scriptures given us through Moses, as well as those of the prophets after him. (The last of the prophets, Zacharias by name, flourished in the reign of Darius.)

Again, all the legislators turn out to have legislated afterwards. For if anyone should mention Solon the Athenian, he lived in the times of the kings Cyrus and Darius and in the time of the prophet Zacharias, just mentioned, who was many years later than Moses. Or if anyone should speak of the legislators Lycurgus or Draco or Minos,[1] the sacred books are more ancient than they, since the scriptures of the divine law given us through Moses actually antedate not only the reign of Zeus in Crete but also the Trojan war.

In order for us to give a more accurate demonstration of periods and times, by God's help—not only recording the events after the deluge but also those before the deluge, so that we can state the total number of all the years as well as possible—we now proceed to do so, going back to the first beginning of the creation of the world, which Moses the minister of God described through the Holy Spirit. For when he spoke of the creation and origin of the world, of the first-formed man, and of the events that came next [II. 10–30], he also indicated the years which passed before the

23. [1] Solon and Lycurgus are mentioned by Josephus, *C. Ap.* ii. 154; for Draco see i. 21; for Minos, ii. 161.

ἔτη γενόμενα. ἐγὼ δ' αἰτοῦμαι χάριν παρὰ τοῦ μόνου θεοῦ, εἰς τὸ τἀληθῆ κατὰ τὸ θέλημα αὐτοῦ πάντα ἀκριβῶς εἰπεῖν, ὅπως καὶ σὺ καὶ πᾶς ὁ τούτοις ἐντυγχάνων ὁδηγῆται ὑπὸ τῆς ἀληθείας καὶ χάριτος αὐτοῦ. ἄρξομαι δὴ πρῶτον ἀπὸ τῶν ἀναγεγραμμένων γενεαλογιῶν, λέγω δὲ ἀπὸ τοῦ πρωτοπλάστου ἀνθρώπου τὴν ἀρχὴν ποιησάμενος.

24. Ἀδὰμ ἕως οὗ ἐτέκνωσεν ἔζησεν ἔτη σλ΄, υἱὸς δὲ τούτου Σὴθ ἔτη σε΄, υἱὸς δὲ τούτου Ἐνῶς ἔτη ρϟ΄, υἱὸς δὲ τούτου Καϊνὰν ἔτη ρο΄, υἱὸς δὲ τούτου Μαλελεὴλ ἔτη ρξε΄,[1] υἱὸς δὲ τούτου Ἰάρεθ ἔτη ρξβ΄, υἱὸς δὲ τούτου Ἐνὼχ ἔτη ρξε΄, υἱὸς δὲ τούτου Μαθουσάλα ἔτη ρξζ΄, υἱὸς δὲ τούτου Λάμεχ ἔτη ρπη΄. τούτῳ δὲ υἱὸς ἐγενήθη ὁ προειρημένος Νῶε, ὃς ἐτέκνωσεν τὸν Σὴμ ὢν ἐτῶν φ΄. ἐπὶ τούτου ἐγένετο ὁ κατακλυσμὸς ὄντος αὐτοῦ ἐτῶν χ΄. τὰ πάντα οὖν μέχρι κατακλυσμοῦ γεγένηται ἔτη ͵βσμβ΄.

Μετὰ δὲ τὸν κατακλυσμὸν εὐθέως ὁ Σὴμ ὢν ἐτῶν ρ΄ ἐτέκνωσεν τὸν Ἀρφαξάθ, Ἀρφαξὰθ δὲ ἐτέκνωσεν Σαλὰ ὢν ἐτῶν ρλε΄, ὁ δὲ Σαλὰ ἐτέκνωσεν ὢν ἐτῶν ρλ΄, τούτου δὲ υἱὸς Ἕβερ ὢν ἐτῶν ρλδ΄, ἀφ' οὗ καὶ τὸ γένος αὐτῶν Ἑβραῖοι προσηγορεύθησαν, τούτου δὲ υἱὸς Φαλὲγ ὢν ἐτῶν ρλ΄, τούτου δὲ υἱὸς Ῥαγαῦ ὢν ἐτῶν ρλβ΄, τούτου δὲ υἱὸς Σερούχ ὢν ἐτῶν ρλ΄, τούτου δὲ υἱὸς Ναχὼρ ὢν ἔτων οε΄, τούτου δὲ υἱὸς Θάρρα ὢν ἔτων ο΄, τούτου δὲ υἱὸς Ἀβραὰμ ὁ πατριάρχης ἡμῶν ἐτέκνωσεν τὸν Ἰσαὰκ ὢν ἐτῶν ρ΄. Γίνονται οὖν μέχρι Ἀβραὰμ ἔτη ͵γσοη΄.

Ἰσαὰκ ὁ προειρημένος ἕως τεκνογονίας ἔζησεν ἔτη ξ΄, ὃς ἐγέννησεν τὸν Ἰακώβ· ἔζησεν ὁ Ἰακὼβ ἕως τῆς μετοικησίας τῆς ἐν Αἰγύπτῳ γενομένης, ἧς ἐπάνω προειρήκαμεν, ἔτη ρλ΄, ἡ δὲ παροίκησις τῶν Ἑβραίων ἐν Αἰγύπτῳ ἐγενήθη ἔτη υλ΄, καὶ μετὰ τὸ ἐξελθεῖν αὐτοὺς ἐκ γῆς Αἰγύπτου ἐν τῇ ἐρήμῳ καλουμένῃ διέτριψαν ἔτη μ΄. γίνεται οὖν τὰ πάντα ἔτη ͵γλη΄,[2] ᾧ καιρῷ τοῦ Μωσέως τελευτήσαντος διεδέξατο ἄρχειν Ἰησοῦς υἱὸς Ναυῆ, ὃς προέστη αὐτῶν ἔτεσιν κζ΄.

Μετὰ δὲ τὸν Ἰησοῦν τοῦ λαοῦ παραβάντος ἀπὸ τῶν ἐντολῶν τοῦ θεοῦ ἐδούλευσαν βασιλεῖ Μεσοποταμίας Χουσαράθων ὄνομα ἔτεσιν ὀκτώ. εἶτα μετανοήσαντος τοῦ λαοῦ κριταὶ ἐγενήθησαν αὐτοῖς.

24. [1] ρξε΄] P; cf. Gen. 5: 15: ρξ΄ V   [2] ͵γλη΄] Fell: γλη΄ V

deluge. I ask favour from the only God that I may speak the whole truth exactly, in accordance with his will, so that you and everyone who reads these books may be led by his truth and grace. I shall begin, then, from the recorded genealogies, starting from the first-formed man.

Biblical Chronology

From Adam to Samuel

24. Adam until he had issue lived 230 years, his son Seth 205 years, his son Enos 190 years, his son Kainan 170 years, his son Maleleel 165 years, his son Iareth 162 years, his son Enoch 165 years, his son Mathousala 167 years, his son Lamech 188 years. His son was the previously mentioned Noah [III. 19], who begot Sem at the age of 500. In the time of Noah was the deluge, when he was 600 years old. The total to the deluge, then, is 2,242 years.

Immediately after the deluge Sem, who was 100 years old, begot Arphaxath; Arphaxath, 135 years old, begot Sala; Sala, 130 years old, had issue; his son Heber, from whom the Hebrew race took its name, was 134 years old. His son Phaleg was 130 years old, his son Ragau 132, his son Seruch 130, his son Nachor 75, his son Tharra 70; his son Abraham, our patriarch, was 100 years old when he begot Isaac. Up to Abraham, then, there were 3,278 years.

The Isaac just mentioned lived 60 years until he had issue and begot Jacob; Jacob lived 130 years before the migration to Egypt which we have already mentioned [III. 20-1]. The sojourning of the Hebrews in Egypt lasted 430 years, and after their exodus from the land of Egypt they lived in what is called the desert for 40 years. The total, then, is 3,938 years to the time when Moses died and Jesus the son of Nave succeeded him.

He was their leader for 27 years. After Jesus, the people transgressed from the commandments of God and were slaves of the king of Mesopotamia, Chousarathon by name, for 8 years. Then,

Γοθονεὴλ ἔτεσιν τεσσαράκοντα, Ἐκλὼν ἔτεσιν ιη΄, Ἀὼθ ἔτεσιν η΄. ἔπειτα πταισάντων αὐτῶν ἀλλόφυλοι ἐκράτησαν ἔτεσιν κ΄. ἔπειτα Δεββώρα ἔκρινεν αὐτοὺς ἔτεσιν μ΄· ἔπειτα Μαδιανῖται ἐκράτησαν αὐτῶν ἔτεσιν ζ΄. εἶτα Γεδεὼν ἔκρινεν αὐτοὺς ἔτεσιν μ΄, Ἀβιμέλεχ ἔτεσιν γ΄, Θωλὰ ἔτεσιν κγ΄,³ Ἰαεὶρ ἔτεσιν κβ΄. ἔπειτα Φυλιστιεὶμ καὶ Ἀμμανῖται ἐκράτησαν αὐτῶν ἔτεσιν ιη΄. εἶτα Ἰεφθάε ἔκρινεν αὐτοὺς ἔτεσιν ἕξ, Ἐσβὼν ἔτεσιν ζ΄, Αἰλὼν ἔτεσιν ι΄, Ἀβδὼν ἔτεσιν η΄. ἔπειτα ἀλλόφυλοι ἐκράτησαν αὐτῶν ἔτεσιν μ΄. εἶτα Σαμψὼν ἔκρινεν αὐτοὺς ἔτεσιν κ΄. ἔπειτα εἰρήνη ἐν αὐτοῖς ἐγένετο ἔτεσιν μ΄. εἶτα Σαμηρὰ ἔκρινεν αὐτοὺς ἐνιαυτόν, Ἠλὶς ἔτεσιν κ΄, Σαμουὴλ ἔτεσιν ιβ΄.

25. Μετὰ δὲ τοὺς κριτὰς ἐγένοντο βασιλεῖς ἐν αὐτοῖς, πρῶτος ὀνόματι Σαούλ, ὃς ἐβασίλευσεν ἔτη κ΄, ἔπειτα Δαυὶδ ὁ πρόγονος ἡμῶν ἔτη μ΄. γίνεται οὖν μέχρι τῆς τοῦ Δαυὶδ βασιλείας τὰ πάντα ἔτη υϟη΄.¹

Μετὰ δὲ τούτους ἐβασιλεύει Σολομών, ὁ καὶ τὸν ναὸν τὸν ἐν Ἱεροσολύμοις κατὰ βουλὴν θεοῦ πρῶτος οἰκοδομήσας,² δι' ἐτῶν μ΄, μετὰ δὲ τοῦτον Ῥοβοὰμ ἔτεσιν ιζ΄, καὶ μετὰ τοῦτον Ἀβίας ἔτεσιν ζ΄, καὶ μετὰ τοῦτον Ἀσα ἔτεσιν μα΄, καὶ μετὰ τοῦτον Ἰωσαφὰτ ἔτεσιν κε΄, μετὰ δὲ τοῦτον Ἰωρὰμ ἔτη η΄, μετὰ δὲ τοῦτον Ὀχοζίας ἐνιαυτόν, καὶ μετὰ τοῦτον Γοθολία³ ἔτεσιν ἕξ, μετὰ δὲ ταύτην Ἰωὰς⁴ ἔτεσιν μ΄, καὶ μετὰ τοῦτον Ἀμεσίας ἔτεσιν λθ΄, καὶ μετὰ τοῦτον Ὀζίας ἔτεσιν νβ΄, μετὰ δὲ τοῦτον Ἰωαθὰμ ἔτεσιν ις΄, μετὰ δὲ τοῦτον Ἄχαζ ἔτεσιν ιζ΄, καὶ μετὰ τοῦτον Ἐζεκίας ἔτεσιν κθ΄, μετὰ δὲ τοῦτον Μανασσὴς ἔτεσιν νε΄, μετὰ δὲ τοῦτον Ἀμὼς ἔτεσιν β΄, μετὰ δὲ τοῦτον Ἰωσίας ἔτεσιν λα΄, μετὰ δὲ τοῦτον Ὠχὰς μῆνας γ΄, μετὰ δὲ τοῦτον Ἰωακεὶμ ἔτη ια΄, ἔπειτα Ἰωακεὶμ ἕτερος μῆνας γ΄ ἡμέρας ι΄, μετὰ δὲ τοῦτον Σεδεκίας ἔτη ια΄. μετὰ δὲ τούτους τοὺς βασιλεῖς, διαμένοντος τοῦ λαοῦ ἐπὶ τοῖς ἁμαρτήμασιν καὶ μὴ μετανοοῦντος, κατὰ προφητείαν Ἰερεμίου ἀνέβη εἰς τὴν Ἰουδαίαν βασιλεὺς Βαβυλῶνος, ὄνομα Ναβουχοδονόσορ. οὗτος μετῴκησεν τὸν λαὸν τῶν Ἰουδαίων εἰς Βαβυλῶνα καὶ τὸν ναὸν κατέστρεψεν, ὃν ᾠκοδομήκει Σολομών. ἐν δὲ τῇ μετοικεσίᾳ Βαβυλῶνος, ὁ λαὸς ἐποίησεν ἔτη ο΄.

³ κγ΄] Fell; cf. Iudic. 10 : 2 : κβ΄ V
25. ¹ υϟη΄] Fell: υλς΄ V　　² οἰκοδομήσας] Humphry: ἐν Ἱεροσολύμοις ᾠκοδόμησεν (οἰκοδομήσας V²) V　　³ Γοθολία] Fell; cf. 4 Regn. 11 : 1 : Γοθονιὴλ V　　⁴ ταύτην Ἰωὰς] Fell: τοῦτον Ἰωσίας V

when the people repented, they were ruled by judges: Gothoneel for 40 years, Eklon for 18 years, and Aoth for 8 years. Then, when they sinned, foreigners governed them for 20 years. Then Debbora judged them for 40 years. Then the Midianites governed them for 7 years. Then Gideon judged them for 40 years, Abimelech for 3 years, Thola for 23 years, Iaeir for 22 years. Then the Phylistieim and the Ammanites governed them for 18 years. Then Jephthah judged them for 6 years, Esbon for 7 years, Ailon for 10 years, Abdon for 8 years. Then foreigners governed them for 40 years. Then Samson judged them for 20 years. Then there was peace among them for 40 years.[1] Then Samera judged them for one year,[2] Eli for 20 years, Samuel for 12 years.

From the Kings through the Exile

25. After the judges there were kings among them; the first was named Saul, who reigned 20 years; then David our ancestor, 40 years. The total to the reign of David, then, is 498 years.

After these Solomon, who first built, in accordance with the will of God, the temple in Jerusalem, reigned 40 years, and after him Roboam for 17 years, and after him Abias for 7 years, and after him Asa for 41 years, and after him Iosaphat for 25 years, and after him Ioram for 8 years, and after him Ochozias for a year, and after him Gotholia for 6 years, and after her Ioas for 40 years, and after him Amesias for 39 years, and after him Ozias for 52 years, and after him Ioatham for 16 years, and after him Achaz for 17 years, and after him Ezekias for 29 years, and after him Manasses for 55 years, and after him Amos for 2 years, and after him Iosias for 31 years, and after him Ochas for 3 months, and after him Ioakeim for 11 years; then another Ioakeim for 3 months and 10 days; and after him Sedekias for 11 years. After these kings, since the people remained in their sins and did not repent, in accordance with the prophecy of Jeremiah [6: 22; 16: 15] a king of Babylon named Nabouchodonosor went up to Judaea. He transferred the people of the Jews to Babylon and destroyed the temple which Solomon had built. The people remained in the

---

24. [1] This period of 'peace' seems necessary to reach a total for Joshua and the judges (438 years) comparable to the '450 years' of Acts 13: 19. The forty years may come from the years missing from Eli and Saul (see page xxiv).

[2] Samera may be the Samegar of Judges 3: 31, assigned a year in the *Chronography* of Julius Africanus; cf. M. J. Routh, *Reliquiae Sacrae* (ed. 2, Oxford, 1846), ii. 281.

γίνεται οὖν μέχρι τῆς παροικεσίας ἐν γῇ Βαβυλῶνος τὰ πάντα ἔτη υ̅ν̅δ̅ μῆνες ϛ′ ἡμέραι ι′.

Ὃν τρόπον δὲ ὁ θεὸς προεῖπεν διὰ Ἰερεμίου τοῦ προφήτου τὸν λαὸν αἰχμαλωτισθῆναι εἰς Βαβυλῶνα, οὕτως προεσήμανεν καὶ τὸ πάλιν ἐπανελθεῖν αὐτοὺς εἰς τὴν γῆν αὐτῶν μετὰ ο′ ἔτη. τελειουμένων οὖν ο′[5] ἐτῶν γίνεται Κῦρος βασιλεὺς Περσῶν, ὃς κατὰ τὴν προφητείαν Ἰερεμίου δευτέρῳ ἔτει τῆς βασιλείας αὐτοῦ ἐκήρυξεν κελεύων δι' ἐγγράφων τοὺς Ἰουδαίους πάντας, τοὺς ὄντας ἐν τῇ βασιλείᾳ αὐτοῦ ἐπιστρέφειν εἰς τὴν ἑαυτῶν[6] χώραν καὶ τῷ θεῷ ἀνοικοδομεῖν τὸν ναόν, ὃν καθῃρήκει βασιλεὺς Βαβυλῶνος ὁ προειρημένος. πρὸς τούτοις δὲ ὁ Κῦρος κατ' ἐγκέλευσιν τοῦ θεοῦ προσέταξεν Σαβεσσάρῳ καὶ Μιθριδάτῃ, τοῖς ἰδίοις σωματοφύλαξιν, τὰ σκεύη τὰ ἐκ τοῦ ναοῦ τοῦ τῆς Ἰουδαίας ληφθέντα ὑπὸ τοῦ Ναβουχοδονόσορ ἀποκομισθῆναι καὶ ἀποτεθῆναι εἰς τὸν ναόν. ἐν τῷ οὖν δευτέρῳ ἔτει Κύρου[7] πληροῦται τὰ ο′ ἔτη, τὰ προειρημένα ὑπὸ τοῦ Ἰερεμίου.

26. Ἐντεῦθεν ὁρᾶν ἔστιν πῶς ἀρχαιότερα καὶ ἀληθέστερα δείκνυται τὰ ἱερὰ γράμματα τὰ καθ' ἡμᾶς εἶναι τῶν καθ' Ἕλληνας καὶ Αἰγυπτίους, ἢ εἰ καί τινας ἑτέρους ἱστοριογράφους. ἤτοι γὰρ Ἡρόδοτος καὶ Θουκυδίδης ἢ καὶ Ξενοφῶν ἢ ὅπως οἱ ἄλλοι ἱστοριογράφοι, οἱ πλείους ἤρξαντο σχεδὸν ἀπὸ τῆς Κύρου καὶ Δαρείου βασιλείας ἀναγράφειν, μὴ ἐξισχύσαντες τῶν παλαιῶν καὶ προτέρων χρόνων τὸ ἀκριβὲς εἰπεῖν. τί γὰρ μέγα ἔφασαν εἰ περὶ Δαρείου καὶ Κύρου τῶν κατὰ βαρβάρους βασιλέων εἶπον, ἢ κατὰ Ἕλληνας Ζωπύρου καὶ Ἱππίου, ἢ τοὺς Ἀθηναίων καὶ Λακεδαιμονίων πολέμους, ἢ τὰς Ξέρξου πράξεις ἢ Παυσανίου τοῦ ἐν τῷ τεμένει τῆς Ἀθηνᾶς λιμῷ κινδυνεύσαντος διαφθαρῆναι, ἢ τὰ περὶ Θεμιστοκλέα καὶ τὸν πόλεμον τὸν Πελοποννησίων, ἢ τὰ περὶ Ἀλκιβιάδην καὶ Θρασύβουλον;

Οὐ γὰρ πρόκειται ἡμῖν ὕλη πολυλογίας, ἀλλὰ εἰς τὸ φανερῶσαι τὴν τῶν χρόνων ἀπὸ καταβολῆς κόσμου ποσότητα καὶ ἐλέγξαι τὴν ματαιοπονίαν καὶ φλυαρίαν τῶν συγγραφέων, ὅτι οὐκ εἰσὶν ἐτῶν οὔτε δισμυρίαι μυριάδες, ὡς Πλάτων ἔφη, καὶ ταῦτα ἀπὸ κατακλυσμοῦ ἕως τῶν αὐτοῦ χρόνων τοσαῦτα ἔτη γεγενῆσθαι δογματίζων, οὔτε

[5] ο′] Fell: ν′ VB: πεντήκοντα P: λ′ Otto [6] ἑαυτῶν] P: ἑαυτοῦ VB
[7] Κύρου] Fell: Δαρείου VBP

Babylonian captivity for 70 years. The total, then, to the sojourning in the land of Babylon is 4,954 years, 6 months, and 10 days.

Just as God foretold through the prophet Jeremiah that the people would be led captive to Babylon, so he indicated in advance that they would come back again to their own land after 70 years. When 70 years were past, Cyrus was king of the Persians, and in accordance with the prophecy of Jeremiah he issued written decrees in the second year of his reign, commanding all the Jews who were in his kingdom to return to their own land and rebuild for God the temple which the previously mentioned king of Babylon had demolished. In addition to these decrees, in accordance with the injunction of God Cyrus commanded Sabessaros and Mithridates [cf. 2 Esd. 1 : 8], his bodyguards, to restore the vessels taken out of the temple of Judaea by Nabouchodonosor and replace them in the temple. In the second year of Cyrus, then, the 70 years predicted by Jeremiah were completed.

The Sacred Books are Superior to those of Historians

26. It is obvious how our sacred writings are proved to be more ancient and more true than the writings of Greeks and Egyptians or any other historiographers. For most writers, such as Herodotus and Thucydides or Xenophon and the other historiographers, begin their accounts at about the reigns of Cyrus and Darius, since they are unable to make accurate statements about the ancient times prior to them.[1] What remarkable information did they provide if they spoke of the barbarian kings Darius and Cyrus or, on the Greek side, of Zopyrus and Hippias,[2] or the wars of Athenians and Spartans, or the deeds of Xerxes or of Pausanias, who almost died of hunger in the shrine of Athena,[3] or the events related to Themistocles and the Peloponnesian war, or those concerning Alcibiades and Thrasybulus?[4]

Our concern is not with material for loquacity but with setting forth the number of years from the creation of the world and with exposing the pointless labour and nonsense of these writers. There are not two myriads of myriads of years, even though Plato said that such a period had elapsed between the deluge and his own

---

26. [1] Theophilus' model is Josephus (*C. Ap.* i. 66), who says that neither Herodotus nor Thucydides mentioned Rome, already powerful; cf. III. 27.

[2] Theophilus apparently has in mind the Zopyrus who deserted from the Persians to Athens (Herodotus iii. 160) and the Greek tyrant Hippias (Thucydides vi. 59).

[3] Pausanias was starved in the temple but taken outside to die (Thucydides i. 134).

[4] Alcibiades and Thrasybulus are mentioned together in Thucydides viii. 81.

μὴν ιε΄ μυριάδες καὶ ͵γοε΄ ἔτη, κατὰ προειρήκαμεν Ἀπολλώνιον τὸν Αἰγύπτιον ἱστορεῖν· οὐδὲ ἀγένητος ὁ κόσμος ἐστὶν καὶ αὐτοματισμὸς τῶν πάντων, καθὼς Πυθαγόρας καὶ οἱ λοιποὶ πεφλυαρήκασιν, ἀλλὰ μὲν οὖν γενητὸς καὶ προνοίᾳ διοικεῖται ὑπὸ τοῦ ποιήσαντος τὰ πάντα θεοῦ· καὶ ὁ πᾶς χρόνος καὶ τὰ ἔτη δείκνυται τοῖς[1] βουλομένοις πείθεσθαι τῇ ἀληθείᾳ. μήπως οὖν δόξωμεν μέχρι Κύρου δεδηλωκέναι, τῶν δὲ μεταξὺ χρόνων ἀμελεῖν, ὡς μὴ ἔχοντες ἀποδεῖξαι, θεοῦ παρέχοντος καὶ τῶν ἑξῆς χρόνων τὴν τάξιν πειράσομαι κατὰ τὸ δυνατὸν ἐξηγήσασθαι.

27. Κύρου οὖν βασιλεύσαντος ἔτεσιν κη΄[1] καὶ ἀναιρεθέντος ὑπὸ Τομύριδος ἐν Μασσαγετίᾳ,[2] τότε οὔσης ὀλυμπιάδος ἑξηκοστῆς δευτέρας· ἔκτοτε ἤδη οἱ Ῥωμαῖοι ἐμεγαλύνοντο τοῦ θεοῦ κρατύνοντος αὐτούς, ἐκτισμένης τῆς Ῥώμης ὑπὸ Ῥωμύλου, τοῦ παιδὸς ἱστορουμένου Ἄρεως καὶ Ἰλίας, ὀλυμπιάδι ζ΄, τῇ πρὸ ι΄ καὶ α΄[3] καλανδῶν Μαίων, τοῦ ἐνιαυτοῦ τότε δεκαμήνου ἀριθμουμένου· τοῦ οὖν Κύρου τελευτήσαντος, ὡς ἔφθημεν εἰρηκέναι, ὀλυμπιάδι ἑξηκοστῇ καὶ δευτέρᾳ, γίνεται ὁ[4] καιρὸς ἀπὸ κτίσεως Ῥώμης ἔτη σκ΄, ᾧ καὶ Ῥωμαίων ἦρξεν Ταρκύνιος Σούπερβος τοὔνομα, ὃς πρῶτος ἐξώρισεν Ῥωμαίους τινὰς καὶ παῖδας διέφθειρεν καὶ σπάδοντας ἐγχωρίους ἐποίησεν· ἔτι μὴν καὶ τὰς παρθένους διαφθείρων πρὸς γάμον ἐδίδου. διὸ οἰκείως Σούπερβος ἐκλήθη τῇ ῥωμαϊκῇ γλώσσῃ· ἑρμηνεύεται δὲ ὑπερήφανος. αὐτὸς γὰρ πρῶτος ἐδογμάτισε τοὺς ἀσπαζομένους αὐτὸν ὑπὸ ἑτέρου ἀντασπάζεσθαι. ὃς ἐβασίλευσεν ἔτεσιν κε΄.

Μεθ᾽ ὃν ἦρξαν ἐνιαύσιοι ὕπατοι, χιλίαρχοι ἢ ἀγορανόμοι ἔτεσιν υξγ΄,[5] ὧν τὰ ὀνόματα καταλέγειν πολὺ καὶ περισσὸν ἡγούμεθα. εἰ γάρ τις βούλεται μαθεῖν, ἐκ τῶν ἀναγραφῶν εὑρήσει ὧν ἀνέγραψεν Χρύσερως ὁ νομεγκλάτωρ, ἀπελεύθερος γενόμενος Μ. Αὐρηλίου Οὐήρου, ὃς ἀπὸ κτίσεως Ῥώμης μέχρι τελευτῆς τοῦ ἰδίου πάτρωνος αὐτοκράτορος Οὐήρου σαφῶς πάντα ἀνέγραψεν καὶ τὰ ὀνόματα καὶ τοὺς χρόνους.

26. [1] τοῖς] Maran: τούτοις V
27. [1] κη΄] Jacoby: κθ΄ Fell: τριάκοντα ὀκτώ V   [2] Τομύριδος ἐν Μασσαγετίᾳ] Fell: μυριάδος ἐν μεσσαγγίαι V   [3] ι΄ καὶ α΄] Fell: ι΄ καὶ ζ΄ V   [4] ὁ] Grant: ὅτε VP: om. B   [5] υξγ΄] Jacoby: υνγ΄ V

time; nor are there 153,075 years, as we have already stated to be the view of Apollonius the Egyptian [III. 16]. The world is not uncreated nor is there spontaneous production of everything, as Pythagoras and the others have babbled [III. 7]; instead, the world is created and is providentially governed by the God who made everything [III. 9]. And the whole period of time and the years can be demonstrated to those who wish to learn the truth. So that it may not be thought that I have presented matters down to Cyrus but am neglecting the subsequent periods as being unable to provide evidence, by God's help I shall try to set forth as well as possible an orderly account of the rest of the times.

Roman Chronology

27. After Cyrus had reigned for 28 years he was killed by Tomyris in Massagetia [cf. Herodotus i. 214]; it was then the 62nd Olympiad. At that time the Romans were already becoming powerful because God was making them strong. Rome had been founded by Romulus, said to have been the son of Ares and Ilia, in the 7th Olympiad and on the 11th day before the Kalends of May on the basis of a ten-month calendar. When Cyrus died, as we have just said, in the 62nd Olympiad, two hundred and twenty years had elapsed from the foundation of Rome to the beginning of the reign over the Romans by Tarquin, surnamed Superbus, who was the first to exile Romans and corrupt boys and make eunuchs of natives; in addition, he would defile virgins and marry them off. For this reason he was rightly called Superbus, which in Latin means 'haughty': he was the first to decree that those who saluted him should have their salutation answered by someone else. He reigned for 25 years.

After him came the rule of consuls appointed annually with tribunes and aediles and this lasted for 463 years; we regard listing their names as time-consuming and unnecessary. If anyone wants to learn them, he can find them in the records compiled by Chryseros the Nomenclator, a freedman of M. Aurelius Verus. He lucidly compiled a record of everything, with names and dates, from the foundation of Rome to the death of his patron the emperor Verus.

Ἐκράτησαν οὖν Ῥωμαίων ἐνιαύσιοι, ὥς φαμεν, ἔτεσιν υξγ΄.[6] ἔπειτα οὕτως ἦρξαν οἱ αὐτοκράτορες καλούμενοι· πρῶτος Γάϊος Ἰούλιος, ὃς ἐβασίλευσεν ἔτη γ΄ μῆνας ζ΄[7] ἡμέρας ἕξ. ἔπειτα Αὔγουστος ἔτη νς΄ μῆνας δ΄ ἡμέραν μίαν. Τιβέριος ἔτη κβ΄ ⟨μῆνας ς΄ ἡμέρας κς΄⟩.[8] εἶτα Γάϊος ἕτερος ἔτη γ΄ μῆνας ι΄[9] ἡμέρας ζ΄. Κλαύδιος ἔτη ιγ΄[10] μῆνας η΄ ἡμέρας κ΄.[11] Νέρων ἔτη ιγ΄ μῆνας ζ΄ ἡμέρας κζ΄.[12] Γάλβας μῆνας[13] ἑπτὰ ἡμέρας ς΄. Ὄθων μῆνας γ΄ ἡμέρας ε΄. Οὐϊτέλλιος μῆνας η΄ ἡμέρας β΄.[14] Οὐεσπασιανὸς ἔτη θ΄ μῆνας ια΄ ἡμέρας κβ΄. Τίτος ἔτη β΄ μῆνας β΄ ἡμέρας κ΄.[15] Δομετιανὸς ἔτη ιε΄ ἡμέρας ε΄.[16] Νερούας ἐνιαυτὸν μῆνας δ΄ ἡμέρας ι΄. Τραϊανὸς ἔτη ιθ΄ μῆνας ἓξ ἡμέρας ιδ΄.[17] Ἁδριανὸς ἔτη κ΄ μῆνας ι΄ ἡμέρας κη΄. Ἀντωνῖνος ἔτη κβ΄ μῆνας ζ΄ ἡμέρας κς΄.[18] Οὐῆρος ἔτη ιθ΄ ἡμέρας ι΄. γίνεται οὖν ὁ χρόνος τῶν Καισάρων μέχρι Οὐήρου αὐτοκράτορος τελευτῆς ἔτη σκε΄.[19] ἀπὸ οὖν τῆς Κύρου ἀρχῆς μέχρι τελευτῆς[20] αὐτοκράτορος Οὐήρου, οὗ προειρήκαμεν, ὁ πᾶς χρόνος συνάγεται ἔτη ψμα΄.[21]

28. Ἀπὸ δὲ καταβολῆς κόσμου ὁ πᾶς χρόνος κεφαλαιωδῶς οὕτως κατάγεται. ἀπὸ κτίσεως κόσμου ἕως κατακλυσμοῦ ἐγένοντο ἔτη ͵βσμβ΄. ἀπὸ δὲ τοῦ κατακλυσμοῦ ἕως τεκνογονίας Ἀβραὰμ τοῦ προπάτορος ἡμῶν ἔτη ͵αλς΄. ἀπὸ δὲ Ἰσαὰκ τοῦ παιδὸς Ἀβραὰμ ἕως οὗ ὁ λαὸς σὺν Μωσῇ ἐν τῇ ἐρήμῳ διέτριβεν ἔτη χζ΄. ἀπὸ δὲ τῆς Μωσέως τελευτῆς, ἀρχῆς Ἰησοῦ υἱοῦ Ναυῆ, μέχρι τελευτῆς Δαυὶδ τοῦ πατριάρχου ἔτη υ϶η΄. ἀπὸ δὲ τῆς τελευτῆς Δαυίδ, βασιλείας δὲ Σολομῶνος, μέχρι τῆς παροικίας τοῦ λαοῦ ἐν γῇ Βαβυλῶνος ἔτη φιη΄ μῆνες ς΄[1] ἡμέραι ι΄. ἀπὸ δὲ τῆς Κύρου ἀρχῆς μέχρι αὐτοκράτορος Αὐρηλίου Οὐήρου τελευτῆς ἔτη ψμα΄.[2] Ὁμοῦ ἀπὸ κτίσεως

[6] υξγ΄] Jacoby: υνγ΄ V   [7] μῆνας ζ΄] Grant: μῆνας δ΄ V   [8] ⟨μῆνας ς΄ ἡμέρας κς΄⟩] Grant: om. V   [9] μῆνας ι΄] Grant: μῆνας η΄ V   [10] ἔτη ιγ΄] Otto: ἔτη κγ΄ V   [11] ἡμέρας κ΄] Grant: ἡμέρας κδ΄ V   [12] μῆνας ζ΄ ἡμέρας κζ΄] Grant: μῆνας ς΄ ἡμέρας κη΄ V   [13] Γάλβας μῆνας] Otto: Γάλβας ἔτη β΄ μῆνας V   [14] μῆνας η΄ ἡμέρας β΄] Grant: μῆνας ς΄ ἡμέρας κβ΄ V   [15] μῆνας β΄ ἡμέρας κ΄] Grant: ἡμέρας κβ΄ V   [16] ἡμέρας ε΄] Grant: μῆνας ε΄ ἡμέρας ς΄ V   [17] ἡμέρας ιδ΄] Grant: ἡμέρας ις΄ V   [18] ἡμέρας κς΄] Grant: ἡμέρας ς΄ V   [19] σκε΄] Otto: κη΄ VB: τκς΄ P   [20] ἀρχῆς μέχρι τελευτῆς] Grant: τελευτῆς Ῥωμαίων δὲ ἀρχῆς Ταρκυνίου Σουπέρβου μέχρι τελευτῆς V   [21] ψμα΄] Otto: ψμδ΄ V
28. [1] μῆνες ς΄] Otto: μῆνες γ΄ V   [2] ψμα΄] Otto: ψμδ΄ V

Magistrates appointed annually ruled the Romans, as we are saying, for 463 years. Then came the reigns of those who are called emperors: first Gaius Julius, who reigned for 3 years, 7 months, 6 days. Then Augustus for 56 years, 4 months, 1 day. Tiberius for 22 years, 6 months, 26 days. Then another Gaius for 3 years, 10 months, 7 days. Claudius for 13 years, 8 months, 20 days. Nero for 13 years, 7 months, 27 days. Galba for 7 months, 6 days. Otho for 3 months, 5 days. Vitellius for 8 months, 2 days. Vespasian for 9 years, 11 months, 22 days. Titus for 2 years, 2 months, 20 days. Domitian for 15 years, 5 days. Nerva for 1 year, 4 months, 10 days. Trajan for 19 years, 6 months, 14 days. Hadrian for 20 years, 10 months, 28 days. Antoninus for 22 years, 7 months, 26 days. Verus for 19 years, 10 days. The period of the Caesars to the death of the emperor Verus is thus 225 years, and from the reign of Cyrus to the death of the aforementioned emperor Verus the total is 741 years.

Summary

28. From the creation of the world the whole time may be summed up as follows: from the creation of the world to the deluge, 2,242 years; from the deluge to the time when our forefather Abraham had issue, 1,036 years; from Isaac the child of Abraham until the people stayed in the desert with Moses, 660 years; from the death of Moses and the reign of Jesus son of Nave to the death of the patriarch David, 498 years; from the death of David and the reign of Solomon to the sojourning of the people in the land of Babylon, 518 years, 6 months, 10 days; from the reign of Cyrus to the death of the emperor Aurelius Verus, 741 years. The total number of

κόσμου συνάγονται τὰ πάντα ἔτη ͵εχϟε΄[3] καὶ οἱ ἐπιτρέχοντες μῆνες καὶ ἡμέραι.

29. Τῶν οὖν χρόνων καὶ τῶν εἰρημένων ἁπάντων συνηρασμένων,[1] ὁρᾶν ἔστιν τὴν ἀρχαιότητα τῶν προφητικῶν γραμμάτων καὶ τὴν θειότητα τοῦ παρ' ἡμῖν λόγου, ὅτι οὐ πρόσφατος ὁ λόγος, οὔτε μὴν τὰ καθ' ἡμᾶς, ὡς οἴονταί τινες, μυθώδη καὶ ψευδῆ ἐστιν, ἀλλὰ μὲν οὖν ἀρχαιότερα καὶ ἀληθέστερα.

Καὶ γὰρ Βήλου τοῦ Ἀσσυρίων βασιλεύσαντος καὶ Κρόνου τοῦ Τιτᾶνος Θάλλος μέμνηται, φάσκων τὸν Βῆλον πεπολεμηκέναι σὺν τοῖς Τιτᾶσι πρὸς τὸν Δία καὶ τοὺς σὺν αὐτῷ θεοὺς λεγομένους, ἔνθα φησίν, "Καὶ Ὤγυγος[2] ἡττηθεὶς ἔφυγεν εἰς Ταρτησσόν, τότε μὲν τῆς χώρας ἐκείνης Ἀκτῆς κληθείσης, νυνὶ δὲ Ἀττικῆς προσαγορευομένης, ἧς Ὤγυγος[3] τότε ἦρξεν." καὶ τὰς λοιπὰς δὲ χώρας καὶ πόλεις ἀφ' ὧν τὰς προσωνυμίας ἔσχον, οὐκ ἀναγκαῖον ἡγούμεθα καταλέγειν, μάλιστα πρὸς σὲ τὸν ἐπιστάμενον τὰς ἱστορίας. ὅτι μὲν οὖν ἀρχαιότερος ὁ Μωσῆς δείκνυται ἀπάντων συγγραφέων (οὐκ αὐτὸς δὲ μόνος ἀλλὰ καὶ οἱ πλείους μετ' αὐτὸν προφῆται γενόμενοι) καὶ Κρόνου καὶ Βήλου καὶ τοῦ Ἰλιακοῦ πολέμου, δηλόν ἐστιν. κατὰ γὰρ τὴν Θάλλου ἱστορίαν ὁ Βῆλος προγενέστερος εὑρίσκεται τοῦ Ἰλιακοῦ πολέμου ἔτεσι τκβ΄. ὅτι δὲ πρός που ἔτεσι ϡ΄ ἢ καὶ ͵α προάγει ὁ Μωσῆς τῆς τοῦ Ἰλίου ἁλώσεως, ἐν τοῖς ἐπάνω δεδηλώκαμεν.

Τοῦ δὲ Κρόνου καὶ τοῦ Βήλου συνακμασάντων ὁμόσε, οἱ πλείους οὐκ ἐπίστανται τίς ἐστιν ὁ Κρόνος ἢ τίς ὁ Βῆλος. ἔνιοι μὲν σέβονται τὸν Κρόνον καὶ τοῦτον αὐτὸν ὀνομάζουσι Βὴλ καὶ Βάλ, μάλιστα οἱ οἰκοῦντες τὰ ἀνατολικὰ κλίματα, μὴ γινώσκοντες μήτε τίς ἐστιν ὁ Κρόνος μήτε τίς ἐστιν ὁ Βῆλος. παρὰ δὲ Ῥωμαίοις Σατοῦρνος ὀνομάζεται· οὐδὲ γὰρ αὐτοὶ γινώσκουσιν τίς ἐστιν αὐτῶν, πότερον ὁ Κρόνος ἢ ὁ Βῆλος.

Ἡ μὲν οὖν ἀρχὴ τῶν ὀλυμπιάδων ἀπὸ Εἰφίτου, φασίν, ἔσχεκεν τὴν θρησκείαν, κατὰ δέ τινας ἀπὸ Αἵμονος,[4] ὃς καὶ Ἡλεῖος[5] ἐπεκλήθη. ὁ μὲν οὖν ἀριθμὸς τῶν ἐτῶν καὶ ὀλυμπιάδων ὡς ἔχει τὴν τάξιν, ἐν τοῖς ἐπάνω δεδηλώκαμεν.

---

[3] ͵εχϟε΄] V: ͵εχϟη΄ Fell
29. [1] συνηρασμένων] V: συνηθροισμένων P   [2] Ὤγυγος] Jacoby: ὁ Γύγος V
[3] Ὤγυγος] Wolf: ὁ Γύγος V   [4] Αἵμονος] Grant; cf. Pausan. v. 4. 6: Λιμοῦ V   [5] Ἡλεῖος] Wolf; cf. Pausan. v. 4. 6: Ἴλιος V

years from the creation of the world is 5,695, with the additional months and days.

Chronological Epilogue

29. From the compilation of the periods of time and from all that has been said, the antiquity of the prophetic writings and the divine nature of our message are obvious. This message is not recent in origin, nor are our writings, as some suppose, mythical and false. They are actually more ancient and more trustworthy.

In fact, Thallus mentioned Belos, who reigned over the Assyrians, and the Titan Kronos, and said that with the Titans Belos waged war against Zeus and the so-called gods on his side. Then he says: 'And Ogygos in defeat fled to Tartessus; the country which Ogygos then ruled was at that time named Akte and is now called Attica.' [*FGrHist* II B 256, 2.] We do not consider it necessary to list the other lands and cities and the persons from whom they received their names, especially for you who know the history. But it is obvious that Moses proves to be more ancient than all writers (not only he, but also most of the prophets after him) and Kronos and Belos and the Trojan war; for according to the history of Thallus, Belos antedated the Trojan war by 322 years, while we have already shown that Moses antedates the capture of Troy by 900 or 1,000 years [III. 21].

Since Kronos and Belos were contemporaries, most people do not know which is Kronos and which is Belos. Some worship Kronos and call him Bel and Bal, especially those who inhabit the eastern regions; they do not know which is Kronos and which is Belos. Among the Romans he is called Saturn; they too do not know which of them he is, whether Kronos or Belos.

The foundation of the Olympiads, they say, received religious observance from the time of Iphitus, although according to some it was from Haimon, who was also called 'of Elis'. The number of the years and the sequence of the Olympiads we have explained above [III. 27].

Τῆς μὲν οὖν ἀρχαιότητος τῶν παρ' ἡμῖν πραγμάτων καὶ τῶν χρόνων τὸν πάντα ἀριθμὸν κατὰ τὸ δύνατον οἶμαι τὰ νῦν ἀκριβῶς εἰρῆσθαι. εἰ γὰρ καὶ ἔλαθεν ἡμᾶς χρόνος, εἰ τύχοι εἰπεῖν ἔτη ν' ἢ ρ' ἢ καὶ σ', οὐ μέντοι μυριάδες ἢ χιλιάδες ἐτῶν, καθὼς προειρήκασιν Πλάτων καὶ Ἀπολλώνιος καὶ οἱ λοιποὶ ψευδῶς ἀναγράψαντες. ὅπερ ἡμεῖς τὸ ἀκριβὲς ἴσως ἀγνοοῦμεν, ἁπάντων τῶν ἐτῶν τὸν ἀριθμόν, διὰ τὸ μὴ ἀναγεγράφθαι ἐν ταῖς ἱεραῖς βίβλοις τοὺς ἐπιτρέχοντας μῆνας καὶ ἡμέρας.

Ἔτι[6] δὲ περὶ ὧν φαμεν χρόνων συνᾴδει καὶ Βήρωσος, ὁ παρὰ Χαλδαίοις φιλοσοφήσας καὶ μηνύσας Ἕλλησιν τὰ χαλδαϊκὰ γράμματα, ὃς ἀκολούθως τινὰ εἴρηκεν τῷ Μωσεῖ περί τε κατακλυσμοῦ καὶ ἑτέρων πολλῶν ἐξιστορῶν. ἔτι μὴν καὶ τοῖς προφήταις Ἰερεμίᾳ καὶ Δανιὴλ σύμφωνα ἐκ μέρους εἴρηκεν· τὰ γὰρ συμβάντα τοῖς Ἰουδαίοις ὑπὸ τοῦ βασιλέως Βαβυλωνίων, ὃν αὐτὸς ὀνομάζει Ναβοπαλάσσαρον, κέκληται δὲ παρὰ Ἑβραίοις Ναβουχοδόνοσορ. μέμνηται καὶ περὶ τοῦ ναοῦ ἐν Ἱεροσολύμοις ὡς ἠρημῶσθαι ὑπὸ τοῦ Χαλδαίων βασιλέως, καὶ ὅτι, Κύρου τὸ δεύτερον ἔτος βασιλεύσαντος τοῦ ναοῦ τῶν θεμελίων τεθέντων, Δαρείου πάλιν βασιλεύσαντος τὸ δεύτερον ἔτος ὁ ναὸς ἐπετελέσθη.

30. Τῶν δὲ τῆς ἀληθείας ἱστοριῶν Ἕλληνες οὐ μέμνηνται, πρῶτον μὲν διὰ τὸ νεωστὶ αὐτοὺς τῶν γραμμάτων τῆς ἐμπειρίας μετόχους γεγενῆσθαι καὶ αὐτοὶ ὁμολογοῦσιν φάσκοντες τὰ γράμματα εὑρῆσθαι, οἱ μὲν παρὰ Χαλδαίων, οἱ δὲ παρὰ Αἰγυπτίων, ἄλλοι δ' αὖ ἀπὸ Φοινίκων· δεύτερον ὅτι ἔπταιον καὶ πταίουσιν περὶ θεοῦ μὴ ποιούμενοι τὴν μνείαν ἀλλὰ περὶ ματαίων καὶ ἀνωφελῶν πραγμάτων. οὕτως μὲν γὰρ καὶ Ὁμήρου καὶ Ἡσιόδου καὶ τῶν λοιπῶν ποιητῶν φιλοτίμως μέμνηνται, τῆς δὲ τοῦ ἀφθάρτου καὶ μόνου θεοῦ δόξης οὐ μόνον ἐπελάθοντο ἀλλὰ καὶ κατελάλησαν· ἔτι μὴν καὶ τοὺς σεβομένους αὐτὸν ἐδίωξαν καὶ τὸ καθ' ἡμέραν διώκουσιν. οὐ μὴν ἀλλὰ καὶ τοῖς εὐφώνως ὑβρίζουσι τὸν θεὸν ἆθλα καὶ τιμὰς τιθέασιν, τοὺς δὲ σπεύδοντας πρὸς ἀρετὴν καὶ ἀσκοῦντας βίον ὅσιον, οὓς μὲν ἐλιθοβόλησαν, οὓς δὲ ἐθανάτωσαν, καὶ ἕως τοῦ δεῦρο ὠμοῖς αἰκισμοῖς περιβάλλουσιν. διὸ οἱ τοιοῦτοι ἀναγκαίως ἀπώλεσαν τὴν σοφίαν τοῦ θεοῦ καὶ τὴν ἀλήθειαν οὐχ εὗρον.

Εἰ οὖν βούλει, ἀκριβῶς ἔντυχε τούτοις, ὅπως σχῇς σύμβουλον καὶ ἀρραβῶνα τῆς ἀληθείας.

[6] ἔτι] Maran: ὅτι V

I think that I have now accurately set forth, as well as possible, the complete accounting of the antiquity of our religion and of the periods of time. If some period has escaped our notice, say 50 or 100 or even 200 years, at any rate it is not myriads or thousands of years as it was for Plato and Apollonius [III. 16, 26] and the rest of those who wrote falsehoods. It may be that we do not know the exact total of all the years simply because the additional months and days are not recorded in the sacred books.

Furthermore, we find agreement concerning the times of which we speak with the words of Berossus, who studied philosophy among the Chaldaeans and informed the Greeks about Chaldaean literature [cf. Josephus, *C. Ap.* i. 129]. He made some statements in agreement with Moses about the deluge and many other matters [ibid., 130]. Furthermore, his statements agree in part with the prophets Jeremiah and Daniel: for example, as to what happened to the Jews under the king of the Babylonians whom he calls Nabopalassaros (the Hebrews call him Nabouchodonosor). He also refers to the temple in Jerusalem and how it was razed by the king of the Chaldaeans and how, after the foundations of the temple had been laid in the second year of Cyrus' reign, later on the temple was completed in the second year of Darius' reign [cf. 1 Esd. 2 : 32].

Conclusion and Final Appeal for Conversion

30. The Greeks made no mention of the true historical narratives, first because they became familiar with writing only recently, as they themselves admit when some of them say that the alphabet was discovered by Chaldaeans, others by Egyptians, still others by Phoenicians, and second because they went astray and still go astray by speaking not of God but of pointless and useless matters. Thus they are eager to speak of Homer and Hesiod and the other poets, but they not only neglect but even slander *the glory of the imperishable* and only *God* [Rom. 1 : 23]; in addition, they have persecuted those who worship him and daily do persecute them. Moreover, they have *appointed prizes and honours for those who euphoniously insult God* [Justin, *Apol.* i. 4. 9], while they have stoned and killed those who are zealous for virtue and practise a holy life, and to this day they afflict them with cruel tortures. Such men necessarily lost the wisdom of God and did not discover the truth.

If you will, read these books carefully so that you may have a counsellor and pledge of the truth.

BIBLICAL QUOTATIONS AND ALLUSIONS

Explicit quotations are marked with an asterisk

OLD TESTAMENT (SEPTUAGINT)

Quotations and allusions from the long passages quoted by Theophilus are noted only once. For the sources of his chronology, see Introduction, pp. xx ff.

Genesis	
1: 1-2	*II. 10
1: 3-2: 3	*II. 11
2: 4-7	*II. 19
2: 8-3: 19	*II. 20-1
4: 1-2	*II. 29
4: 9-14	*II. 29
4: 17-22	*II. 30
7: 11-12	III. 19
7: 20	III. 19
9: 1	II. 32
9: 11	III. 9
10: 5	II. 32
10: 10-14	II. 31
11: 1, 4, 7	II. 31
11: 31	II. 31
14: 1-6	II. 31
14: 18	II. 31
15: 13	III. 10
20: 2	II. 31
23: 10	II. 31
26: 1	II. 31

Exodus	
1: 11	III. 20
4: 11	I. 14
12: 40	III. 10
20: 3-5	*III. 9
20: 7	II. 10
20: 12-17	*III. 9
20: 13-17	II. 35
23: 6-8	*III. 9
23: 9	*III. 10

Deuteronomy	
4: 19	II. 35

18: 15	III. 11

4 Regn.	
15: 29, 17: 3, 18: 13	II. 31

Job	
9: 8	I. 7
9: 9	I. 6
12: 15	I. 6
34: 14-15	I. 7
37: 15	I. 6
38: 10	I. 6
38: 18	I. 7
38: 22	I. 6
38: 31	I. 6
38: 35	I. 6

Psalms	
13: 1, 3	*II. 35
23: 2	I. 7
32: 6	I. 7
32: 7	I. 6
44: 2	II. 10
50: 10	*II. 38
54: 20	II. 10
64: 8	I. 7
88: 10	I. 7
93: 9	I. 14
94: 4	I. 4
95: 5	I. 10
103: 5	I. 4
103: 14	I. 4
109: 3	II. 10
113: 9	I. 14
113: 12-14	I. 1, I. 10, II. 34
113: 16	I. 10

BIBLICAL QUOTATIONS AND ALLUSIONS

134: 7	I. 6	Hosea	
134: 15	I. 10, II. 34	12: 7	*III. 12
134: 18	I. 10	13: 4	*II. 35, *III. 12
146: 4	I. 6	14: 10	*II. 38
146: 8	I. 4		
		Joel	
Proverbs		1: 14	III. 12
3: 8	II. 38	2: 16	*III. 12
3: 19-20	I. 7		
4: 25	*II. 35	Habakkuk	
4: 25-6	*III. 13	2: 18-19	*II. 35
6: 27-9	*III. 13	Zechariah	
8: 22	II. 10	7: 9-10	*III. 12
8: 27-9	*II. 10	9: 9	III. 12
24: 21-2	*I. 11		
		Malachi	
Ecclesiastes		1: 9	*III. 12
11: 7	I. 6	3: 19 (4: 1)	*II. 38
		Baruch	
Isaiah		2: 4	III. 11
1: 16-17	*III. 12		
11: 6-9	II. 17	1 Esdras	
30: 27, 30, 28	*II. 38	2: 32	III. 29
31: 6	*III. 11	2 Esdras	
40: 22	*II. 13	1: 8	III. 25
40: 28	*II. 35		
42: 5-6	*II. 35	2 Macc. 7: 28	I. 4
43: 25	III. 12	NEW TESTAMENT	
45: 3	I. 6		
45: 12	*II. 35	Matthew	
45: 22	*III. 11	3: 15	III. 9
55: 6-7	*III. 11	4: 23	III. 21
58: 6-8	III. 11	5: 8	I. 2 (note)
60: 21	II. 15	5: 28	*III. 13
66: 1	I. 4, II. 22	5: 32	*III. 13
66: 5	*III. 14	5: 44, 46	*III. 14
		6: 3	*III. 14
Jeremiah		13: 32	II. 14
6: 9	*III. 11	19: 17, 25	II. 27
6: 16	*III. 12	Luke	
6: 22	III. 25	1: 2-3	III. 2
6: 29	*II. 35	1: 35	II. 10
9: 23	III. 12	18: 27	II. 13
10: 12-13	I. 6, *II. 35		
10: 14-15	*II. 35	John	
16: 15	III. 25	1: 1-3	*II. 22
28: 15-16	*II. 35	1: 3	II. 10
		14: 26	III. 11
Ezekiel		15: 26	II. 38
18: 21-3	II. 17, *III. 11	16: 8, 13	II. 38, III. 15
		20: 27	I. 14

Acts		Philippians	
15: 20, 29	II. 34	1: 10	I. 2
Romans		3: 19	II. 17
1: 22	II. 35	4: 8	II. 36
1: 23	III. 30	Colossians	
1: 30	I. 2	1: 15	II. 22
2: 6–9	I. 14	5: 2	II. 17
2: 18	I. 7		
5: 18–19	II. 22	1 Thessalonians	
11: 33	II. 12	4: 8	II. 15
13: 1	I. 11	1 Timothy	
13: 1–3	III. 14	1: 10	I. 2
13: 7–8	*III. 14	2: 1–2	I. 11, *III. 14
1 Corinthians		2 Timothy	
1: 18	III. 4	3: 2	I. 2
1: 24	II. 22	3: 8	I. 1
2: 9	I. 14	Titus	
2: 10	II. 34	1: 7	I. 2
3: 18	II. 35	3: 1	*III. 14
6: 8–10	I. 2	3: 5	II. 16
6: 9–10	I. 14		
8: 4	II. 1	Philemon	
9: 17	I. 11	11	I. 1
9: 26	III. 1	Hebrews	
12: 11	I. 13, II. 35	11: 35	II. 27
15: 50	II. 27		
15: 53–4	I. 7	1 Peter	
2 Corinthians		2: 15, 17	I. 11
7: 1	I. 2	3: 20	III. 19
11: 6	II. 1	4: 3	I. 14, II. 34
11: 19	III. 4	Revelation	
Galatians		12: 9	II. 28
4: 19	II. 35	1 Clement	
5: 22	I. 14	14: 3	II. 14
Ephesians		Kerygma Petri	
1: 19	**I. 3**, II. 12	fr. 3	I. 14
3: 10	**I. 6**, II. 16		

NON-BIBLICAL SOURCES AND PARALLELS

Adespoton comicum 148 Kock (iii. 437) = Stob. i. 3. 29	II. 37
Adespoton tragicum 493 Nauck = Stob. i. 3. 27	II. 37
Aeschylus tragicus fr. 22 Nauck = Stob. i. 3. 26	II. 37
fr. 456 = Stob. i. 3. 24	II. 37
Apollonides Horapius, *Semenouthi* (*FGrHist* III C 661)	II. 6
Apollonius Aegyptius (*FHG* iv. 310)	III. 16 (26)
Aratus Stoicus, *Phaen.* 1–9 = Stob. i. 1. 3	II. 8
Sphaerographia	III. 2
Archilochus lyricus fr. 65 Bergk	II. 37
Ariston comicus (cf. Meineke, *FCG* i, pp. ix–x)	III. 7
Aristophanes comicus, *Aves* 695 (cf. Kern, *Orph. fragmenta* 1)	II. 7
Berossus historicus (cf. Josephus)	III. 29
Chryseros nomenclator (*FGrHist* II A 96)	III. 27
Chrysippus Stoicus (*SVF* ii. 1073)	III. 8
Cleanthes Stoicus (*SVF* i. 584)	III. 5
Clitomachus Academicus (cf. Sext. Emp. *Adv. math.* ix. 182–90)	III. 7
Diogenes Cynicus (cf. Diog. Laert. vi. 73)	III. 5
Dionysius tragicus fr. 5 Nauck = Stob. i. 3. 19	II. 37
Doxographi graeci, ed. H. Diels, 567, 13	II. 4
572, 6	III. 7
588, 17–18	II. 4
589, 7–10	III. 7
Epicurea, ed. H. Usener, 323, 7–13	III. 6
Euhemerus historicus (*FGrHist* 1 63)	III. 7
Euripides tragicus, *Iphigenia in Aulis* 394–5 = Stob. iii. 28. 2	II. 37
fr. 303 Nauck = Stob. iii. 2. 13	II. 37
fr. 391	II. 8
fr. 397 = Stob. i. 2. 19	II. 8
fr. 1089	II. 8
fr. 1090–2	II. 37
Herodotus historicus i. 199, iii. 99	III. 5
iii. 60	III. 26
Hesiodus poeta, *Theog.* 73–4, 104–10, 112–15	II. 5
116–23, 126–33	II. 6
139, 185, 207	II. 6
Homerus poeta, *Ilias* v. 31, 340, 455	II. 9
xiv. 201 = 302	II. 5
xvi. 856 = xxii. 362	II. 38
xx. 242 = Stob. i. 1. 4	II. 8
xxi. 196	II. 5
xxiii. 71	II. 38

152 NON-BIBLICAL SOURCES AND PARALLELS

Homerus poeta (*cont.*)	
Odyss. xi. 108	II. 38
xi. 221	II. 38
Josephus historicus, *Contra Apionem* i. 94–7, 102	III. 20
103–4	III. 21
109–26	III. 22
129–32	III. 29
154	III. 25, 29
ii. 154	III. 23
Justinus apologeta, *Apol.* i. 4. 9	III. 30
Manetho historicus (cf. Josephus)	III. 20–1
Menander comicus fr. 752 Kock = *Epitrepontes* 734	II. 8
Menander Ephesius historicus (cf. Josephus)	III. 22–3
Menandri Sententiae, ed. S. Jaekel, 81, 107	II. 4
Orpheus theologus fr. 62 Kern (pp. 145–6)	III. 17
fr. 245 (pp. 255–6)	III. 2
test. 1 (pp. 1–2)	II. 30
Philemon comicus fr. 143 Kock	III. 7
fr. 181	III. 7
Pindarus lyricus, *Nem.* iv. 51–2 = Stob. iv. 5. 8	II. 37
Plato philosophus, *Leg.* iii. 677 a–b	III. 18
677 c–d, 683 b–c	III. 16
Meno 99 e	III. 17
Phaedo 81 e, 82 a, 88 d	III. 7
Rep. v. 457 c, 460 b	III. 6
Protagoras Abderites philosophus (cf. Sext. Emp. *Adv. math.* ix. 56)	III. 7
Pythagoras philosophus	III. 2, 7, 26
Satyrus historicus (*FGrHist* III C 631)	II. 7
Sextus Empiricus, *Adv. math.* ix. 56, 182–90	III. 7
x. 18–19	II. 6
Sibylla vates, *Oracula* iii. 97–103, 105; viii. 5	II. 31
fr. 1 Geffcken (pp. 227–9)	II. 36
fr. 2 (p. 229)	II. 3
fr. 3 (pp. 230–2)	II. 36
Simonides lyricus fr. 61 Bergk = Stob. i. 1. 10	II. 8
fr. 62	II. 37
Simylus comicus fr. falsum 143 Kock (ii. 444)	III. 7
Solon legislator	III. 23
Sophocles tragicus, *Oedip. rex* 978–9 (cf. Stob. i. 7. 5)	II. 8
fr. 876 Nauck = Stob. i. 3. 7	II. 8
fr. 877 = Stob. i. 3. 48a	II. 37
Stobaeus anthologus, *Ecl.* i. 1. 3, 4, 10; i. 2. 19; i. 3. 7	II. 8
i. 3. 19, 24, 26, 27, 29, 48a	II. 37
iii. 2. 13, 28. 2; iv. 5. 8	II. 37
iv. 57. 8	II. 38
Stoicorum veterum fragmenta, ed. H. von Arnim, i. 254 = 584	III. 5
ii. 1033	II. 4

ii. 1073	III. 8
iii. 750	III. 5, 6
Thallus historicus (*FGrHist* II B 256)	III. 29
Thucydides historicus i. 134, vi. 59	III. 26
Timocles comicus fr. 31 Kock = Stob. iv. 57. 8	II. 38
Zeno Stoicus (*SVF* i. 254)	III. 5

PRINTED IN GREAT BRITAIN
AT THE UNIVERSITY PRESS, OXFORD
BY VIVIAN RIDLER
PRINTER TO THE UNIVERSITY